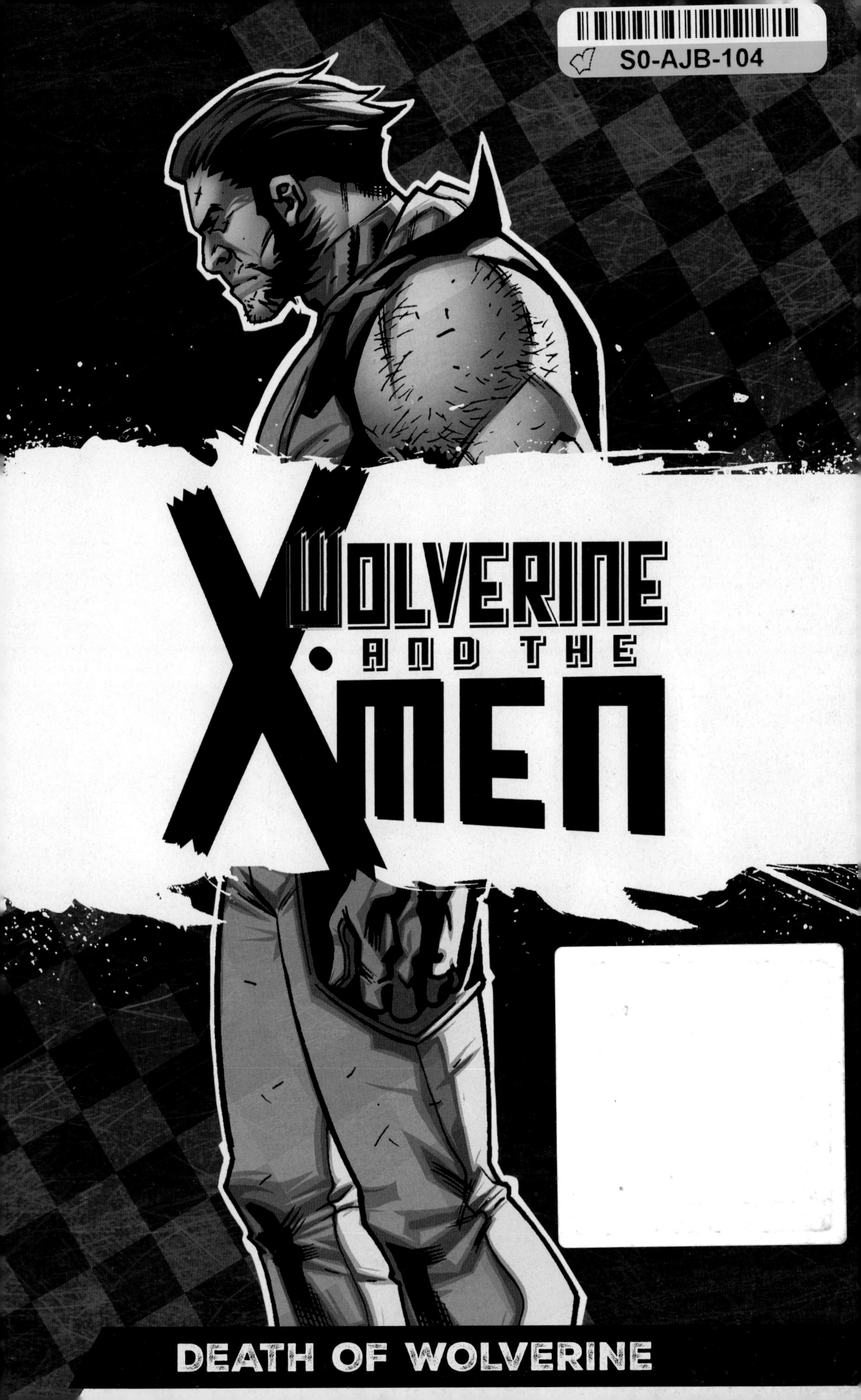
WOLVERINE
AND THE
X-MEN
DEATH OF WOLVERINE

COLLECTION EDITOR: **JENNIFER GRÜNWALD**
ASSISTANT EDITOR: **SARAH BRUNSTAD**
ASSOCIATE MANAGING EDITOR: **ALEX STARBUCK**
EDITOR, SPECIAL PROJECTS: **MARK D. BEAZLEY**
SENIOR EDITOR, SPECIAL PROJECTS: **JEFF YOUNGQUIST**
SVP PRINT, SALES & MARKETING: **DAVID GABRIEL**
BOOK DESIGNER: **NELSON RIBEIRO**

EDITOR IN CHIEF: **AXEL ALONSO**
CHIEF CREATIVE OFFICER: **JOE QUESADA**
PUBLISHER: **DAN BUCKLEY**
EXECUTIVE PRODUCER: **ALAN FINE**

10 9 8 7 6 5 4 3 2 1

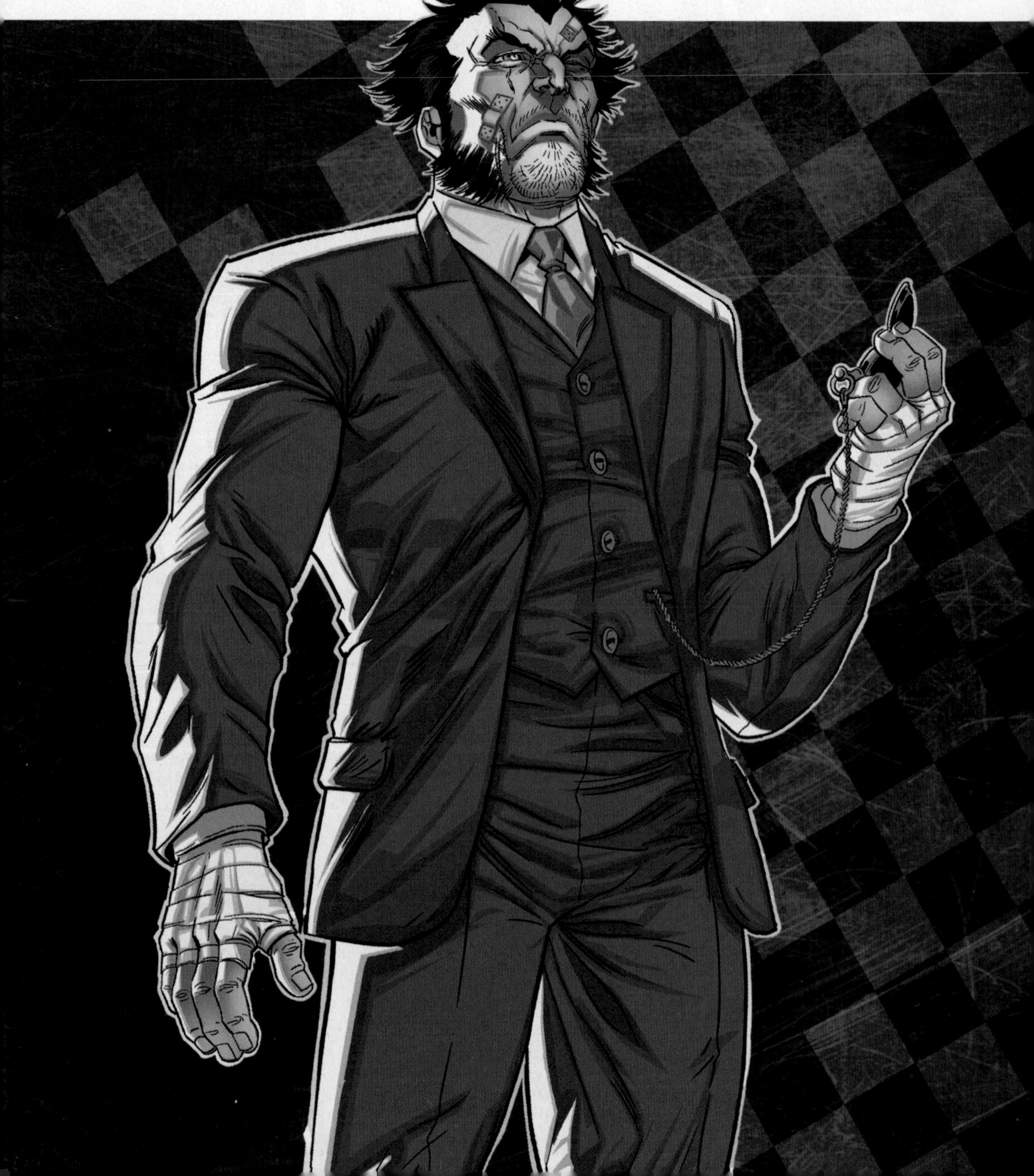

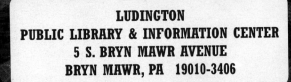

X WOLVERINE AND THE MEN

DEATH OF WOLVERINE

writer:
JASON LATOUR

ISSUE #7
ARTISTS: **MASSIMILIANO VELTRI,
MARC DEERING & DAVID MESSINA**
COLOR ARTISTS: **ISRAEL SILVA &
BRETT SMITH**

ISSUE #8
ARTISTS: **PACO DIAZ** (PP. 1-4) AND
DAVID MESSINA & GAETANO CARLUCCI
(PP. 5-20)
COLOR ARTISTS: **ISRAEL SILVA &
JOHN KALISZ**

ISSUES #9 & #12
ARTIST: **JORGE FORNÉS**
COLOR ARTIST: **ISRAEL SILVA**

ISSUE #10
ARTISTS: **ROBBI RODRIGUEZ &
ISRAEL SILVA, IAN BERTRAM &
IAN HERRING, RONALD WIMBERLY &
SASHA KIMIATEK, KRIS ANKA &
JIM RUGG, ARIELA KRISTANTINA &
SONIA OBACK, DECLAN SHALVEY &
MATTHEW WILSON** AND
JAMES HARREN & MATTHEW WILSON

ISSUE #11
ARTISTS: **BEN CALDWELL;
ROBBI RODRIGUEZ & ISRAEL SILVA;
FAREL DALRYMPLE & RICO RENZI;
VANESSA DEL REY & RICO RENZI;
JASON LATOUR;** AND **CHRIS BRUNNER &
RICO RENZI**
SPECIAL THANKS TO BRITTANY HEINER &
MARTE GRACIA

letterer:
**VC'S CLAYTON
COWLES**

cover:
**MAHMUD ASRAR
& MARTE GRACIA**

assistant editor: **KATIE KUBERT**
group editor: **MIKE MARTS**
X-MEN created by **STAN LEE & JACK KIRBY**

In a world where being born a mutant is a crime, there's only one place where children with super-powers are safe – the Jean Grey School for Higher Learning! Here, students from across the planet and galaxy learn to focus what makes them special into a tool that can be used to make the world a better place. And when trouble strikes the students, they can count on support from their faculty, a group of super heroes known as...

PREVIOUSLY...

Though one of the greatest mutant warriors ever, Wolverine has now unfortunately lost his mutant ability to heal. Every time he unsheathes his claws he's consumed with excruciating pain--a pain that might possibly be dulled by spending some quality time with Storm. Sadly, the companions haven't been able to grab a free moment together for just the two of them...but no matter what, they're in this together.

Idie Okonkwo is a young mutant student at the Jean Grey School...but when she was unexpectedly thrust into the future--she was forced to do the unthinkable! In order to save the world and the fate of her friend Evan, Idie was forced to kill the **Dark Phoenix** of the future--an adult Quentin Quire!

As a result of witnessing his impending death, the teenage **Quentin Quire** of today has fled the school. Leaving behind his fellow X-Men to deal with the ramifications of what they fear is a destiny of death and loss.*

*THESE EVENTS TAKE PLACE PRIOR TO WOLVERINE #1! --K.K.

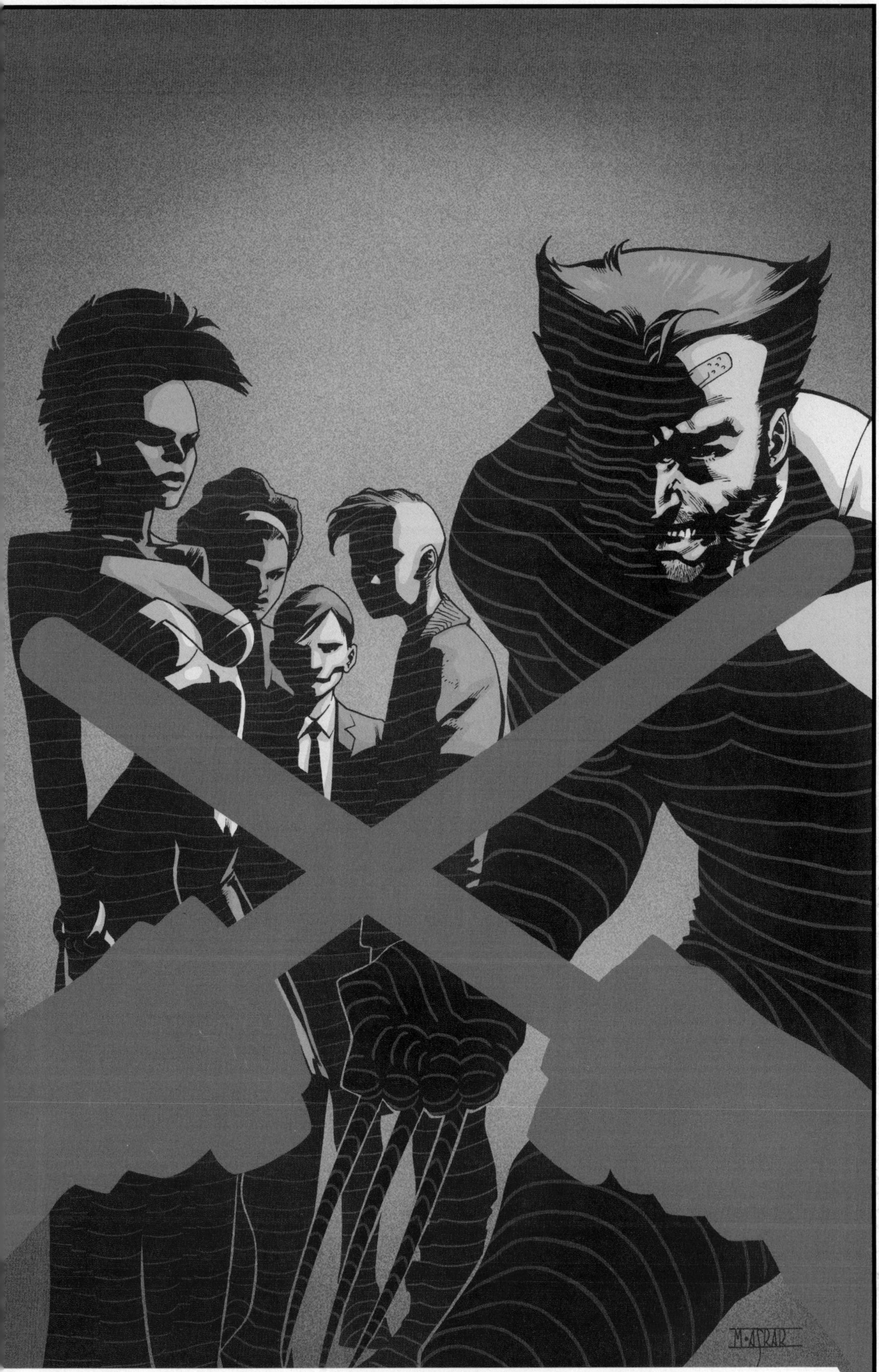
M•ASRAR

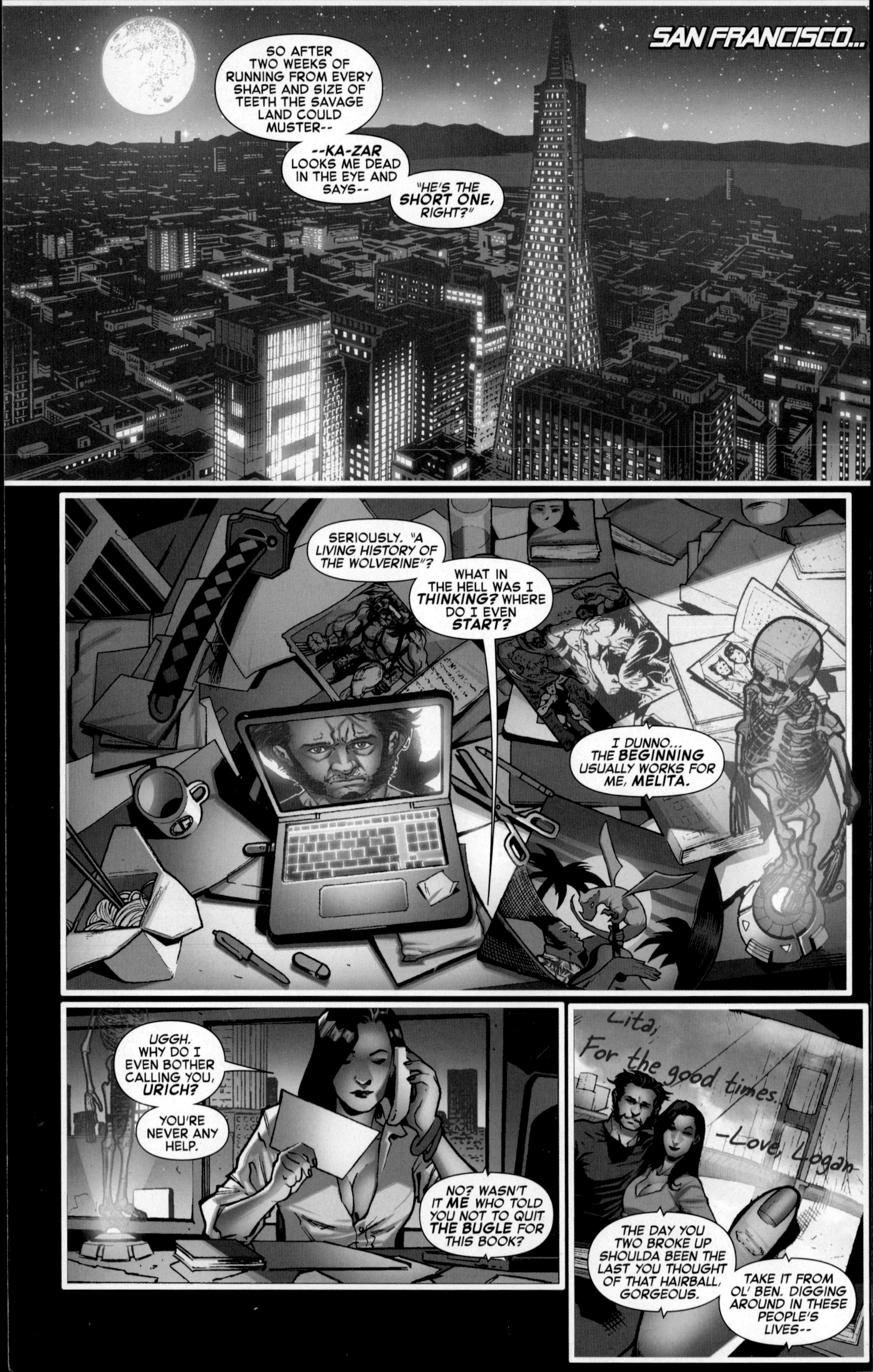
SAN FRANCISCO...
SO AFTER TWO WEEKS OF RUNNING FROM EVERY SHAPE AND SIZE OF TEETH THE SAVAGE LAND COULD MUSTER--
--KA-ZAR LOOKS ME DEAD IN THE EYE AND SAYS--
"HE'S THE SHORT ONE, RIGHT?"
SERIOUSLY. "A LIVING HISTORY OF THE WOLVERINE"?
WHAT IN THE HELL WAS I THINKING? WHERE DO I EVEN START?
I DUNNO... THE BEGINNING USUALLY WORKS FOR ME, MELITA.
UGGH. WHY DO I EVEN BOTHER CALLING YOU, URICH?
YOU'RE NEVER ANY HELP.
NO? WASN'T IT ME WHO TOLD YOU NOT TO QUIT THE BUGLE FOR THIS BOOK?
Lita, For the good times. -Love, Logan
THE DAY YOU TWO BROKE UP SHOULDA BEEN THE LAST YOU THOUGHT OF THAT HAIRBALL, GORGEOUS.
TAKE IT FROM OL' BEN. DIGGING AROUND IN THESE PEOPLE'S LIVES--

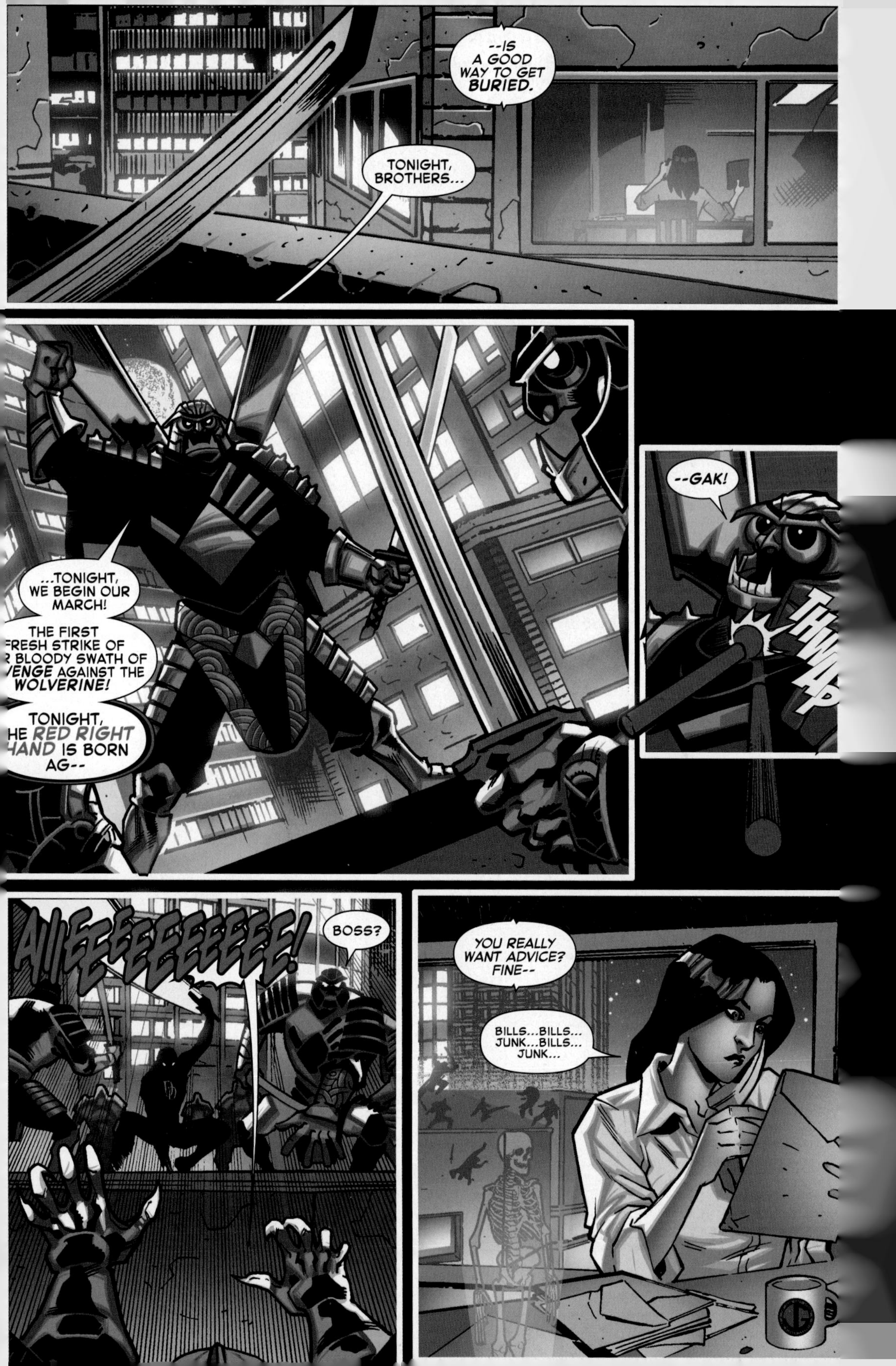

--IS A GOOD WAY TO GET BURIED.
TONIGHT, BROTHERS...
...TONIGHT, WE BEGIN OUR MARCH!
THE FIRST FRESH STRIKE OF R BLOODY SWATH OF VENGE AGAINST THE WOLVERINE!
TONIGHT, HE RED RIGHT HAND IS BORN AG--
--GAK!
THWAP
AIIEEEEEEEEEE!
BOSS?
YOU REALLY WANT ADVICE? FINE--
BILLS...BILLS... JUNK...BILLS... JUNK...

ARRGGGHH!

--IT'S TIME TO STOP SIFTING THROUGH WHATEVER PAST YOU TWO LEFT BACK THERE.

SLLCSSHHH

THE MAN YOU KNEW? WHOEVER HE WAS--

FROM THE LEGAL OFFICES OF **McDUFFIE** and MURDOCK

--HE'S DIFFERENT NOW.

LEGAL OFFICES OF MCDUFFIE AND MURDOCK.

CEASE AND DESIST

LEGAL OFFICES OF MCDUFFIE AND MURDOCK.

YOUR STORY IS WHAT'S COMING.

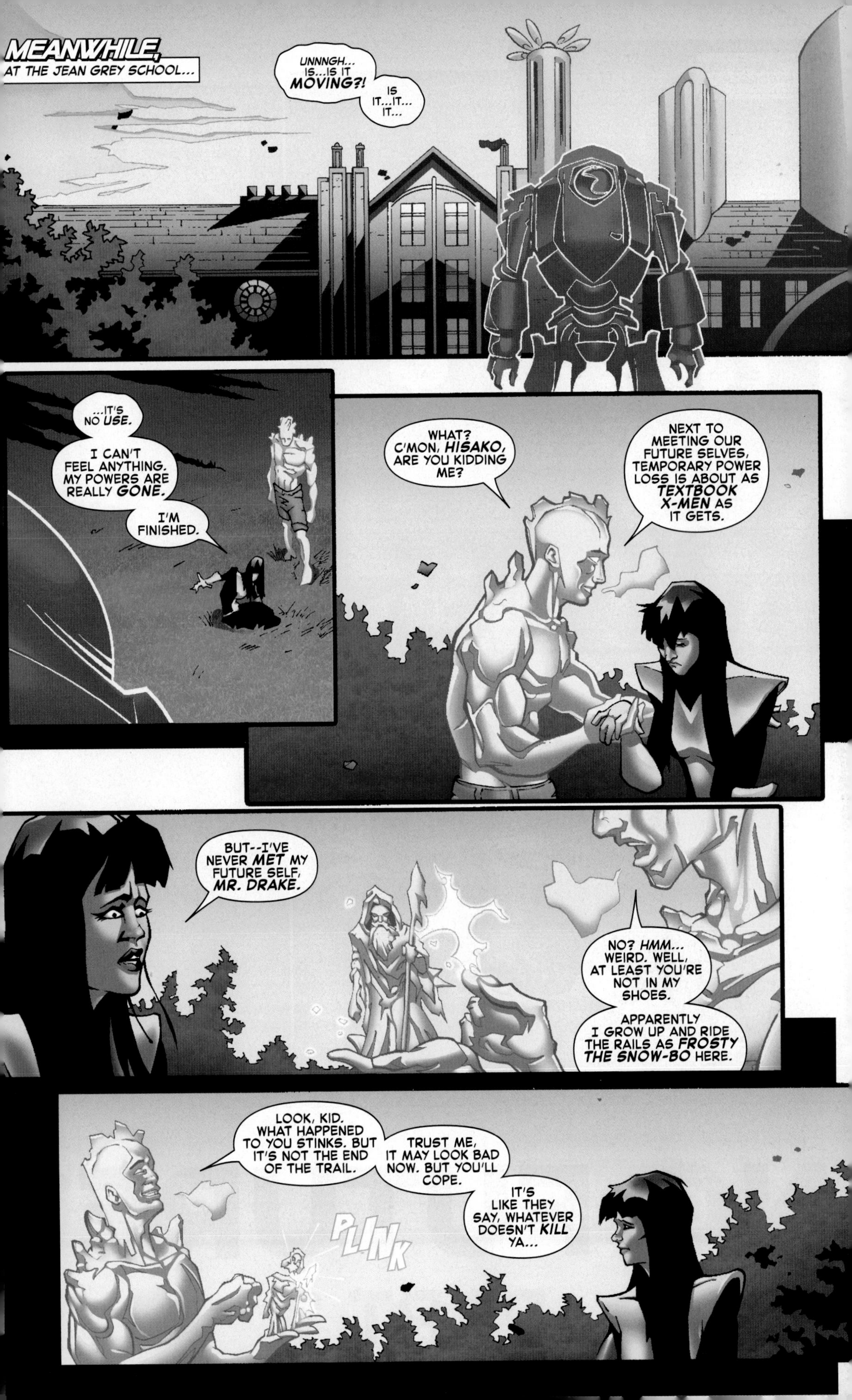
MEANWHILE, AT THE JEAN GREY SCHOOL...
UNNNGH... IS...IS IT MOVING?!
IS IT...IT... IT...
...IT'S NO USE.
I CAN'T FEEL ANYTHING. MY POWERS ARE REALLY GONE.
I'M FINISHED.
WHAT? C'MON, HISAKO, ARE YOU KIDDING ME?
NEXT TO MEETING OUR FUTURE SELVES, TEMPORARY POWER LOSS IS ABOUT AS TEXTBOOK X-MEN AS IT GETS.
BUT--I'VE NEVER MET MY FUTURE SELF, MR. DRAKE.
NO? HMM... WEIRD. WELL, AT LEAST YOU'RE NOT IN MY SHOES.
APPARENTLY I GROW UP AND RIDE THE RAILS AS FROSTY THE SNOW-BO HERE.
LOOK, KID. WHAT HAPPENED TO YOU STINKS. BUT IT'S NOT THE END OF THE TRAIL.
TRUST ME, IT MAY LOOK BAD NOW. BUT YOU'LL COPE.
IT'S LIKE THEY SAY, WHATEVER DOESN'T KILL YA...
PLINK

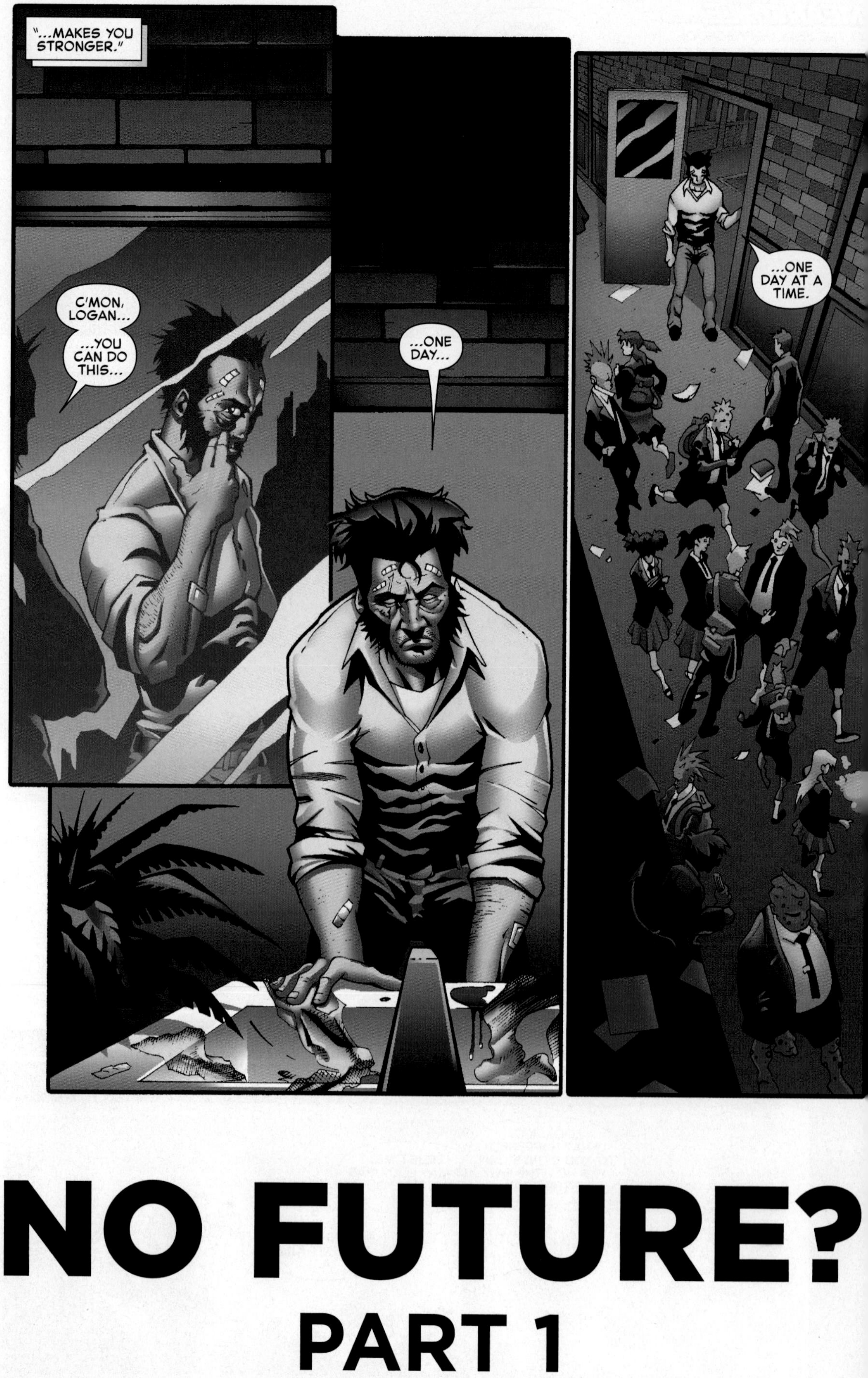
"...MAKES YOU STRONGER."
C'MON, LOGAN...
...YOU CAN DO THIS...
...ONE DAY...
...ONE DAY AT A TIME.

NO FUTURE?
PART 1

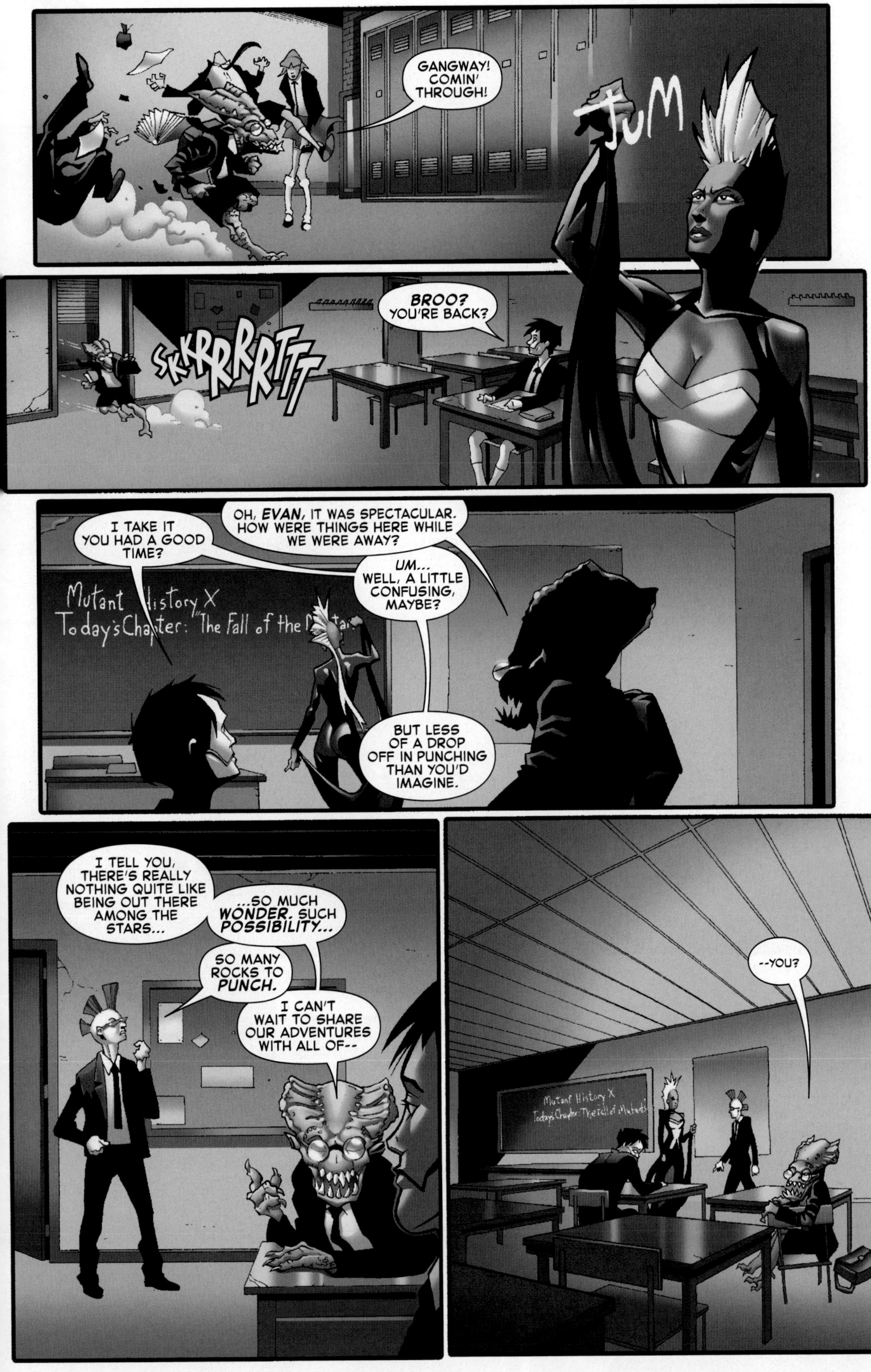

GANGWAY! COMIN' THROUGH!
JUM
SKKRRRRTTT
BROO? YOU'RE BACK?
I TAKE IT YOU HAD A GOOD TIME?
OH, EVAN, IT WAS SPECTACULAR. HOW WERE THINGS HERE WHILE WE WERE AWAY?
UM... WELL, A LITTLE CONFUSING, MAYBE?
BUT LESS OF A DROP OFF IN PUNCHING THAN YOU'D IMAGINE.
Mutant History X
I TELL YOU, THERE'S REALLY NOTHING QUITE LIKE BEING OUT THERE AMONG THE STARS...
...SO MUCH WONDER. SUCH POSSIBILITY...
SO MANY ROCKS TO PUNCH.
I CAN'T WAIT TO SHARE OUR ADVENTURES WITH ALL OF--
--YOU?
Mutant History X
Today's Chapter: The Fall of Mutants

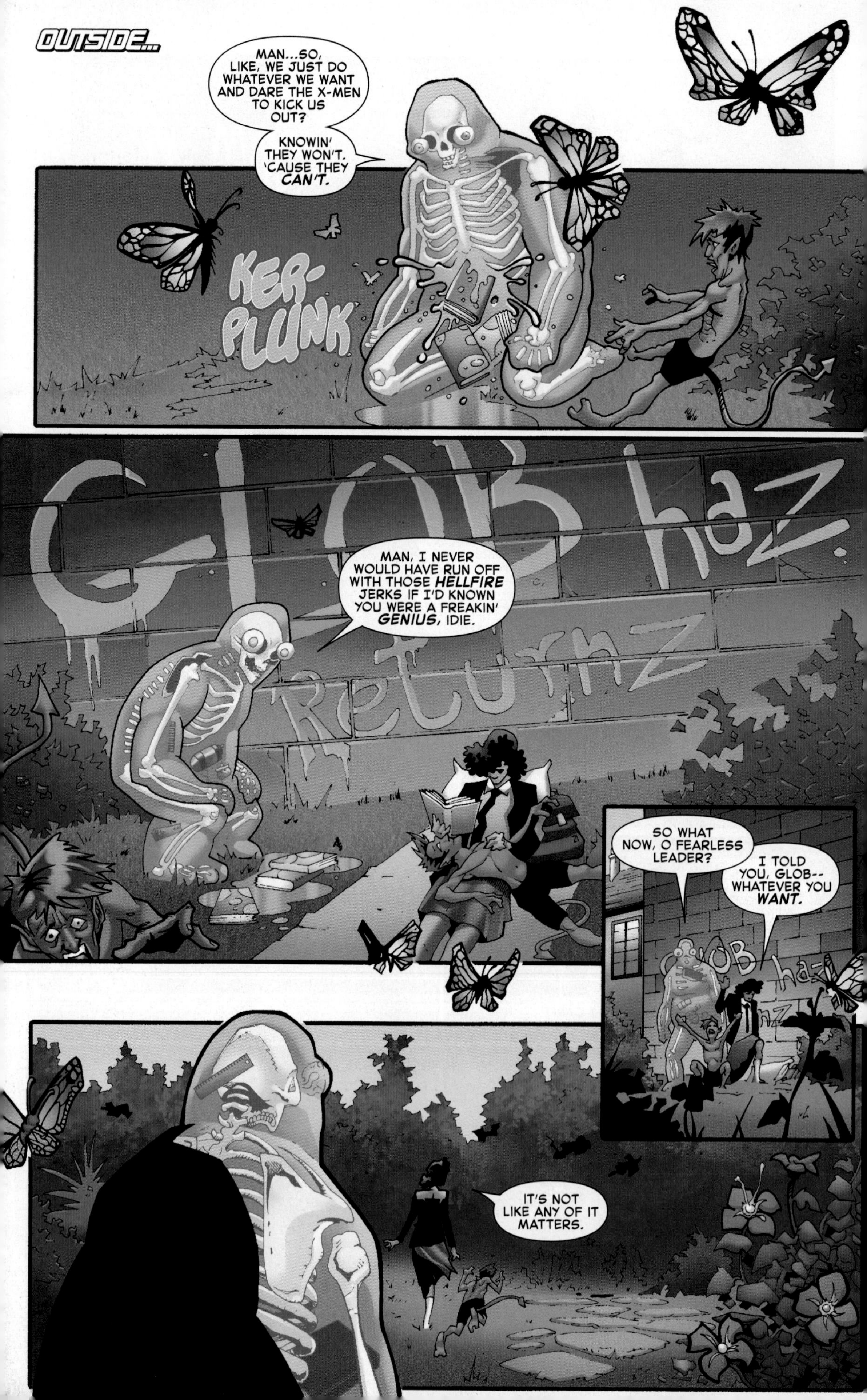
OUTSIDE...
MAN...SO, LIKE, WE JUST DO WHATEVER WE WANT AND DARE THE X-MEN TO KICK US OUT?
KNOWIN' THEY WON'T. 'CAUSE THEY CAN'T.
KER-PLUNK
GLOB haz ReTurnz
MAN, I NEVER WOULD HAVE RUN OFF WITH THOSE HELLFIRE JERKS IF I'D KNOWN YOU WERE A FREAKIN' GENIUS, IDIE.
SO WHAT NOW, O FEARLESS LEADER?
I TOLD YOU, GLOB-- WHATEVER YOU WANT.
IT'S NOT LIKE ANY OF IT MATTERS.

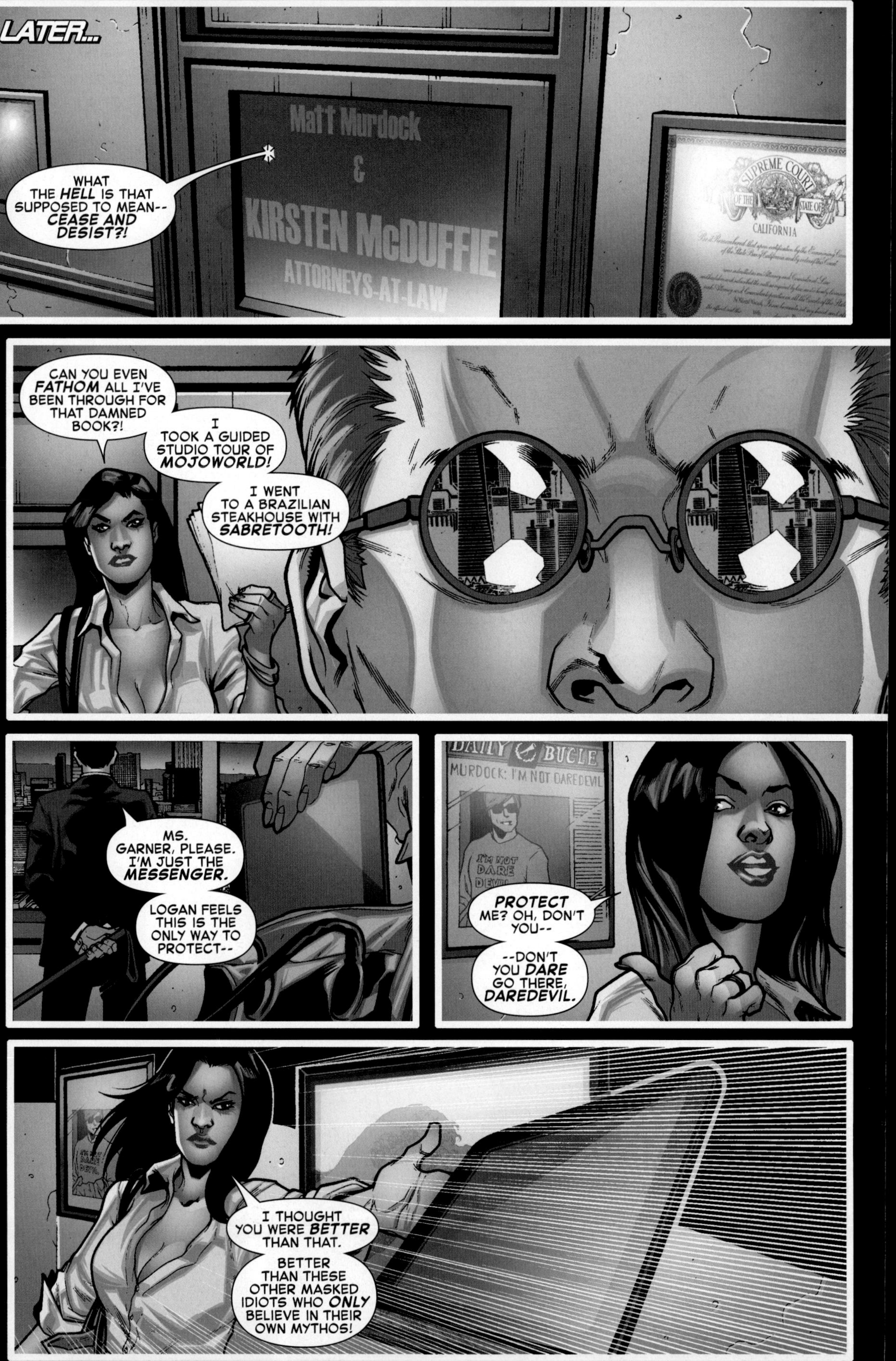
LATER...
Matt Murdock
&
KIRSTEN McDUFFIE
ATTORNEYS-AT-LAW
WHAT THE HELL IS THAT SUPPOSED TO MEAN-- CEASE AND DESIST?!
SUPREME COURT OF THE STATE OF CALIFORNIA
CAN YOU EVEN FATHOM ALL I'VE BEEN THROUGH FOR THAT DAMNED BOOK?!
I TOOK A GUIDED STUDIO TOUR OF MOJOWORLD!
I WENT TO A BRAZILIAN STEAKHOUSE WITH SABRETOOTH!
MS. GARNER, PLEASE. I'M JUST THE MESSENGER.
LOGAN FEELS THIS IS THE ONLY WAY TO PROTECT--
DAILY BUGLE
MURDOCK: I'M NOT DAREDEVIL
I'M NOT DARE DEVIL
PROTECT ME? OH, DON'T YOU--
--DON'T YOU DARE GO THERE, DAREDEVIL.
I THOUGHT YOU WERE BETTER THAN THAT.
BETTER THAN THESE OTHER MASKED IDIOTS WHO ONLY BELIEVE IN THEIR OWN MYTHOS!

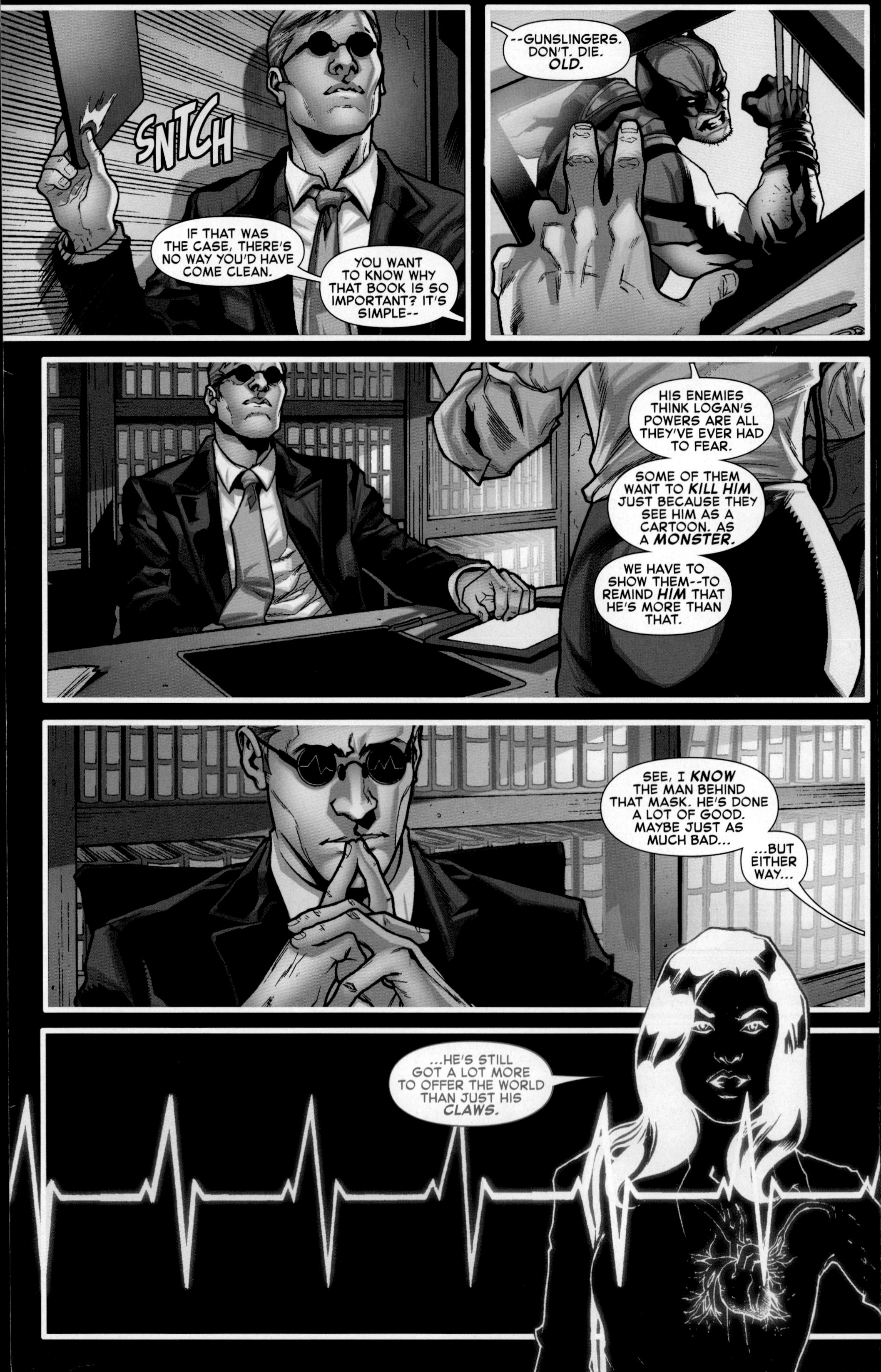
SNTCH
IF THAT WAS THE CASE, THERE'S NO WAY YOU'D HAVE COME CLEAN.
YOU WANT TO KNOW WHY THAT BOOK IS SO IMPORTANT? IT'S SIMPLE--
--GUNSLINGERS. DON'T. DIE. OLD.
HIS ENEMIES THINK LOGAN'S POWERS ARE ALL THEY'VE EVER HAD TO FEAR.
SOME OF THEM WANT TO KILL HIM JUST BECAUSE THEY SEE HIM AS A CARTOON. AS A MONSTER.
WE HAVE TO SHOW THEM--TO REMIND HIM THAT HE'S MORE THAN THAT.
SEE, I KNOW THE MAN BEHIND THAT MASK. HE'S DONE A LOT OF GOOD. MAYBE JUST AS MUCH BAD...
...BUT EITHER WAY...
...HE'S STILL GOT A LOT MORE TO OFFER THE WORLD THAN JUST HIS CLAWS.

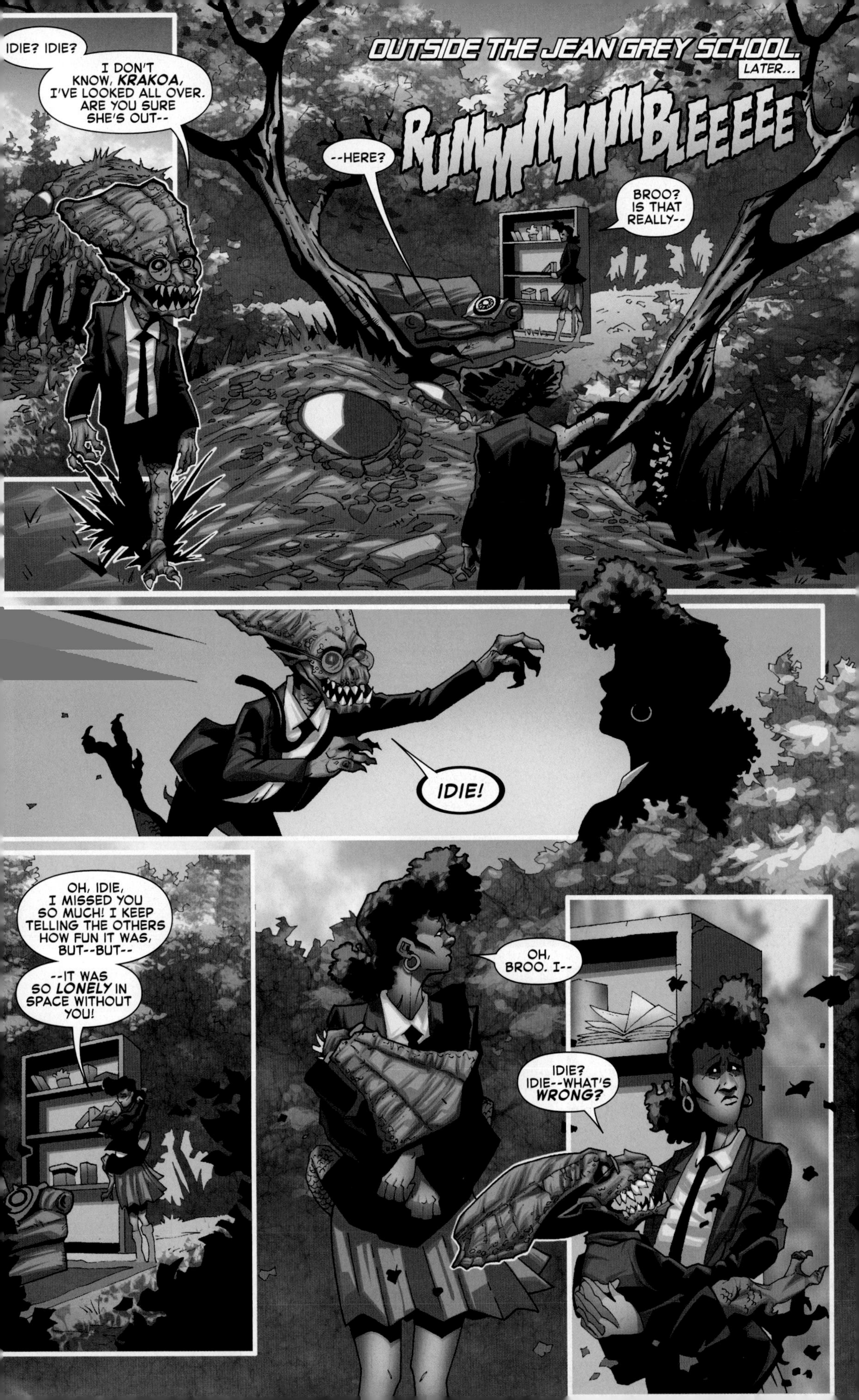
OUTSIDE THE JEAN GREY SCHOOL.
LATER...
IDIE? IDIE?
I DON'T KNOW, KRAKOA, I'VE LOOKED ALL OVER. ARE YOU SURE SHE'S OUT--
--HERE?
RUMMMMMMBLEEEEE
BROO? IS THAT REALLY--
IDIE!
OH, IDIE, I MISSED YOU SO MUCH! I KEEP TELLING THE OTHERS HOW FUN IT WAS, BUT--BUT--
--IT WAS SO LONELY IN SPACE WITHOUT YOU!
OH, BROO. I--
IDIE? IDIE--WHAT'S WRONG?

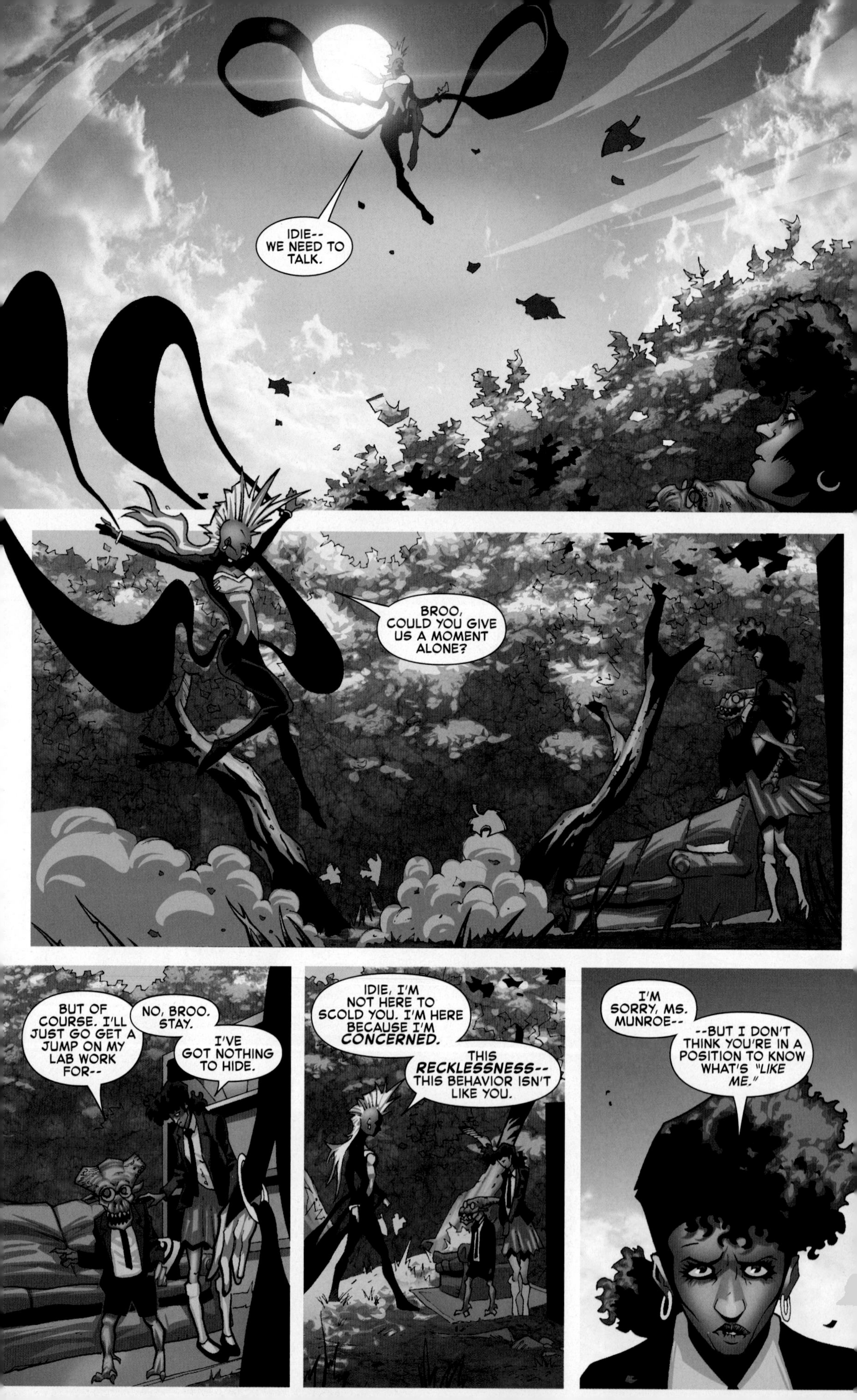
IDIE--
WE NEED TO
TALK.
BROO,
COULD YOU GIVE
US A MOMENT
ALONE?
BUT OF
COURSE. I'LL
JUST GO GET A
JUMP ON MY
LAB WORK
FOR--
NO, BROO.
STAY.
I'VE
GOT NOTHING
TO HIDE.
IDIE, I'M
NOT HERE TO
SCOLD YOU. I'M HERE
BECAUSE I'M
CONCERNED.
THIS
RECKLESSNESS--
THIS BEHAVIOR ISN'T
LIKE YOU.
I'M
SORRY, MS.
MUNROE--
--BUT I DON'T
THINK YOU'RE IN A
POSITION TO KNOW
WHAT'S *"LIKE
ME."*

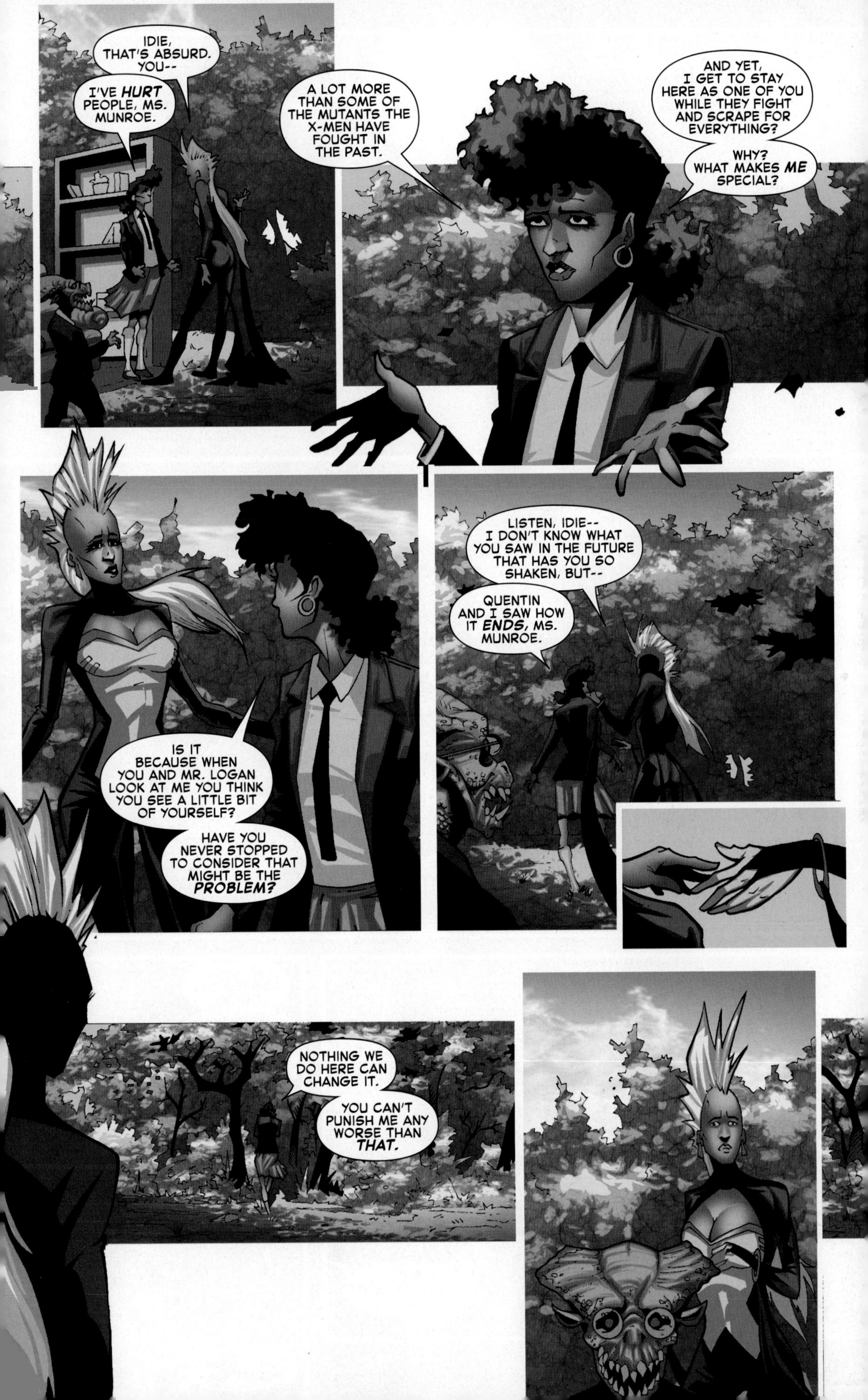
IDIE, THAT'S ABSURD. YOU--
I'VE **HURT** PEOPLE, MS. MUNROE.
A LOT MORE THAN SOME OF THE MUTANTS THE X-MEN HAVE FOUGHT IN THE PAST.
AND YET, I GET TO STAY HERE AS ONE OF YOU WHILE THEY FIGHT AND SCRAPE FOR EVERYTHING?
WHY? WHAT MAKES **ME** SPECIAL?
IS IT BECAUSE WHEN YOU AND MR. LOGAN LOOK AT ME YOU THINK YOU SEE A LITTLE BIT OF YOURSELF?
HAVE YOU NEVER STOPPED TO CONSIDER THAT MIGHT BE THE **PROBLEM?**
LISTEN, IDIE-- I DON'T KNOW WHAT YOU SAW IN THE FUTURE THAT HAS YOU SO SHAKEN, BUT--
QUENTIN AND I SAW HOW IT **ENDS**, MS. MUNROE.
NOTHING WE DO HERE CAN CHANGE IT.
YOU CAN'T PUNISH ME ANY WORSE THAN **THAT.**

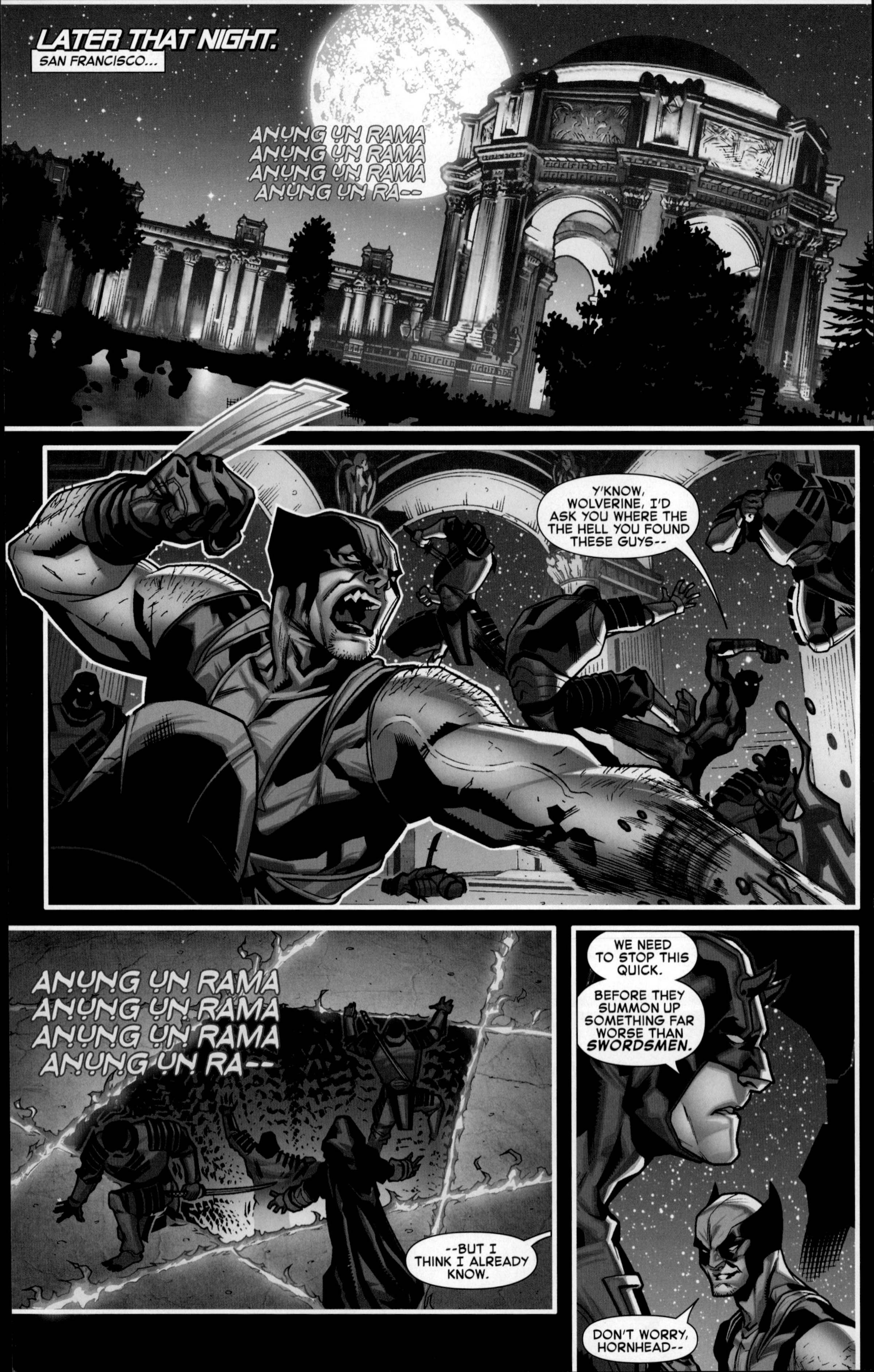
LATER THAT NIGHT.
SAN FRANCISCO...
ANUNG UN RAMA
ANUNG UN RAMA
ANUNG UN RAMA
ANUNG UN RA--
Y'KNOW, WOLVERINE, I'D ASK YOU WHERE THE THE HELL YOU FOUND THESE GUYS--
ANUNG UN RAMA
ANUNG UN RAMA
ANUNG UN RAMA
ANUNG UN RA--
--BUT I THINK I ALREADY KNOW.
WE NEED TO STOP THIS QUICK.
BEFORE THEY SUMMON UP SOMETHING FAR WORSE THAN SWORDSMEN.
DON'T WORRY, HORNHEAD--

--WE GOT A DEMON OF OUR OWN.

ᴖᴖᴖ ᴌᴧ ᴕᴖᴖᴙᴼ ᴳᴖᴑᴑ ᴑᴇ ᴥ ᴥᴖᴖᴖᴖᴧᴧᴧᴛ᷍ᴛ᷍ᴛ᷍ᴦᴦᴦᴦᴼᴼ

ANUNG UN RAMAAAAAAAHHHHHHHHHH!

YOINK

BLOOMPH

MY GOD, LOGAN, THAT PIT SWALLOWED THEM...ARE YOU SURE HE'LL--

DOOP?

DOOP'S FINE.

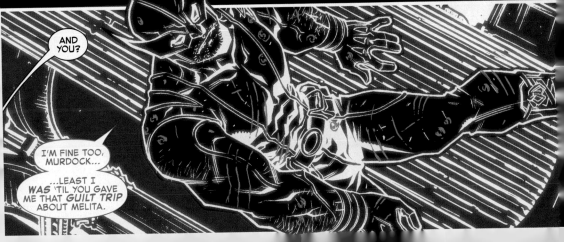

AND YOU?

I'M FINE TOO, MURDOCK...

...LEAST I WAS 'TIL YOU GAVE ME THAT GUILT TRIP ABOUT MELITA.

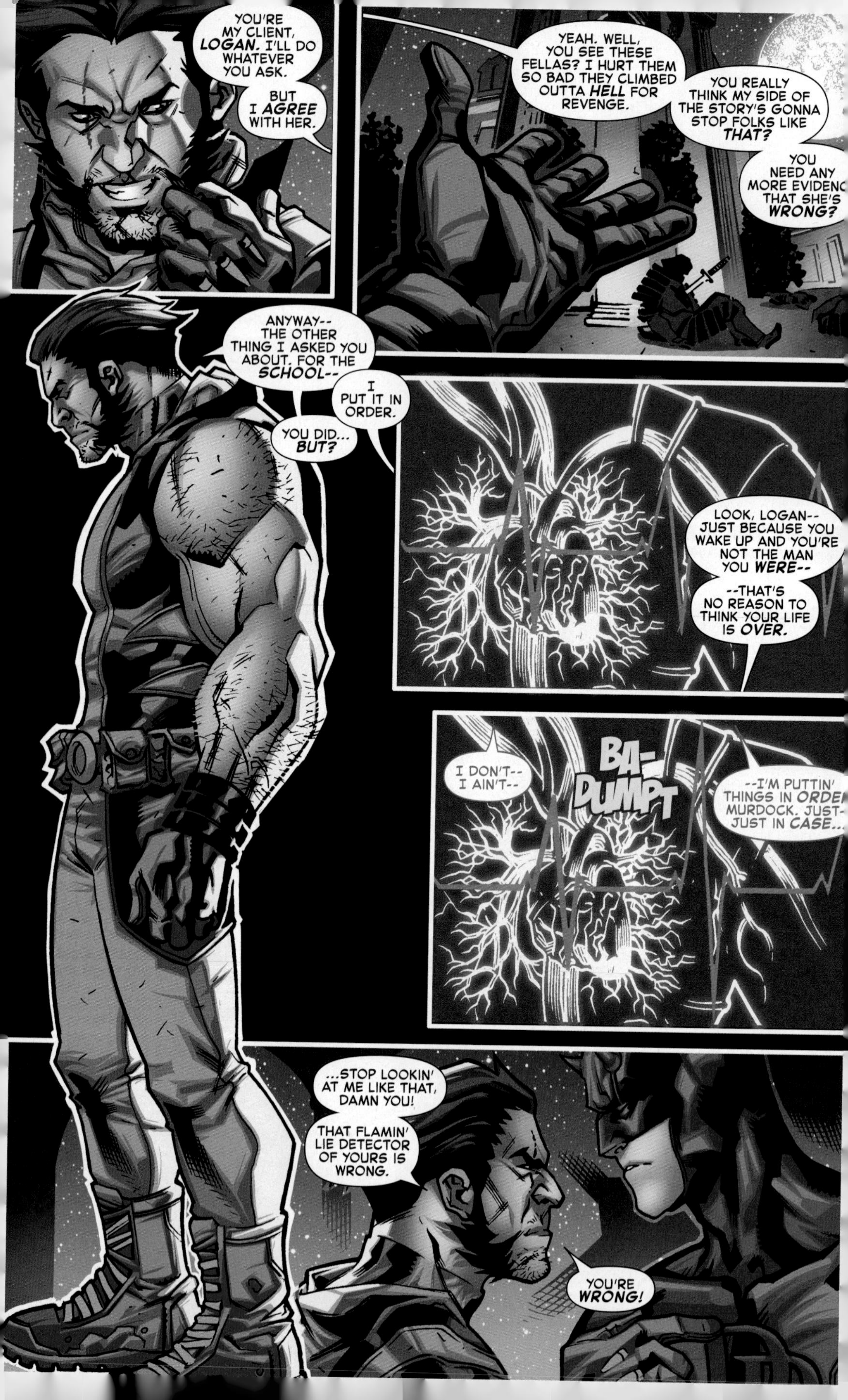
YOU'RE MY CLIENT, LOGAN. I'LL DO WHATEVER YOU ASK.
BUT I AGREE WITH HER.
YEAH. WELL, YOU SEE THESE FELLAS? I HURT THEM SO BAD THEY CLIMBED OUTTA HELL FOR REVENGE.
YOU REALLY THINK MY SIDE OF THE STORY'S GONNA STOP FOLKS LIKE THAT?
YOU NEED ANY MORE EVIDENC THAT SHE'S WRONG?
ANYWAY-- THE OTHER THING I ASKED YOU ABOUT. FOR THE SCHOOL--
I PUT IT IN ORDER.
YOU DID... BUT?
LOOK, LOGAN-- JUST BECAUSE YOU WAKE UP AND YOU'RE NOT THE MAN YOU WERE--
--THAT'S NO REASON TO THINK YOUR LIFE IS OVER.
I DON'T-- I AIN'T--
BA-DUMPT
--I'M PUTTIN' THINGS IN ORDE MURDOCK. JUST-- JUST IN CASE...
...STOP LOOKIN' AT ME LIKE THAT, DAMN YOU!
THAT FLAMIN' LIE DETECTOR OF YOURS IS WRONG.
YOU'RE WRONG!

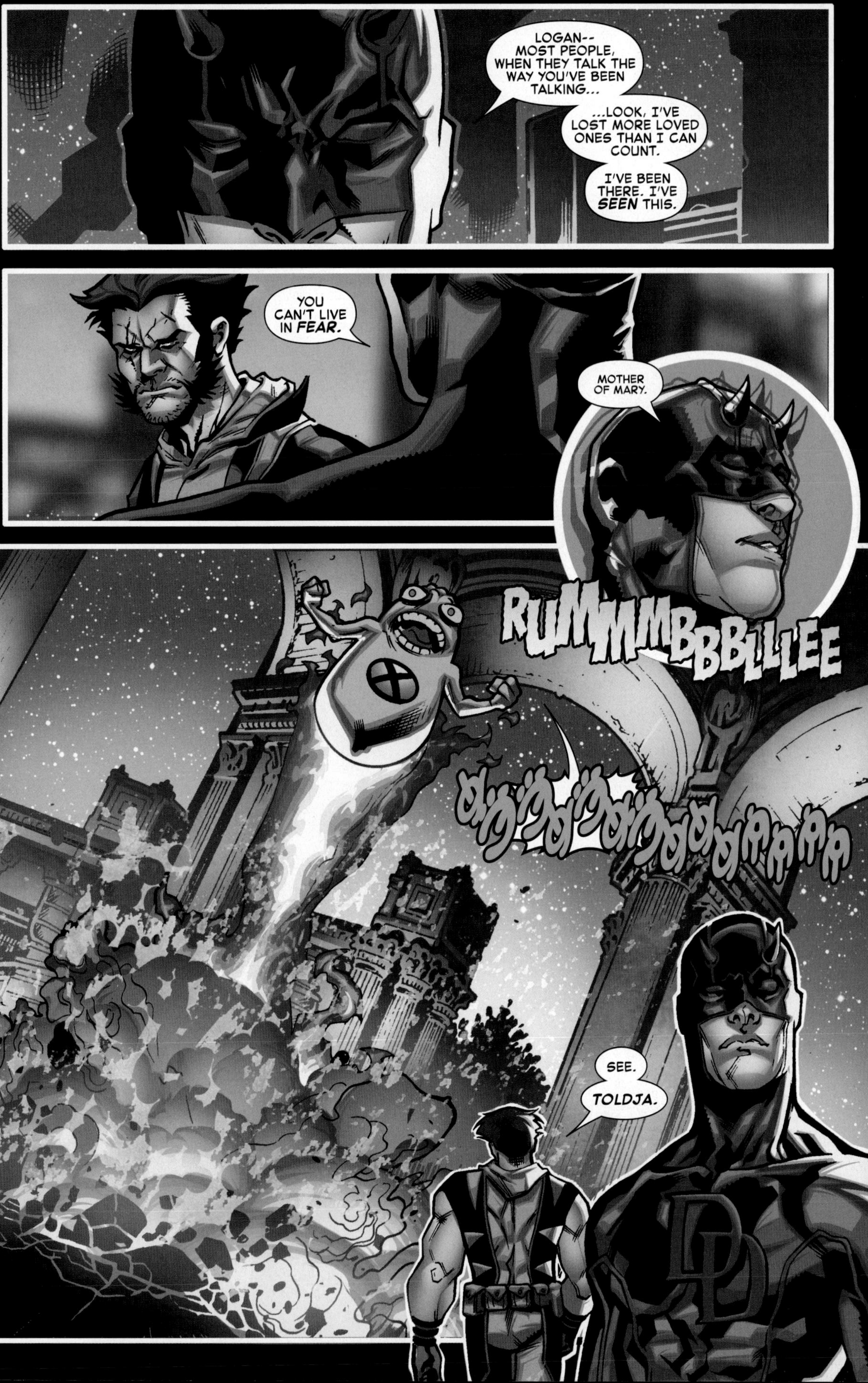
LOGAN-- MOST PEOPLE, WHEN THEY TALK THE WAY YOU'VE BEEN TALKING...
...LOOK, I'VE LOST MORE LOVED ONES THAN I CAN COUNT.
I'VE BEEN THERE. I'VE *SEEN* THIS.
YOU CAN'T LIVE IN *FEAR.*
MOTHER OF MARY.
RUMMMMBBBLLLEE
SEE.
TOLDJA.

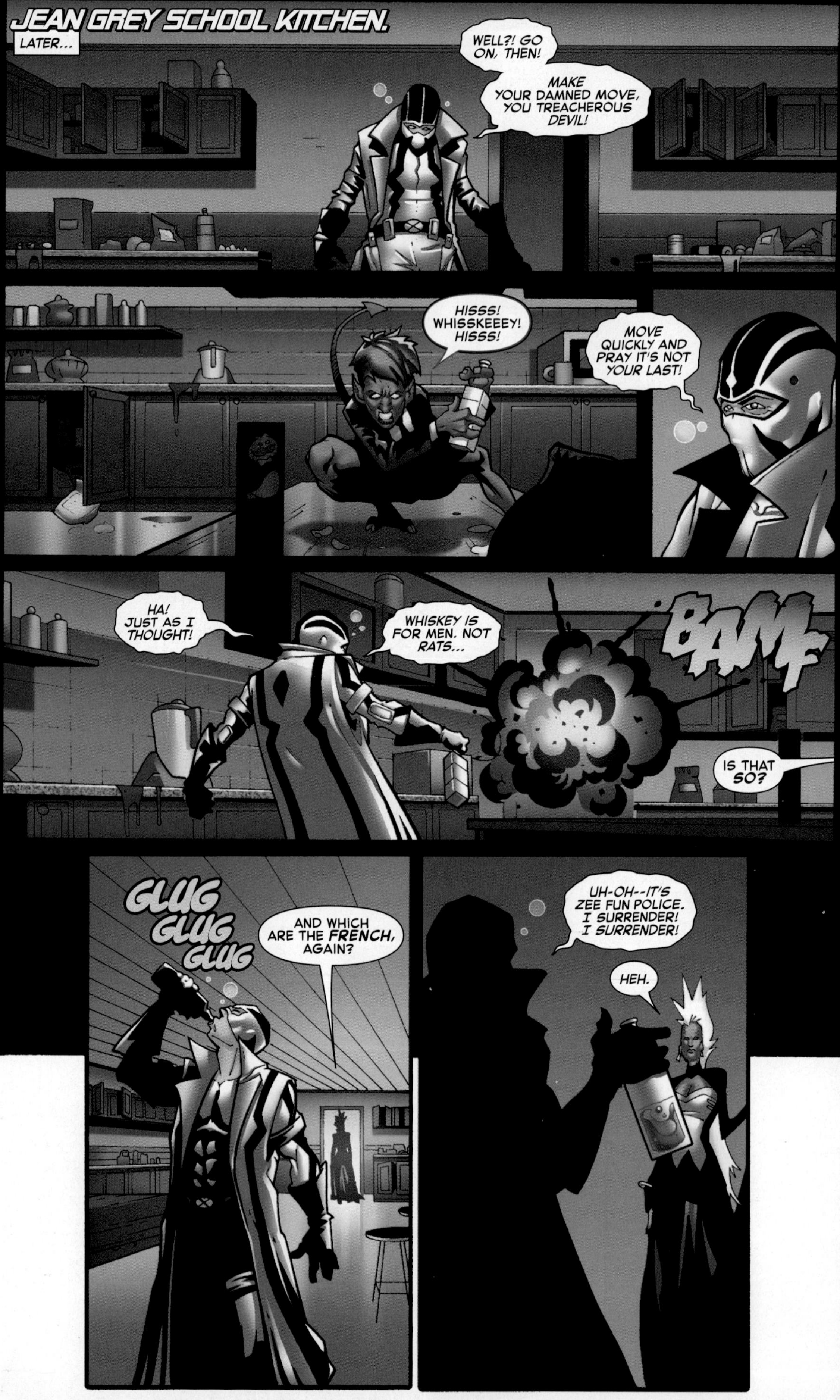
JEAN GREY SCHOOL KITCHEN.
LATER...
WELL?! GO ON, THEN!
MAKE YOUR DAMNED MOVE, YOU TREACHEROUS DEVIL!
HISSS! WHISSKEEEY! HISSS!
MOVE QUICKLY AND PRAY IT'S NOT YOUR LAST!
HA! JUST AS I THOUGHT!
WHISKEY IS FOR MEN. NOT RATS...
BAMF
IS THAT SO?
GLUG GLUG GLUG
AND WHICH ARE THE FRENCH, AGAIN?
UH-OH--IT'S ZEE FUN POLICE. I SURRENDER! I SURRENDER!
HEH.

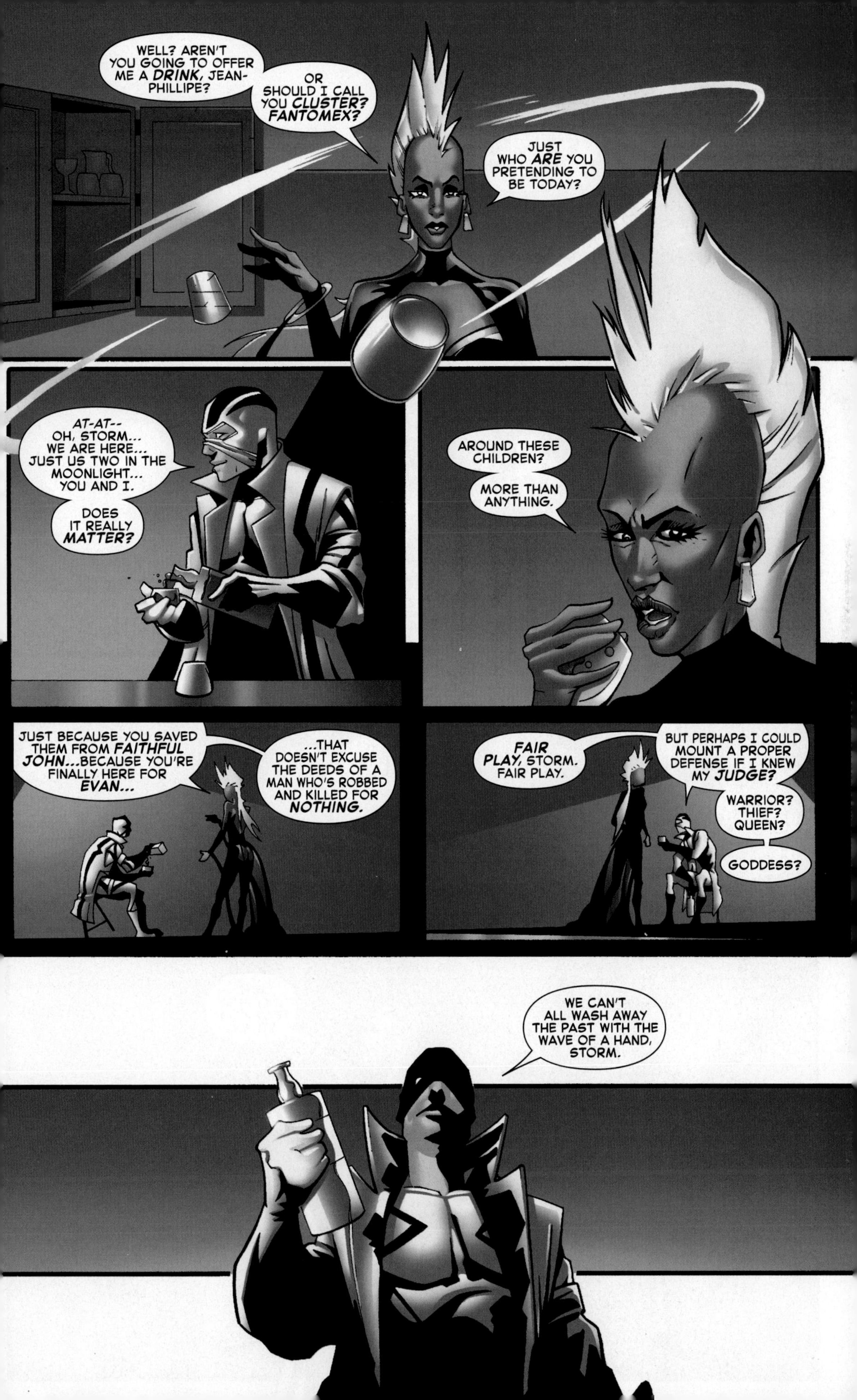
WELL? AREN'T YOU GOING TO OFFER ME A DRINK, JEAN-PHILLIPE?
OR SHOULD I CALL YOU CLUSTER? FANTOMEX?
JUST WHO ARE YOU PRETENDING TO BE TODAY?
AT-AT-- OH, STORM... WE ARE HERE... JUST US TWO IN THE MOONLIGHT... YOU AND I.
DOES IT REALLY MATTER?
AROUND THESE CHILDREN?
MORE THAN ANYTHING.
JUST BECAUSE YOU SAVED THEM FROM FAITHFUL JOHN...BECAUSE YOU'RE FINALLY HERE FOR EVAN...
...THAT DOESN'T EXCUSE THE DEEDS OF A MAN WHO'S ROBBED AND KILLED FOR NOTHING.
FAIR PLAY, STORM. FAIR PLAY.
BUT PERHAPS I COULD MOUNT A PROPER DEFENSE IF I KNEW MY JUDGE?
WARRIOR? THIEF? QUEEN?
GODDESS?
WE CAN'T ALL WASH AWAY THE PAST WITH THE WAVE OF A HAND, STORM.

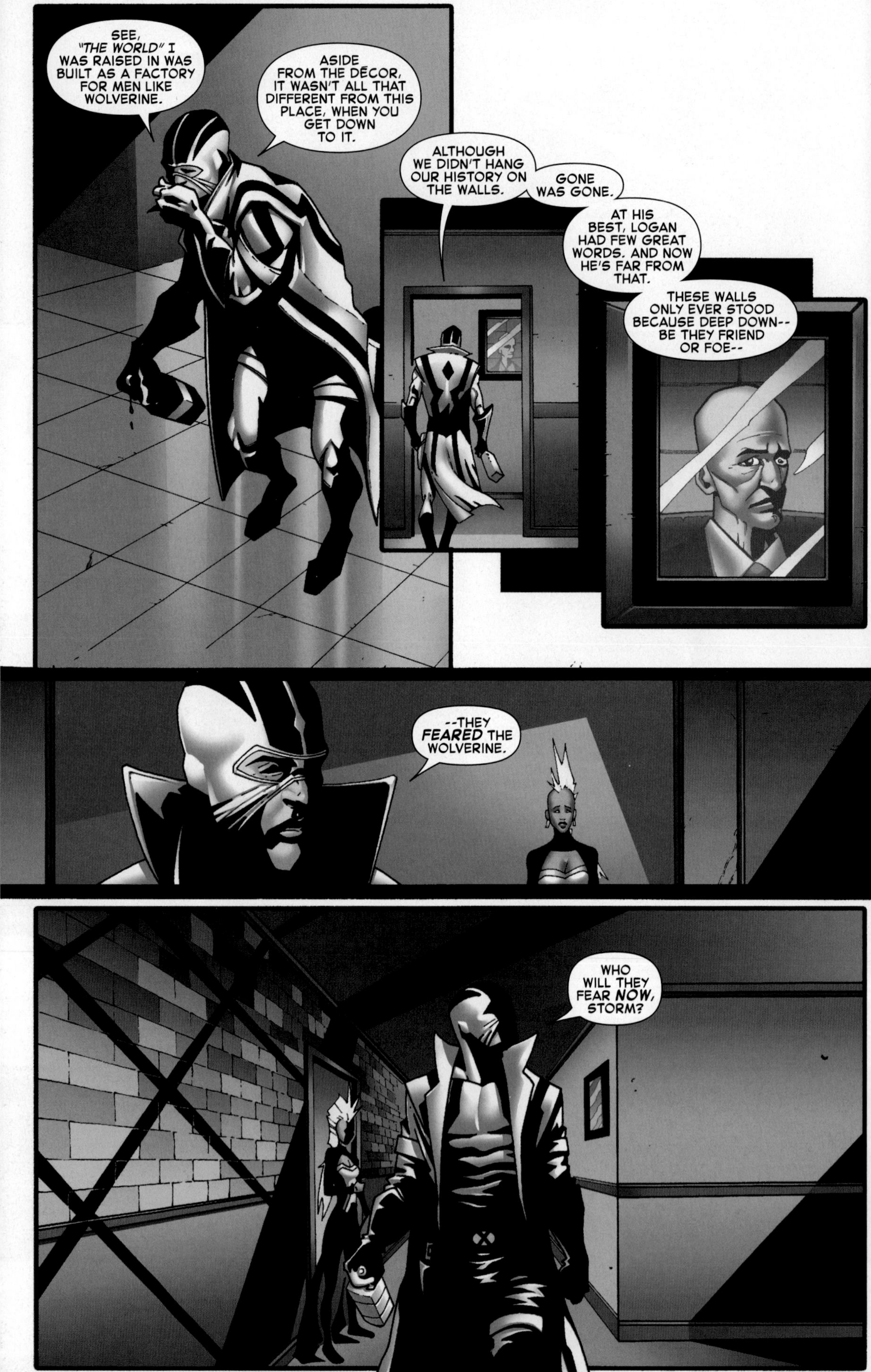
SEE, "THE WORLD" I WAS RAISED IN WAS BUILT AS A FACTORY FOR MEN LIKE WOLVERINE.
ASIDE FROM THE DÉCOR, IT WASN'T ALL THAT DIFFERENT FROM THIS PLACE, WHEN YOU GET DOWN TO IT.
ALTHOUGH WE DIDN'T HANG OUR HISTORY ON THE WALLS.
GONE WAS GONE.
AT HIS BEST, LOGAN HAD FEW GREAT WORDS. AND NOW HE'S FAR FROM THAT.
THESE WALLS ONLY EVER STOOD BECAUSE DEEP DOWN-- BE THEY FRIEND OR FOE--
--THEY FEARED THE WOLVERINE.
WHO WILL THEY FEAR NOW, STORM?

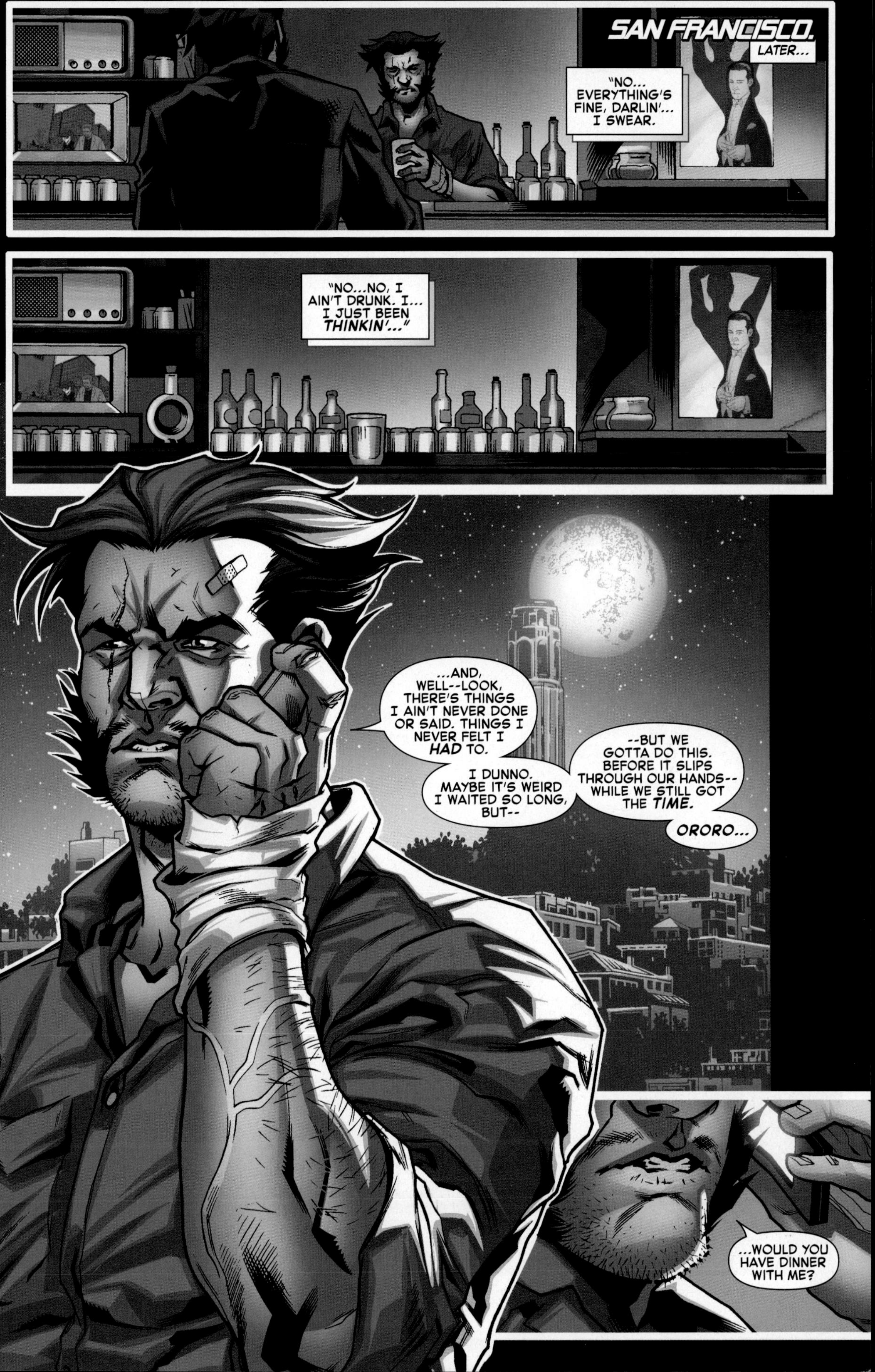
SAN FRANCISCO.
LATER...
"NO... EVERYTHING'S FINE, DARLIN'... I SWEAR.
"NO...NO, I AIN'T DRUNK. I... I JUST BEEN THINKIN'..."
...AND, WELL--LOOK, THERE'S THINGS I AIN'T NEVER DONE OR SAID. THINGS I NEVER FELT I HAD TO.
I DUNNO. MAYBE IT'S WEIRD I WAITED SO LONG, BUT--
--BUT WE GOTTA DO THIS. BEFORE IT SLIPS THROUGH OUR HANDS--WHILE WE STILL GOT THE TIME.
ORORO...
...WOULD YOU HAVE DINNER WITH ME?

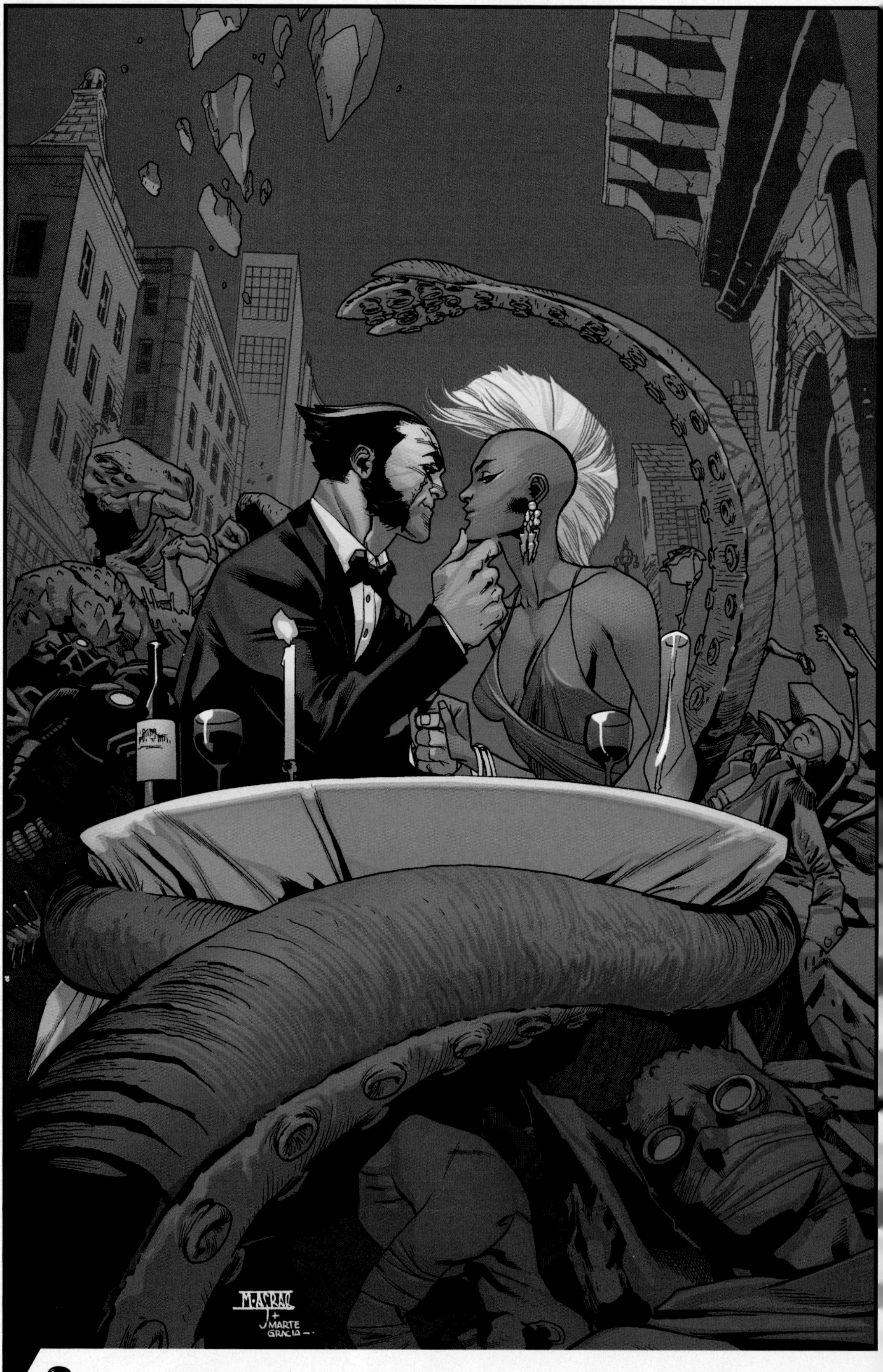
M·ASRAR
+ MARTE GRACIA

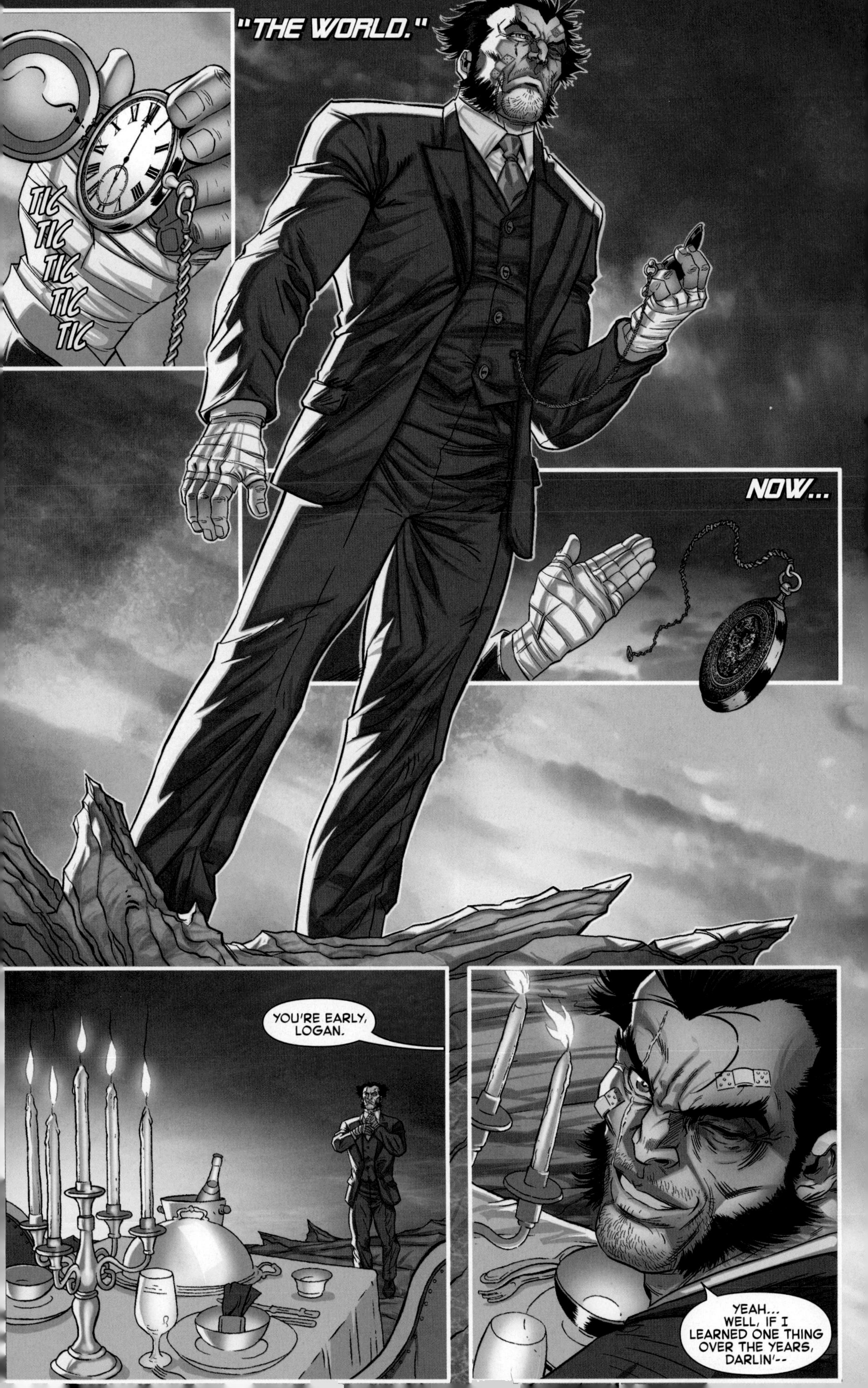
TIC
TIC
TIC
TIC
TIC
"THE WORLD."
NOW...
YOU'RE EARLY, LOGAN.
YEAH... WELL, IF I LEARNED ONE THING OVER THE YEARS, DARLIN'--

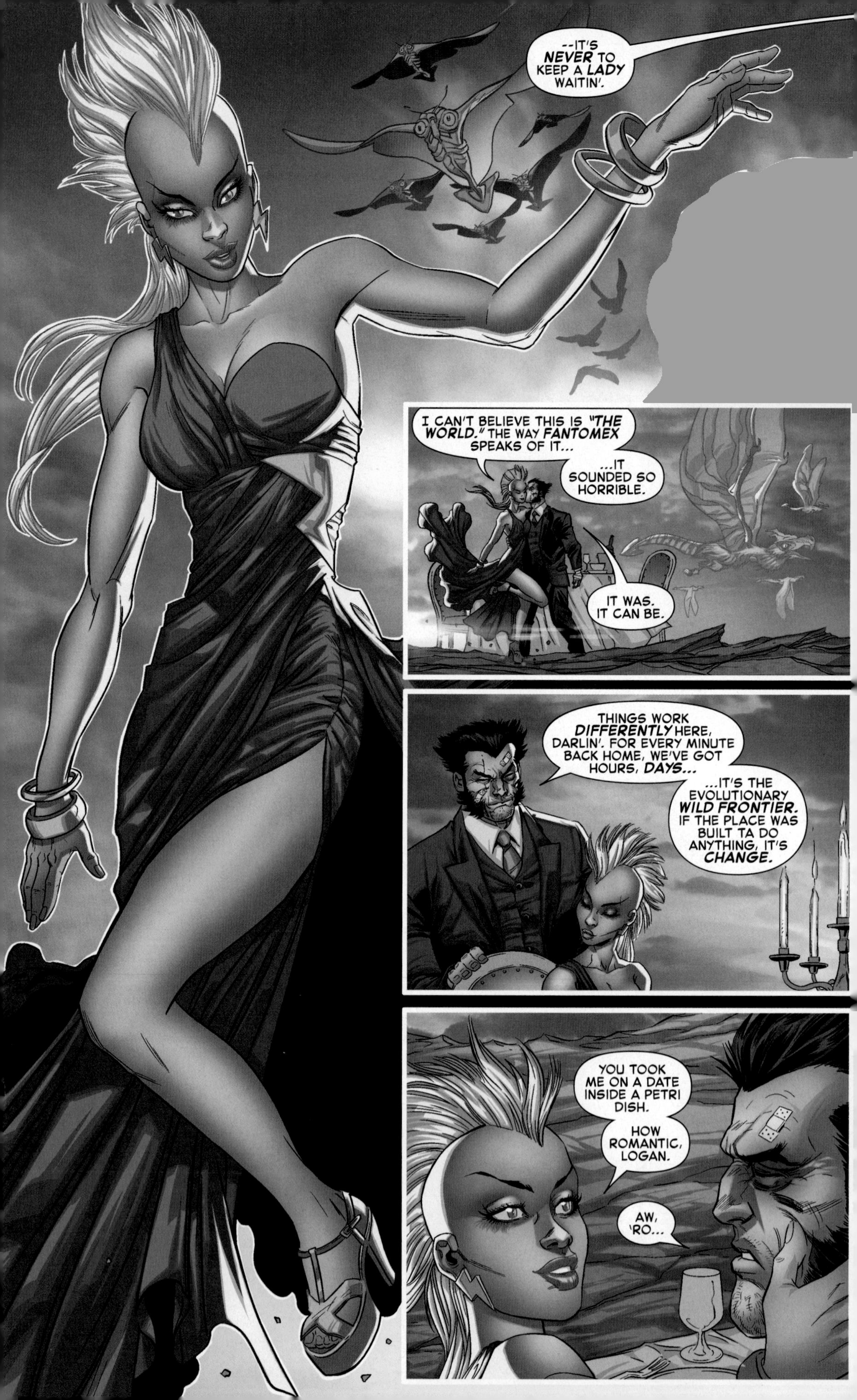
--IT'S NEVER TO KEEP A LADY WAITIN'.
I CAN'T BELIEVE THIS IS "THE WORLD." THE WAY FANTOMEX SPEAKS OF IT...
...IT SOUNDED SO HORRIBLE.
IT WAS. IT CAN BE.
THINGS WORK DIFFERENTLY HERE, DARLIN'. FOR EVERY MINUTE BACK HOME, WE'VE GOT HOURS, DAYS...
...IT'S THE EVOLUTIONARY WILD FRONTIER. IF THE PLACE WAS BUILT TA DO ANYTHING, IT'S CHANGE.
YOU TOOK ME ON A DATE INSIDE A PETRI DISH.
HOW ROMANTIC, LOGAN.
AW, 'RO...

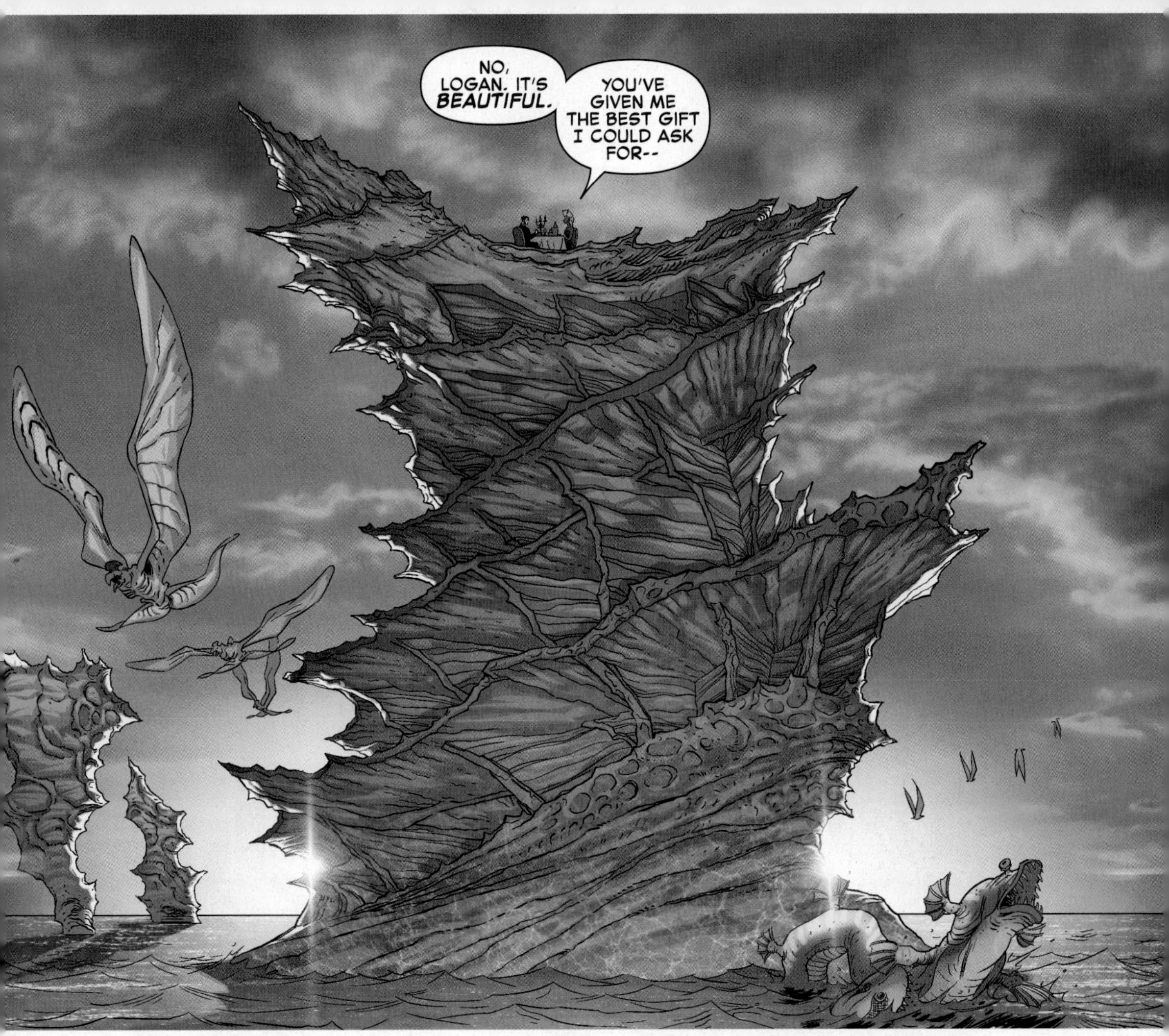
NO, LOGAN. IT'S BEAUTIFUL.
YOU'VE GIVEN ME THE BEST GIFT I COULD ASK FOR--

NO FUTURE?
PART 2

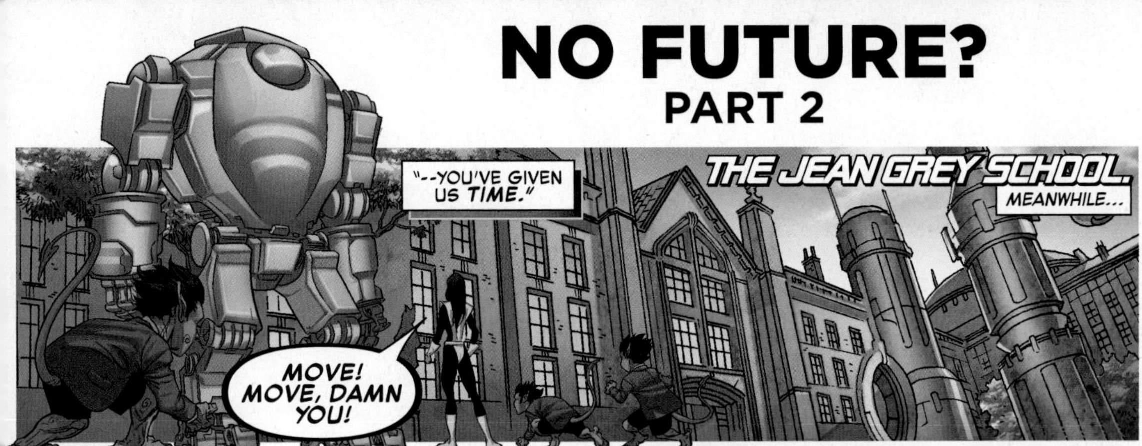
THE JEAN GREY SCHOOL.
MEANWHILE...
"--YOU'VE GIVEN US TIME."
MOVE! MOVE, DAMN YOU!

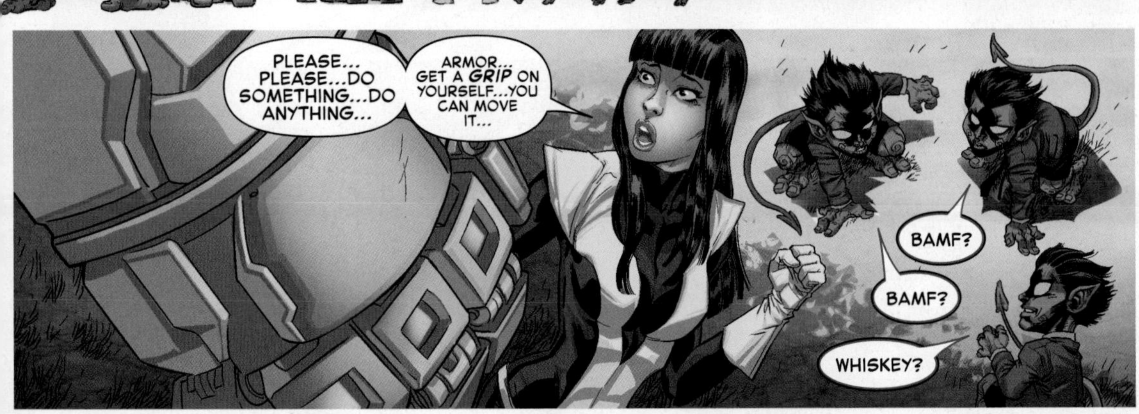
PLEASE... PLEASE...DO SOMETHING...DO ANYTHING...
ARMOR... GET A GRIP ON YOURSELF...YOU CAN MOVE IT...
BAMF?
BAMF?
WHISKEY?

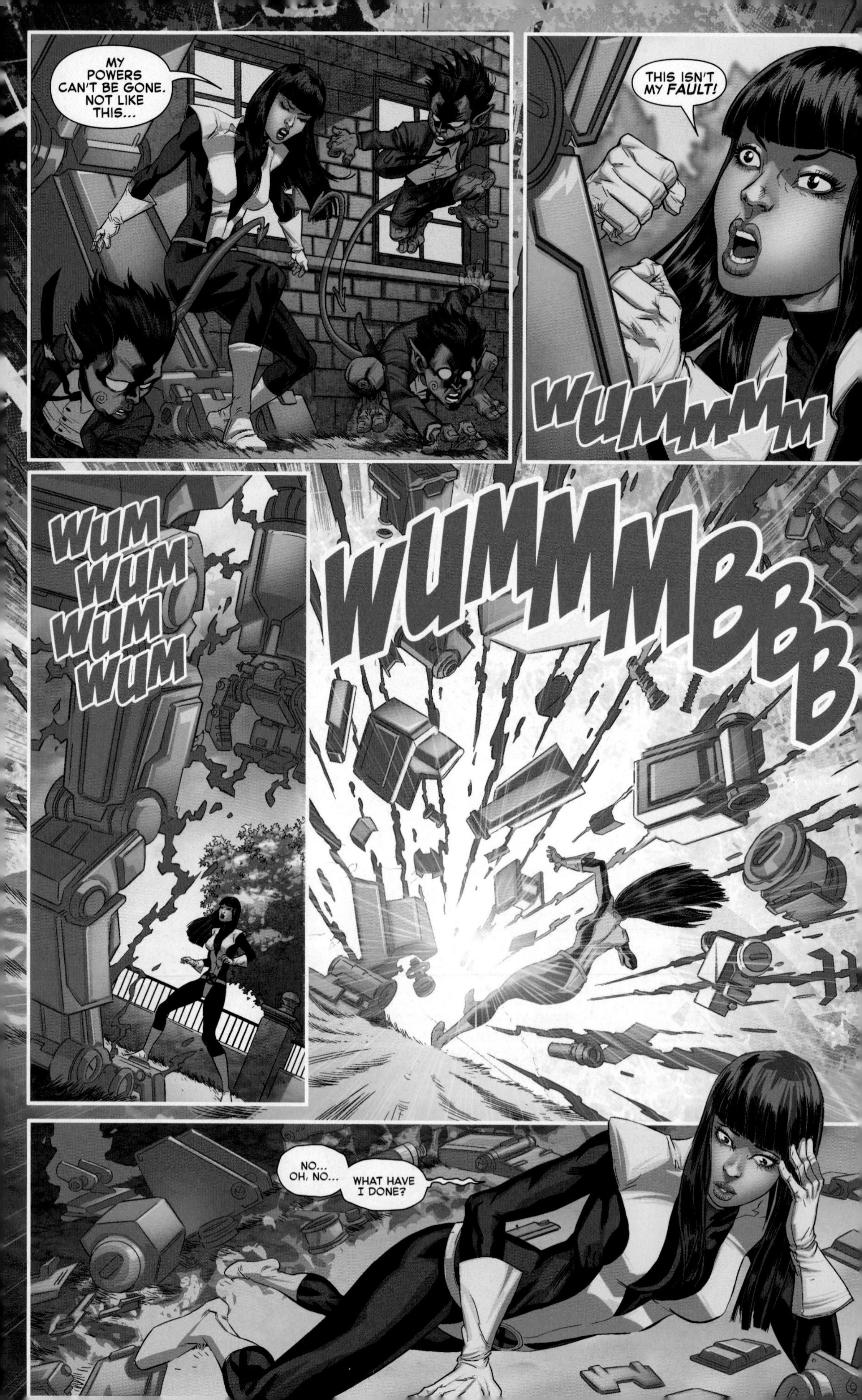

MY POWERS CAN'T BE GONE. NOT LIKE THIS...
THIS ISN'T MY FAULT!
WUMMMMM
WUM WUM WUM WUM
WUMMMBBB
NO... OH, NO...
WHAT HAVE I DONE?

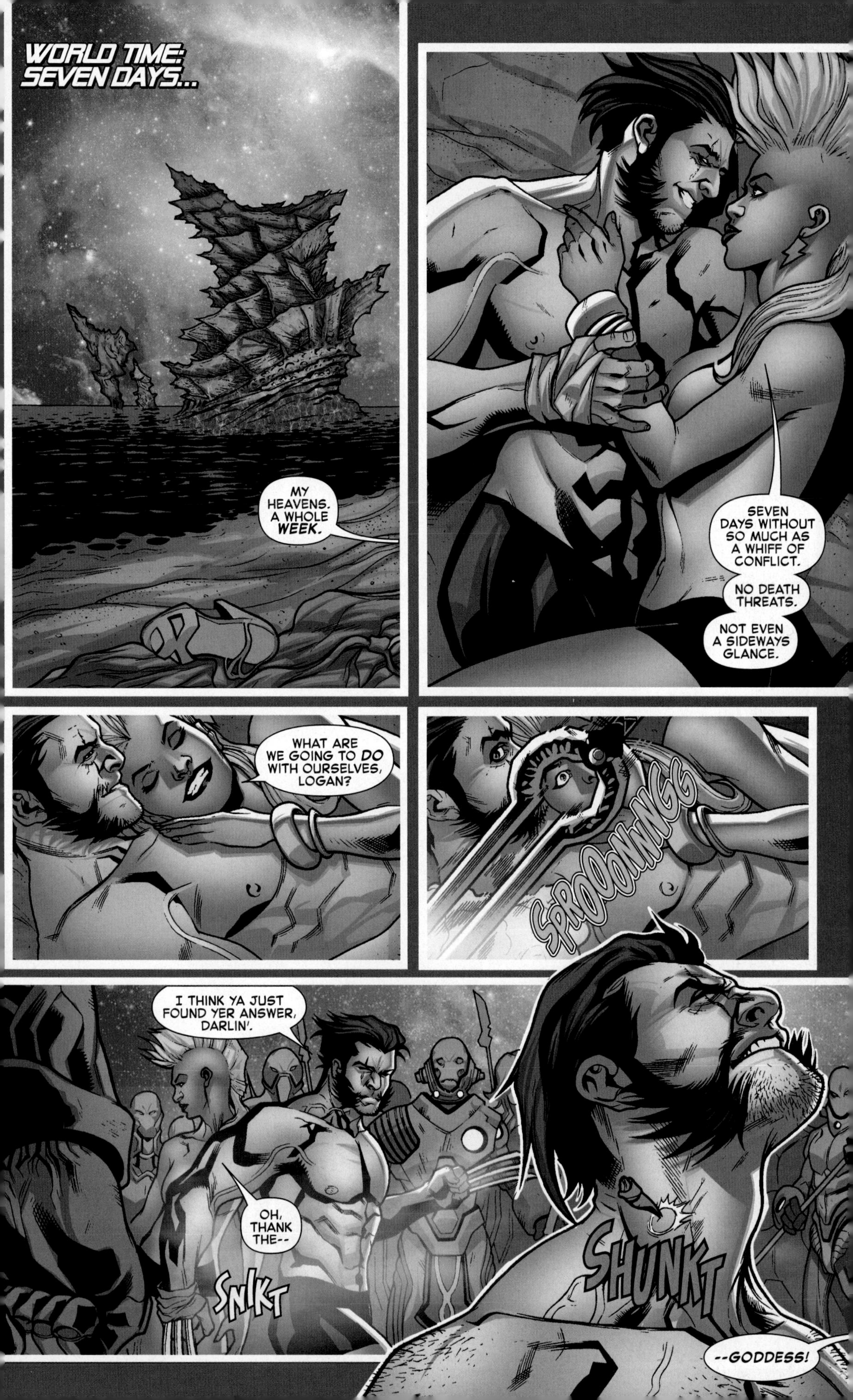
WORLD TIME: SEVEN DAYS...
MY HEAVENS. A WHOLE WEEK.
SEVEN DAYS WITHOUT SO MUCH AS A WHIFF OF CONFLICT.
NO DEATH THREATS.
NOT EVEN A SIDEWAYS GLANCE.
WHAT ARE WE GOING TO DO WITH OURSELVES, LOGAN?
SPROOONNGG
I THINK YA JUST FOUND YER ANSWER, DARLIN'.
OH, THANK THE--
SNIKT
SHUNKT
--GODDESS!

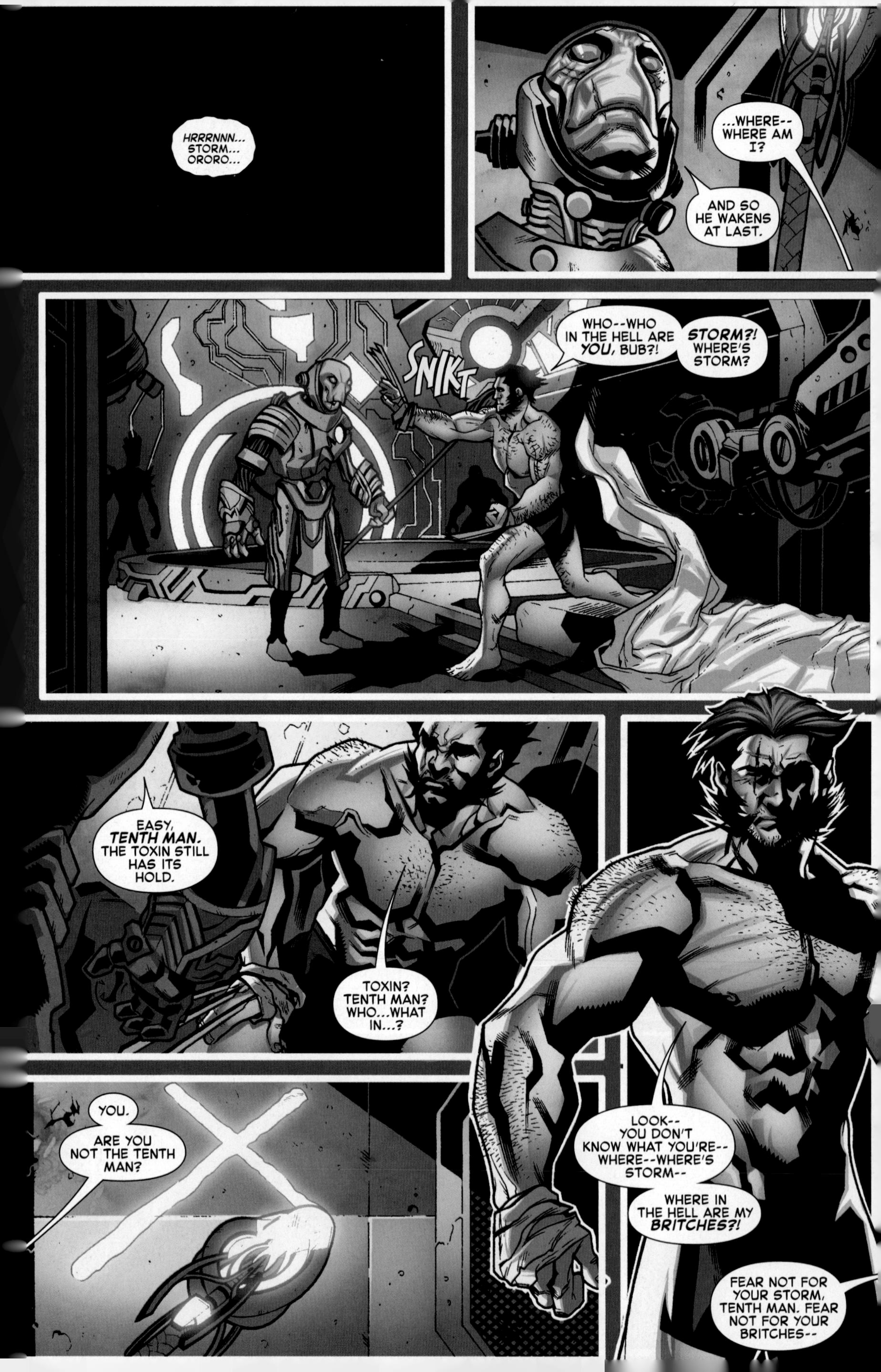
HRRRNNN... STORM... ORORO...
...WHERE-- WHERE AM I?
AND SO HE WAKENS AT LAST.
SNIKT
WHO--WHO IN THE HELL ARE *YOU*, BUB?!
STORM?! WHERE'S STORM?
EASY, *TENTH MAN.* THE TOXIN STILL HAS ITS HOLD.
TOXIN? TENTH MAN? WHO...WHAT IN...?
YOU.
ARE YOU NOT THE TENTH MAN?
LOOK-- YOU DON'T KNOW WHAT YOU'RE-- WHERE--WHERE'S STORM--
WHERE IN THE HELL ARE MY *BRITCHES?!*
FEAR NOT FOR YOUR STORM, TENTH MAN. FEAR NOT FOR YOUR BRITCHES--

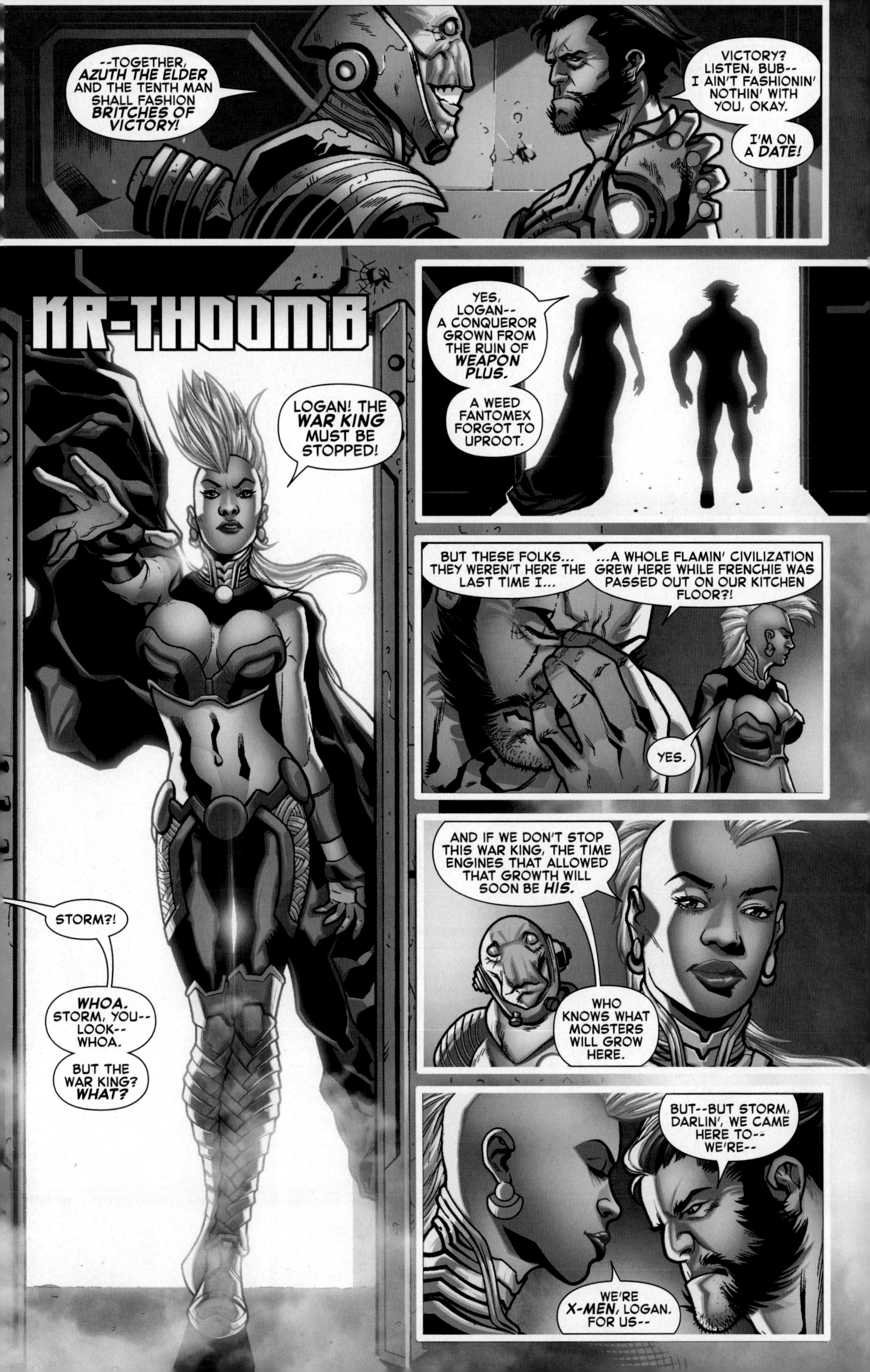

--TOGETHER, AZUTH THE ELDER AND THE TENTH MAN SHALL FASHION BRITCHES OF VICTORY!
VICTORY? LISTEN, BUB-- I AIN'T FASHIONIN' NOTHIN' WITH YOU, OKAY.
I'M ON A DATE!
KR-THOOMB
LOGAN! THE WAR KING MUST BE STOPPED!
STORM?!
WHOA. STORM, YOU-- LOOK-- WHOA.
BUT THE WAR KING? WHAT?
YES, LOGAN-- A CONQUEROR GROWN FROM THE RUIN OF WEAPON PLUS.
A WEED FANTOMEX FORGOT TO UPROOT.
BUT THESE FOLKS... THEY WEREN'T HERE THE LAST TIME I...
...A WHOLE FLAMIN' CIVILIZATION GREW HERE WHILE FRENCHIE WAS PASSED OUT ON OUR KITCHEN FLOOR?!
YES.
AND IF WE DON'T STOP THIS WAR KING, THE TIME ENGINES THAT ALLOWED THAT GROWTH WILL SOON BE HIS.
WHO KNOWS WHAT MONSTERS WILL GROW HERE.
BUT--BUT STORM, DARLIN', WE CAME HERE TO-- WE'RE--
WE'RE X-MEN, LOGAN. FOR US--

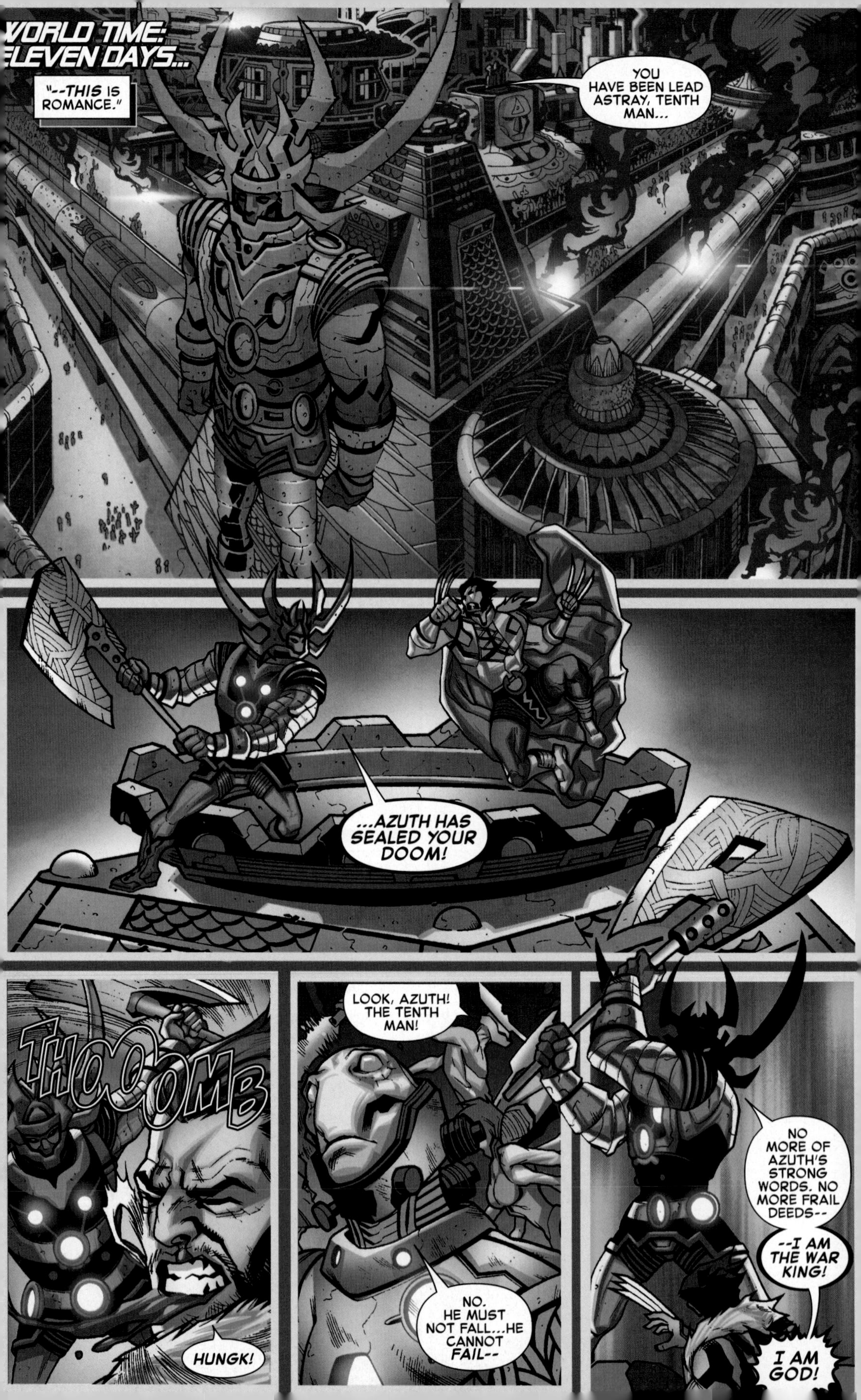
WORLD TIME: ELEVEN DAYS...
"--THIS IS ROMANCE."
YOU HAVE BEEN LEAD ASTRAY, TENTH MAN...
...AZUTH HAS SEALED YOUR DOOM!
THOOOOMB
HUNGK!
LOOK, AZUTH! THE TENTH MAN!
NO. HE MUST NOT FALL...HE CANNOT FAIL--
NO MORE OF AZUTH'S STRONG WORDS. NO MORE FRAIL DEEDS--
--I AM THE WAR KING!
I AM GOD!

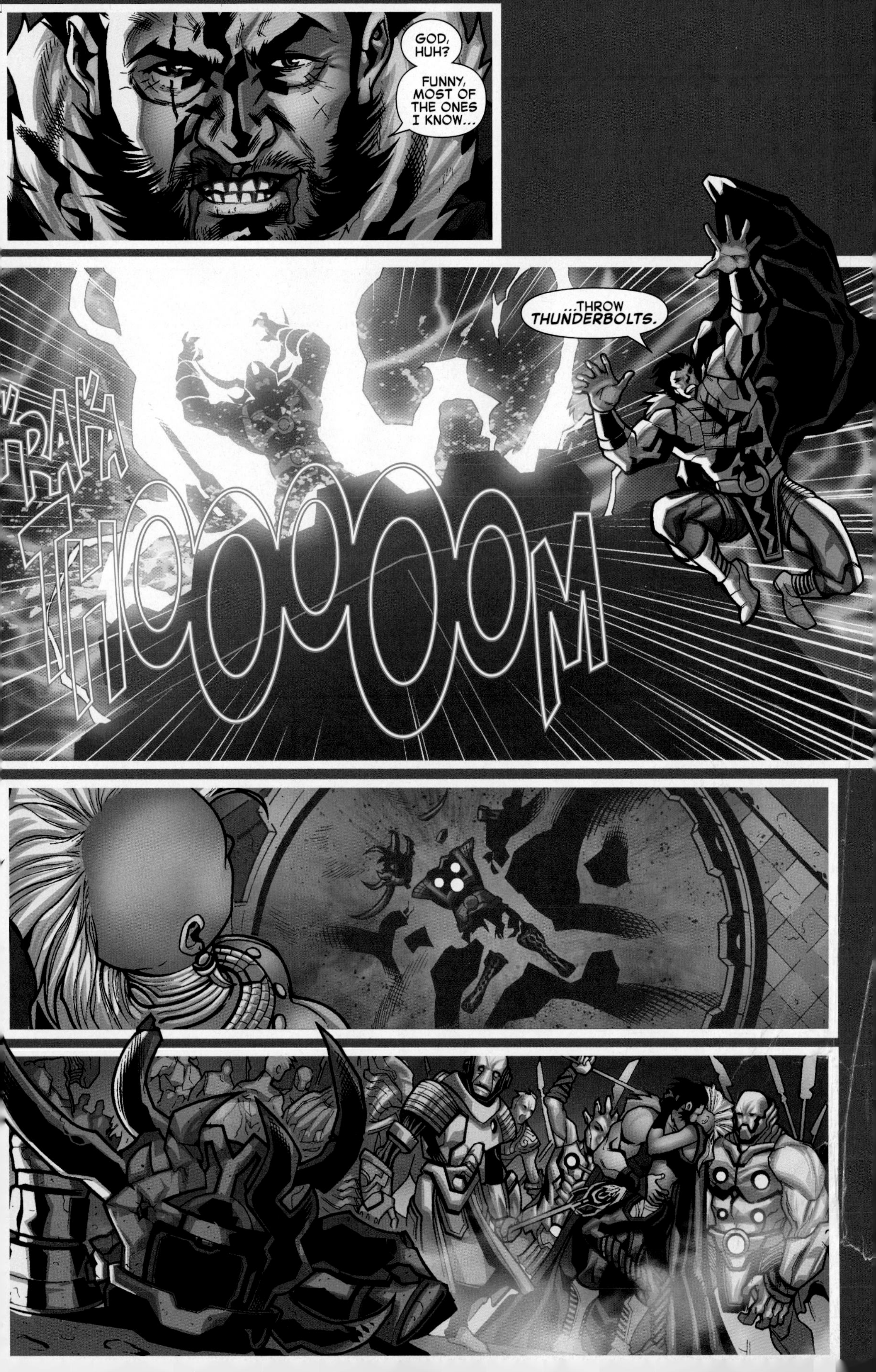
GOD, HUH?
FUNNY, MOST OF THE ONES I KNOW...
...THROW THUNDERBOLTS.
THOOOOOM

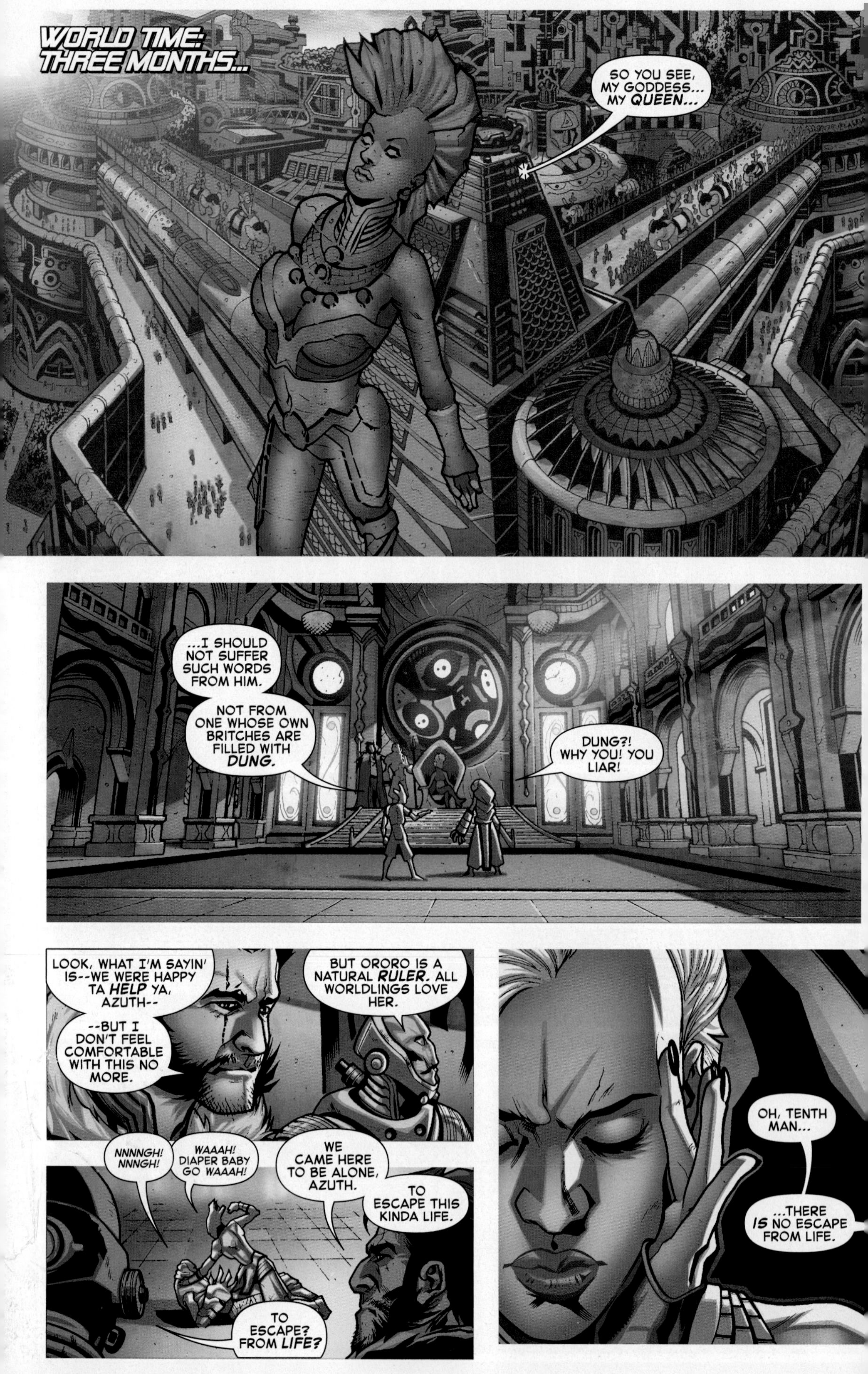
WORLD TIME: THREE MONTHS...
SO YOU SEE, MY GODDESS... MY QUEEN...
...I SHOULD NOT SUFFER SUCH WORDS FROM HIM.
NOT FROM ONE WHOSE OWN BRITCHES ARE FILLED WITH DUNG.
DUNG?! WHY YOU! YOU LIAR!
LOOK, WHAT I'M SAYIN' IS--WE WERE HAPPY TA HELP YA, AZUTH--
--BUT I DON'T FEEL COMFORTABLE WITH THIS NO MORE.
BUT ORORO IS A NATURAL RULER. ALL WORLDLINGS LOVE HER.
NNNNGH! NNNGH!
WAAAH! DIAPER BABY GO WAAAH!
WE CAME HERE TO BE ALONE, AZUTH.
TO ESCAPE THIS KINDA LIFE.
TO ESCAPE? FROM LIFE?
OH, TENTH MAN...
...THERE IS NO ESCAPE FROM LIFE.

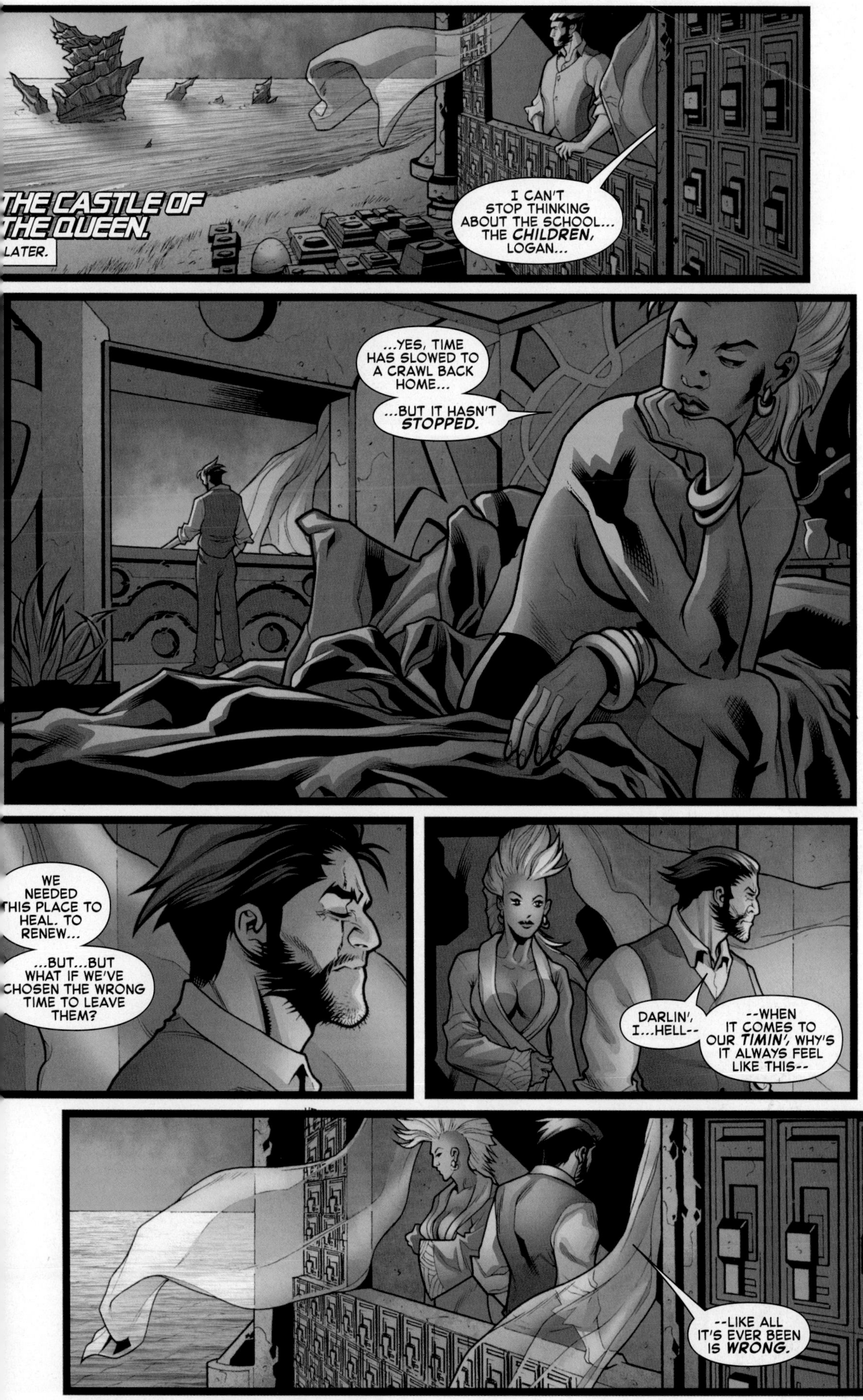
THE CASTLE OF THE QUEEN.
LATER.
I CAN'T STOP THINKING ABOUT THE SCHOOL... THE CHILDREN, LOGAN...
...YES, TIME HAS SLOWED TO A CRAWL BACK HOME...
...BUT IT HASN'T STOPPED.
WE NEEDED THIS PLACE TO HEAL. TO RENEW...
...BUT...BUT WHAT IF WE'VE CHOSEN THE WRONG TIME TO LEAVE THEM?
DARLIN', I...HELL--
--WHEN IT COMES TO OUR TIMIN', WHY'S IT ALWAYS FEEL LIKE THIS--
--LIKE ALL IT'S EVER BEEN IS WRONG.

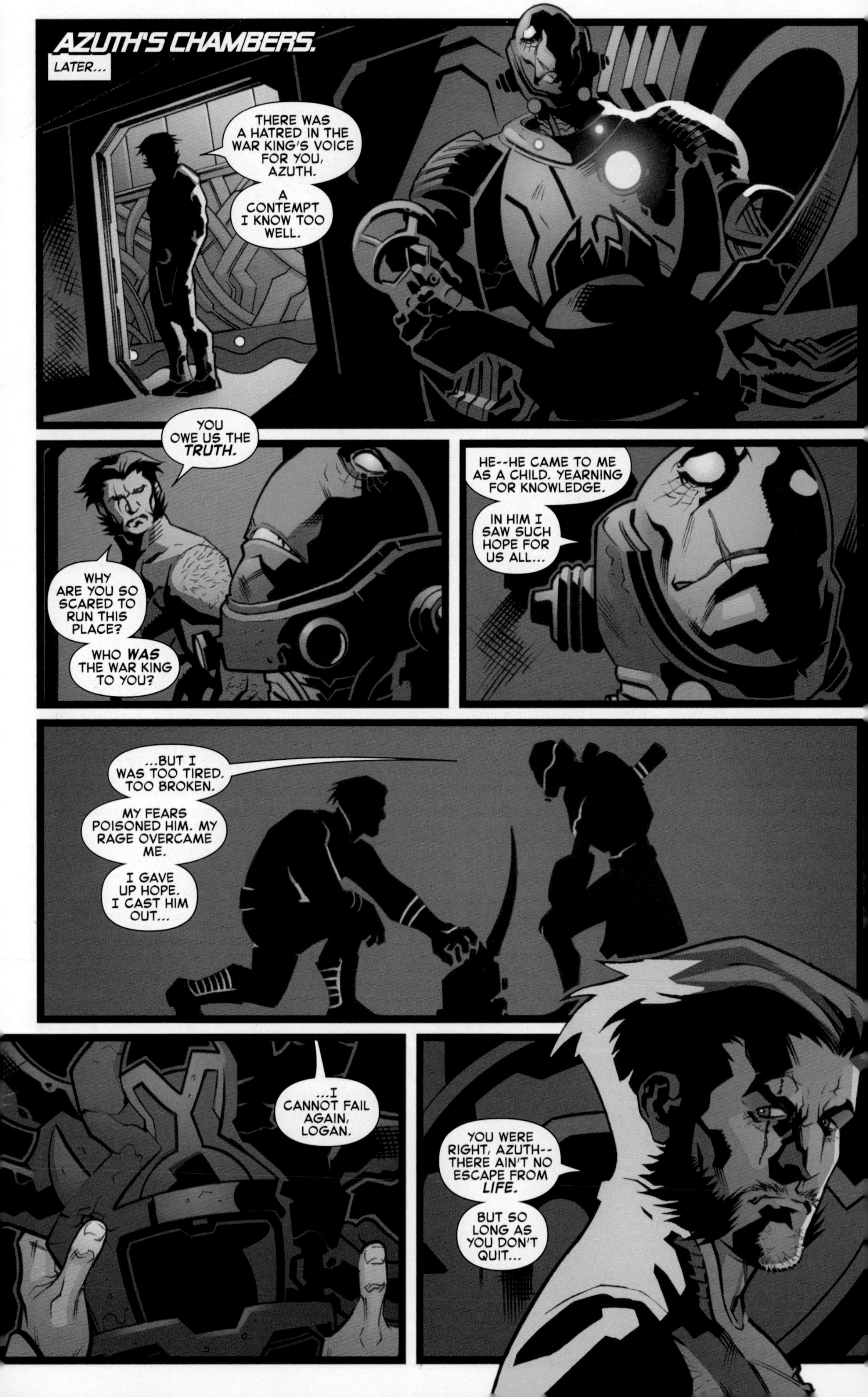
AZUTH'S CHAMBERS.
LATER...
THERE WAS A HATRED IN THE WAR KING'S VOICE FOR YOU, AZUTH.
A CONTEMPT I KNOW TOO WELL.
YOU OWE US THE TRUTH.
WHY ARE YOU SO SCARED TO RUN THIS PLACE?
WHO WAS THE WAR KING TO YOU?
HE--HE CAME TO ME AS A CHILD. YEARNING FOR KNOWLEDGE.
IN HIM I SAW SUCH HOPE FOR US ALL...
...BUT I WAS TOO TIRED. TOO BROKEN.
MY FEARS POISONED HIM. MY RAGE OVERCAME ME.
I GAVE UP HOPE. I CAST HIM OUT...
...I CANNOT FAIL AGAIN, LOGAN.
YOU WERE RIGHT, AZUTH-- THERE AIN'T NO ESCAPE FROM LIFE.
BUT SO LONG AS YOU DON'T QUIT...

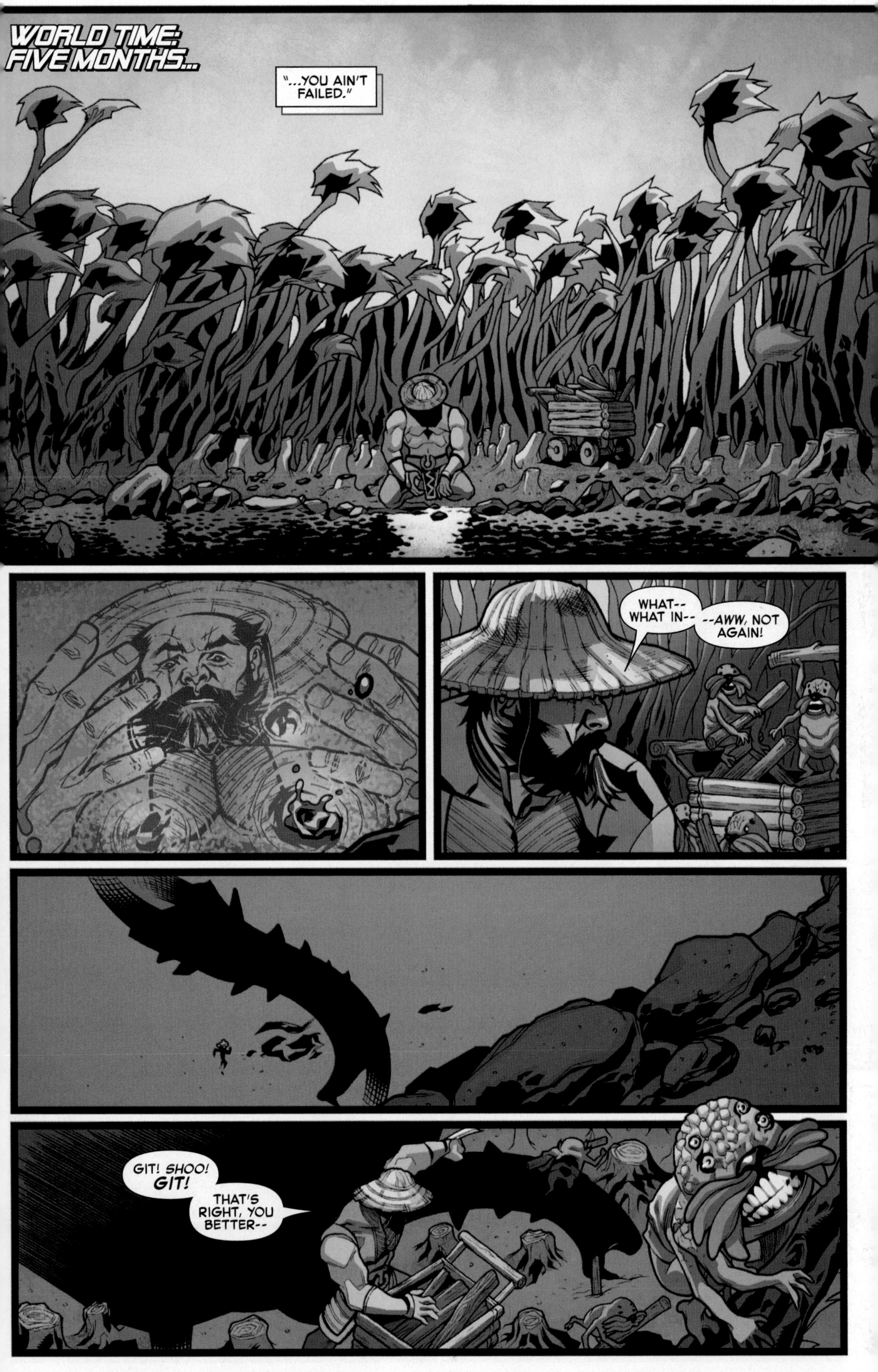
WORLD TIME:
FIVE MONTHS...
"...YOU AIN'T FAILED."
WHAT--
WHAT IN--
--AWW, NOT AGAIN!
GIT! SHOO!
GIT!
THAT'S RIGHT, YOU BETTER--

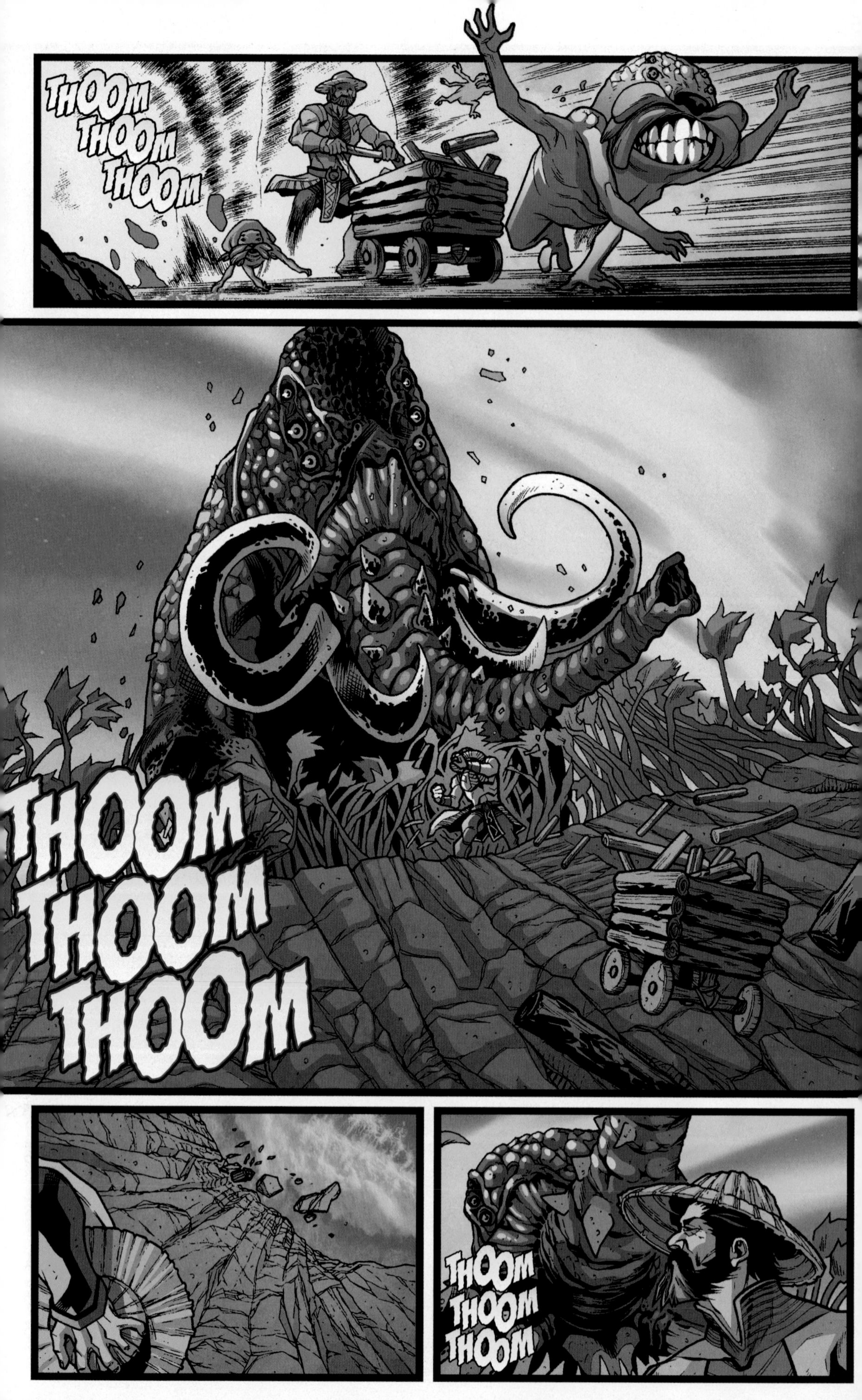
THOOM
THOOM
THOOM
THOOM
THOOM
THOOM
THOOM
THOOM
THOOM

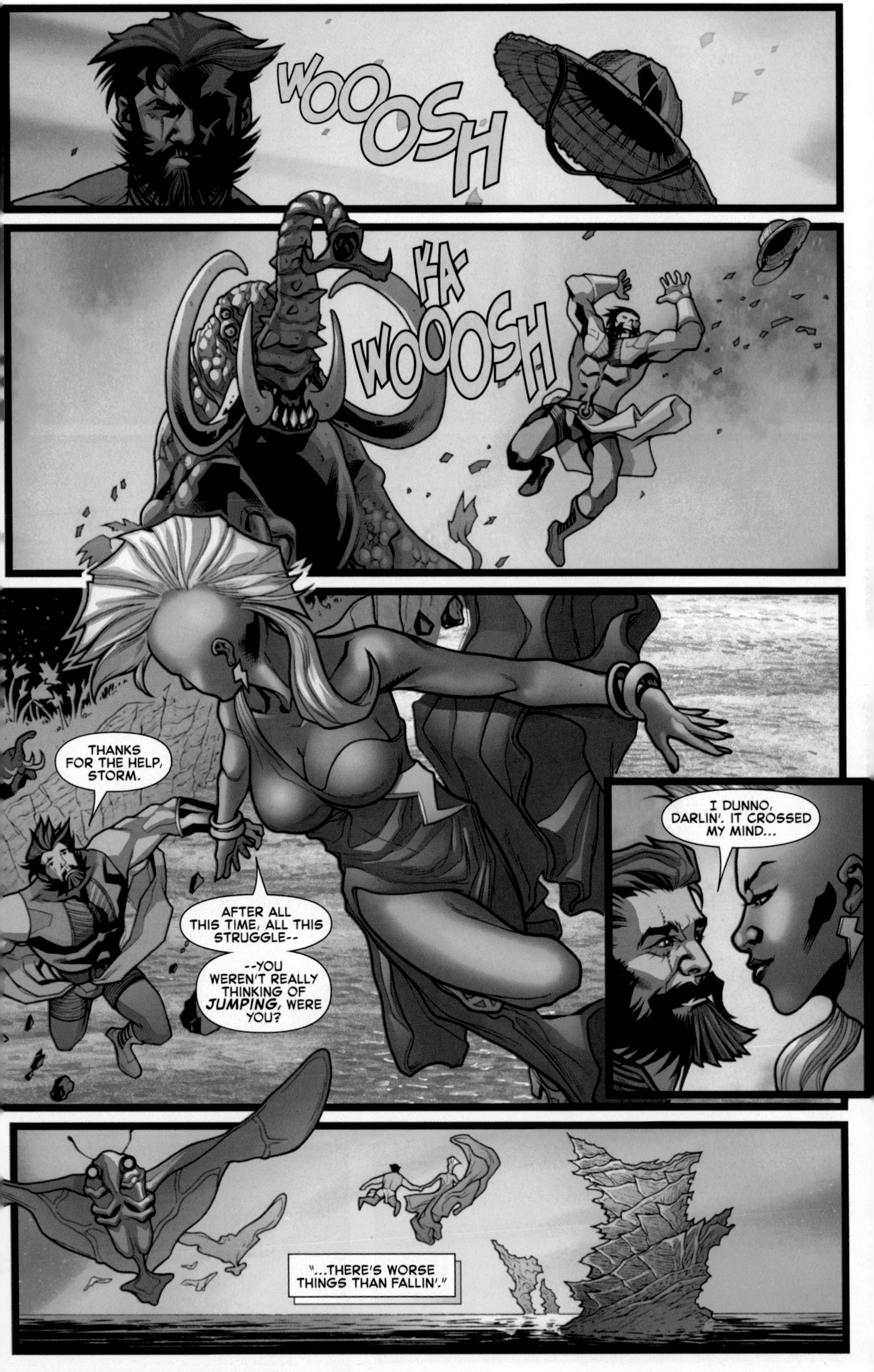
WOOOSH
KA-WOOOSH
THANKS FOR THE HELP, STORM.
AFTER ALL THIS TIME, ALL THIS STRUGGLE--
--YOU WEREN'T REALLY THINKING OF JUMPING, WERE YOU?
I DUNNO, DARLIN'. IT CROSSED MY MIND...
"...THERE'S WORSE THINGS THAN FALLIN'."

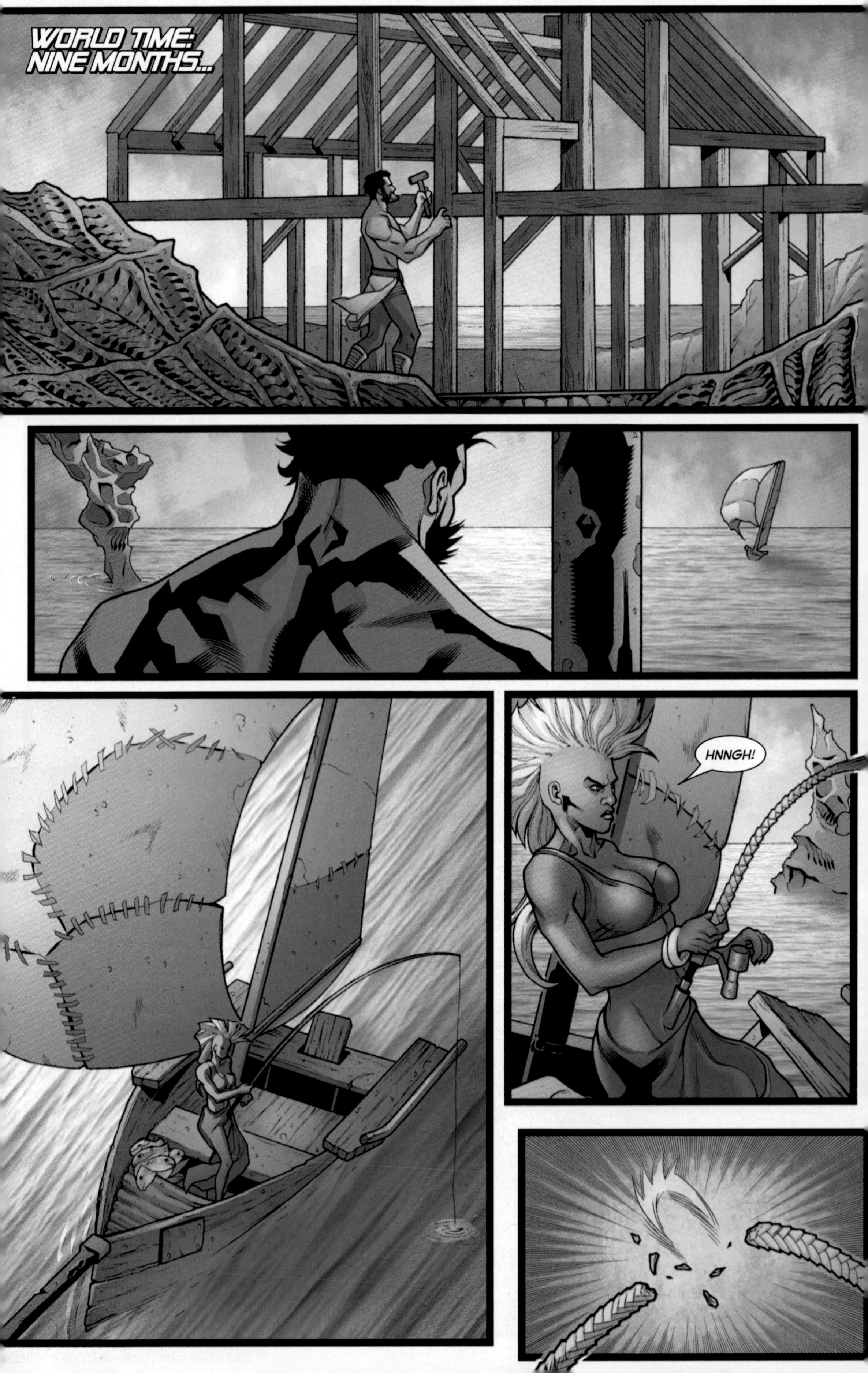
WORLD TIME:
NINE MONTHS...
HNNGH!

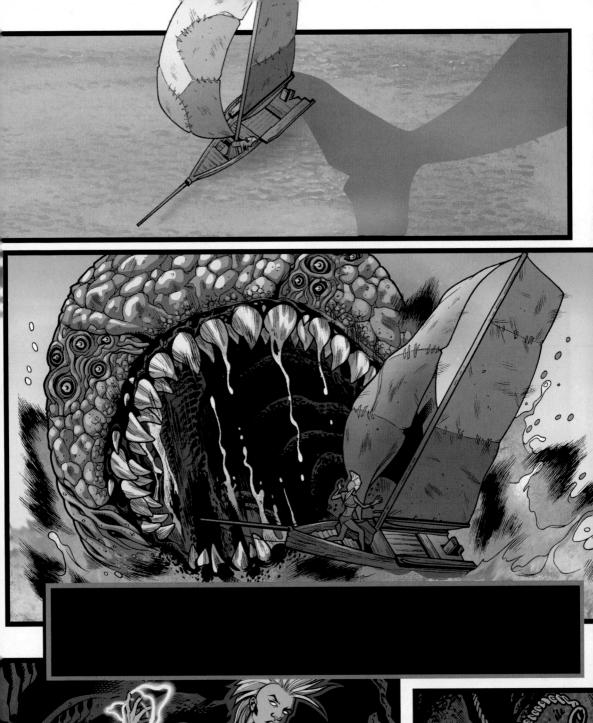

...WHAT THE--?

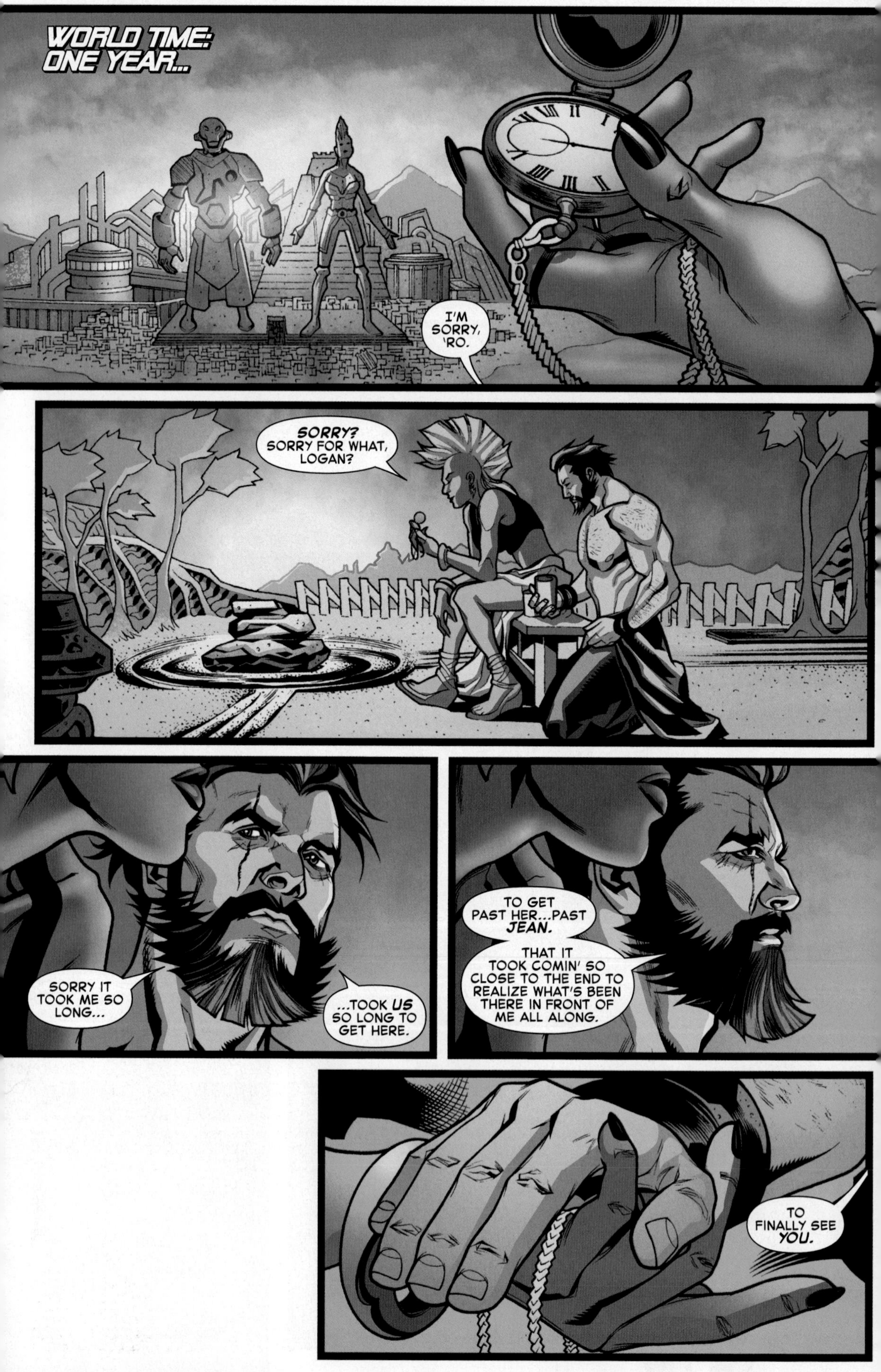
WORLD TIME: ONE YEAR...
I'M SORRY, 'RO.
SORRY? SORRY FOR WHAT, LOGAN?
SORRY IT TOOK ME SO LONG...
...TOOK US SO LONG TO GET HERE.
TO GET PAST HER...PAST JEAN.
THAT IT TOOK COMIN' SO CLOSE TO THE END TO REALIZE WHAT'S BEEN THERE IN FRONT OF ME ALL ALONG.
TO FINALLY SEE YOU.

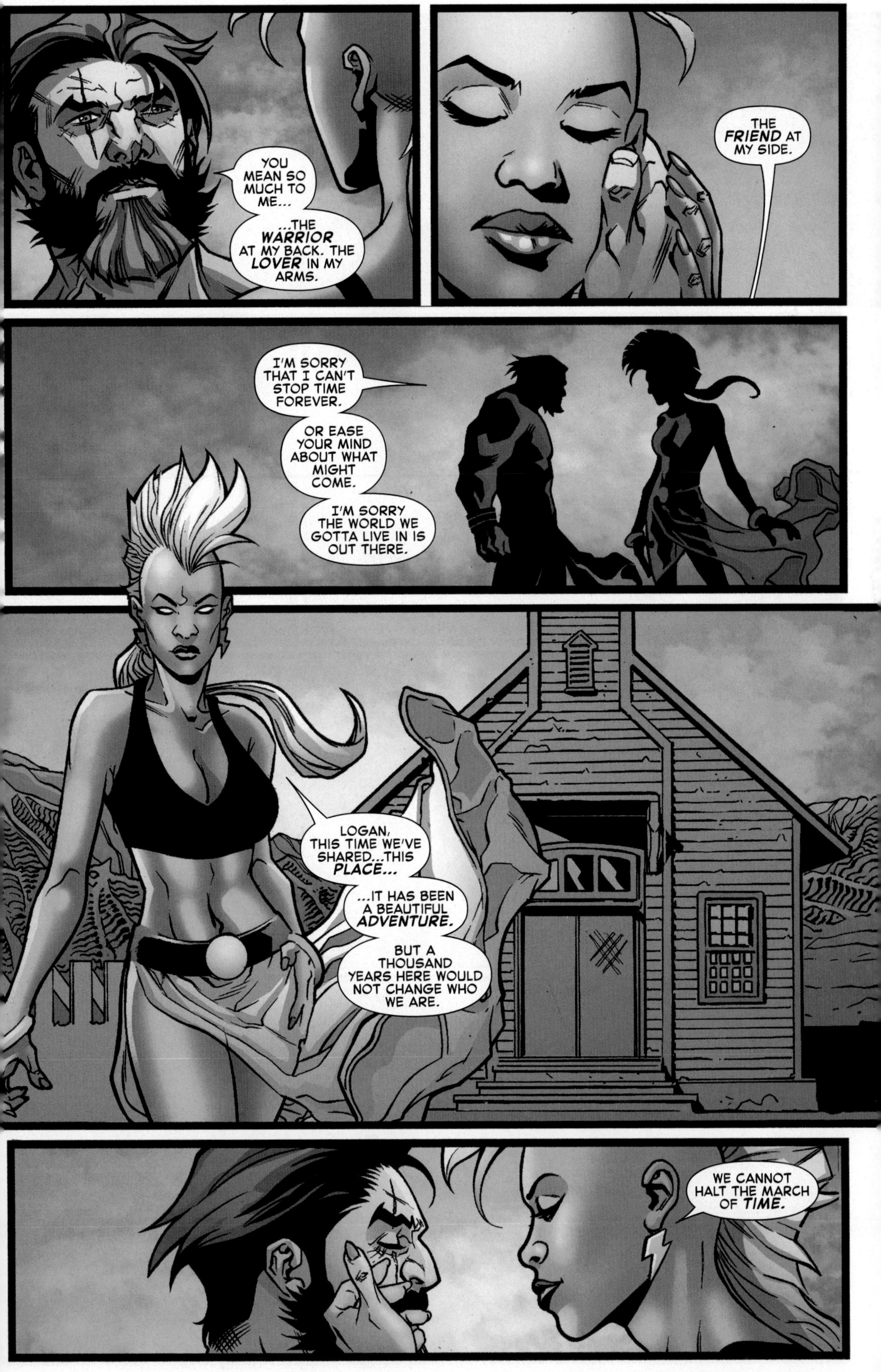
YOU MEAN SO MUCH TO ME...
...THE WARRIOR AT MY BACK. THE LOVER IN MY ARMS.
THE FRIEND AT MY SIDE.
I'M SORRY THAT I CAN'T STOP TIME FOREVER.
OR EASE YOUR MIND ABOUT WHAT MIGHT COME.
I'M SORRY THE WORLD WE GOTTA LIVE IN IS OUT THERE.
LOGAN, THIS TIME WE'VE SHARED...THIS PLACE...
...IT HAS BEEN A BEAUTIFUL ADVENTURE.
BUT A THOUSAND YEARS HERE WOULD NOT CHANGE WHO WE ARE.
WE CANNOT HALT THE MARCH OF TIME.

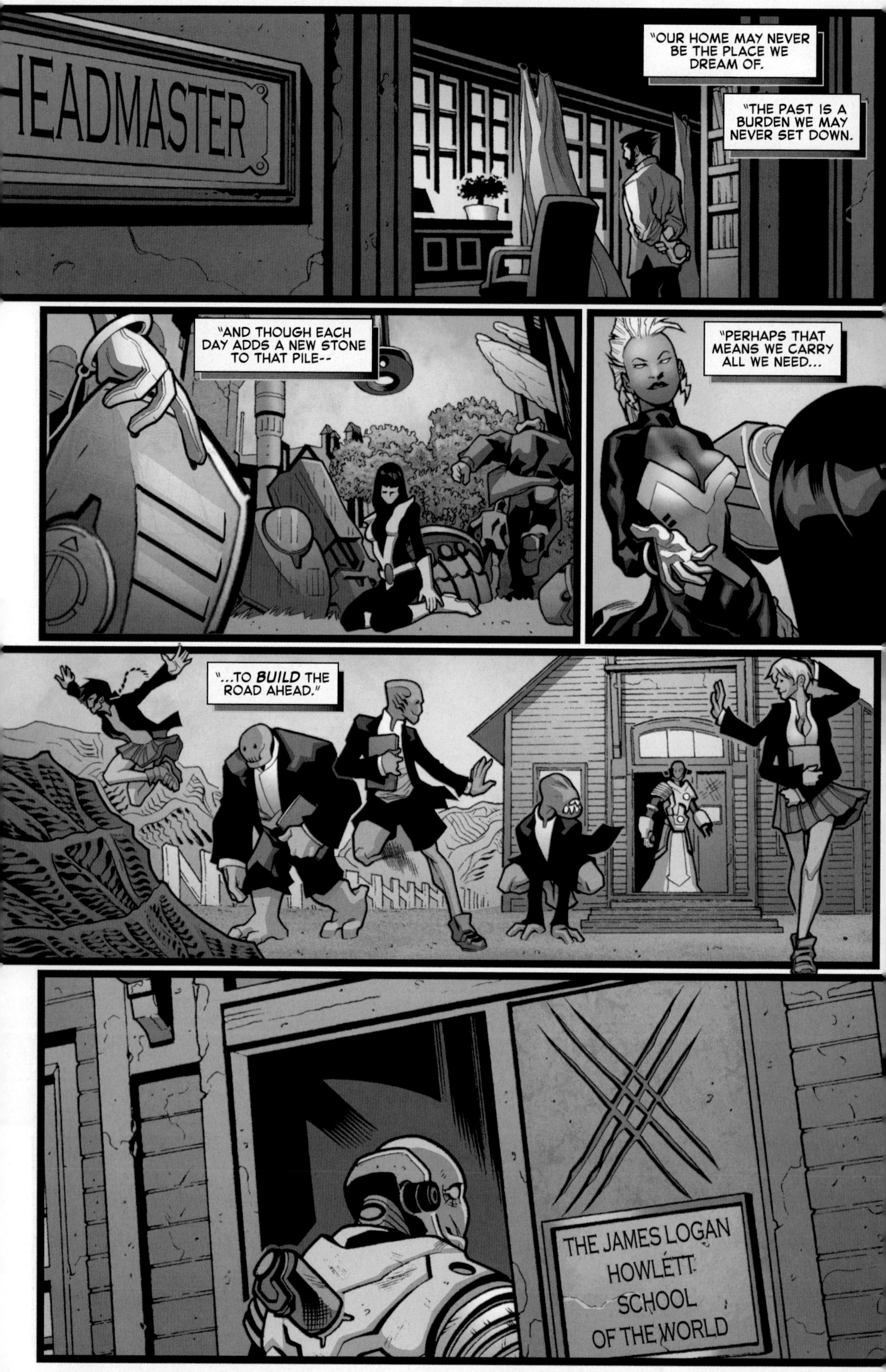
HEADMASTER
"OUR HOME MAY NEVER BE THE PLACE WE DREAM OF.
"THE PAST IS A BURDEN WE MAY NEVER SET DOWN.
"AND THOUGH EACH DAY ADDS A NEW STONE TO THAT PILE--
"PERHAPS THAT MEANS WE CARRY ALL WE NEED...
"...TO BUILD THE ROAD AHEAD."
THE JAMES LOGAN HOWLETT SCHOOL OF THE WORLD

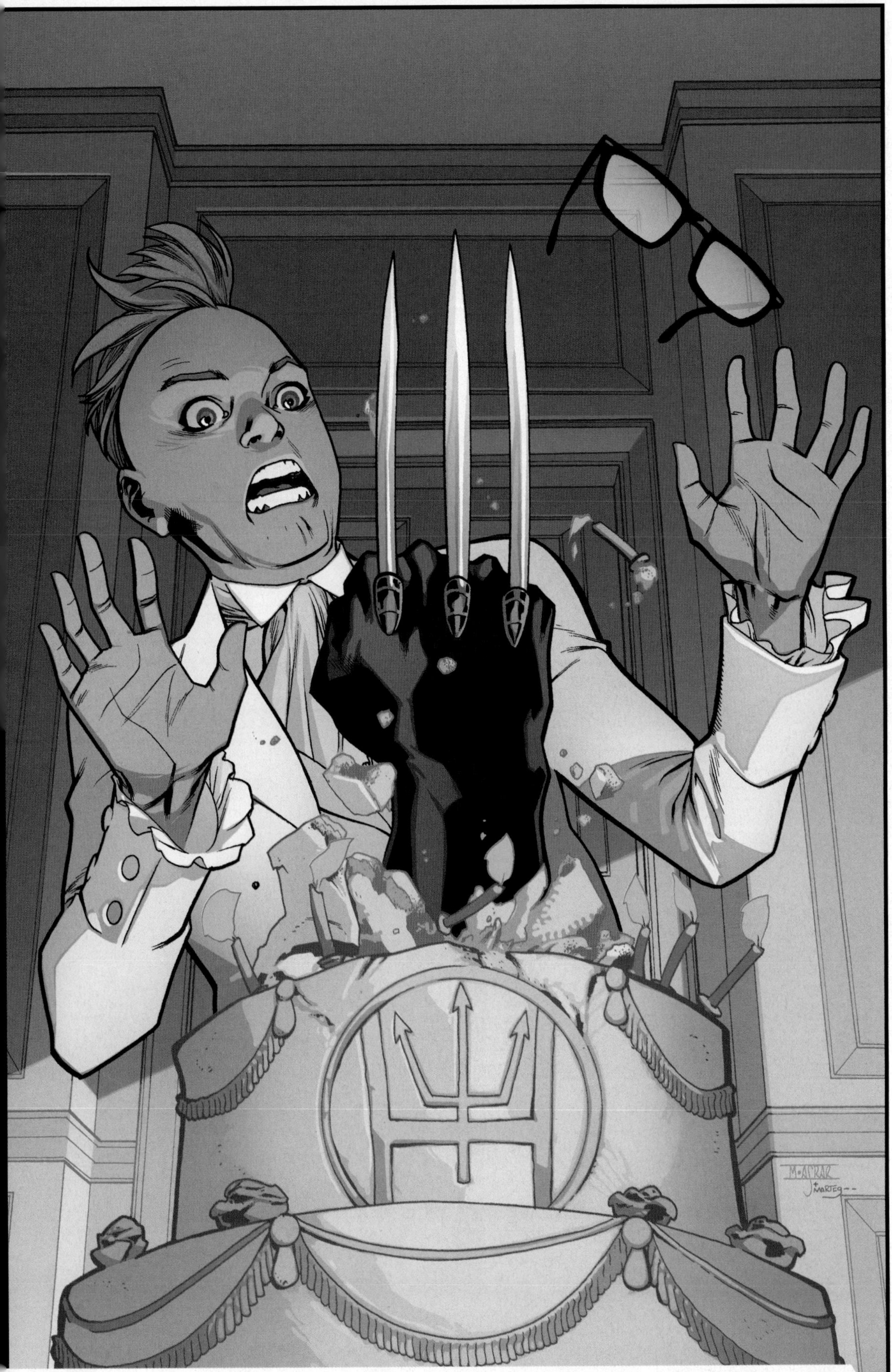

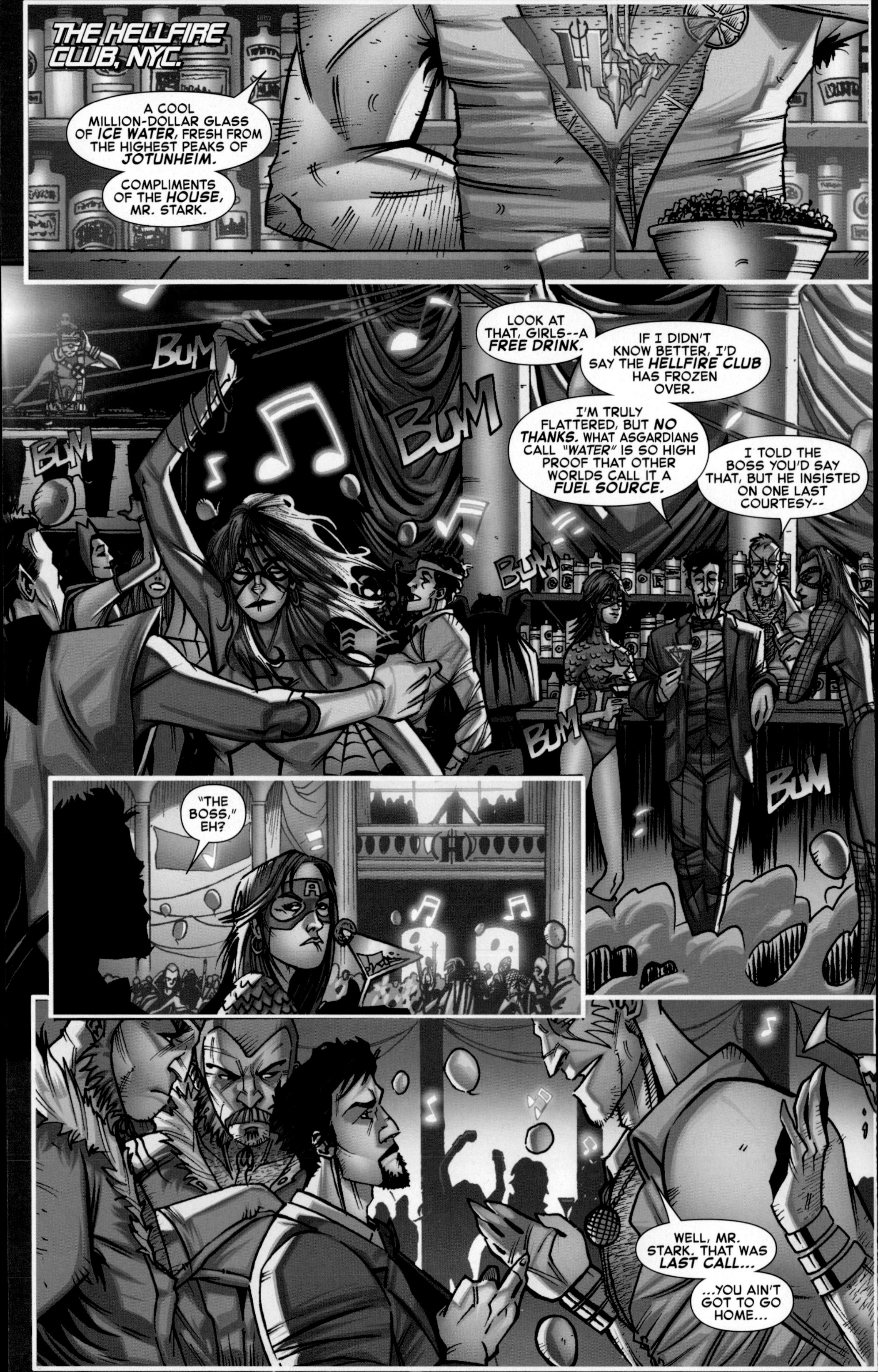
THE HELLFIRE CLUB, NYC.
A COOL MILLION-DOLLAR GLASS OF ICE WATER, FRESH FROM THE HIGHEST PEAKS OF JOTUNHEIM.
COMPLIMENTS OF THE HOUSE, MR. STARK.
BUM
BUM
BUM
LOOK AT THAT, GIRLS--A FREE DRINK.
IF I DIDN'T KNOW BETTER, I'D SAY THE HELLFIRE CLUB HAS FROZEN OVER.
I'M TRULY FLATTERED, BUT NO THANKS. WHAT ASGARDIANS CALL "WATER" IS SO HIGH PROOF THAT OTHER WORLDS CALL IT A FUEL SOURCE.
I TOLD THE BOSS YOU'D SAY THAT, BUT HE INSISTED ON ONE LAST COURTESY--
BUM
BUM
BUM
"THE BOSS," EH?
WELL, MR. STARK. THAT WAS LAST CALL...
...YOU AIN'T GOT TO GO HOME...

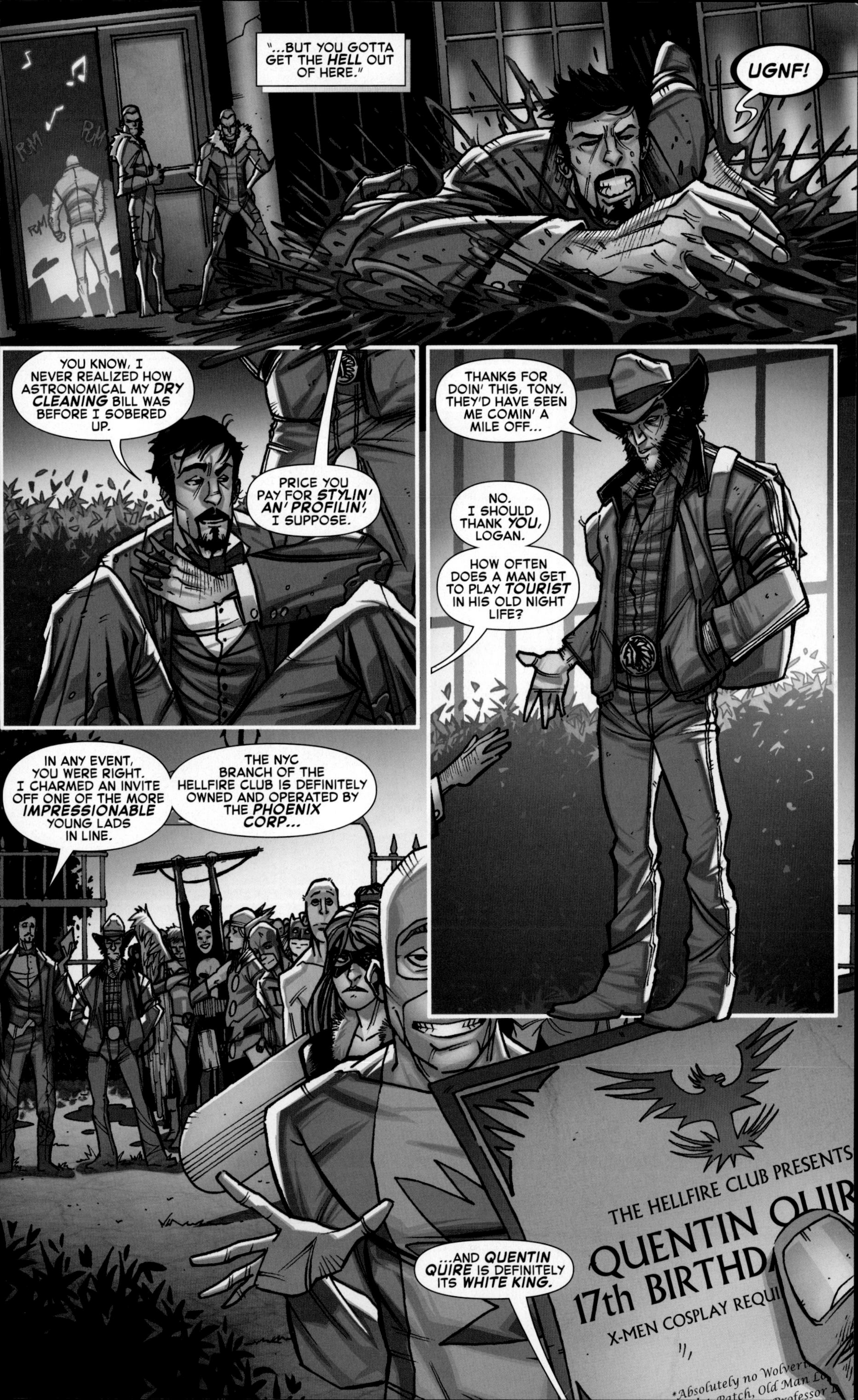
"...BUT YOU GOTTA GET THE HELL OUT OF HERE."
UGNF!
YOU KNOW, I NEVER REALIZED HOW ASTRONOMICAL MY DRY CLEANING BILL WAS BEFORE I SOBERED UP.
PRICE YOU PAY FOR STYLIN' AN' PROFILIN', I SUPPOSE.
THANKS FOR DOIN' THIS, TONY. THEY'D HAVE SEEN ME COMIN' A MILE OFF...
NO. I SHOULD THANK YOU, LOGAN.
HOW OFTEN DOES A MAN GET TO PLAY TOURIST IN HIS OLD NIGHT LIFE?
IN ANY EVENT, YOU WERE RIGHT. I CHARMED AN INVITE OFF ONE OF THE MORE IMPRESSIONABLE YOUNG LADS IN LINE.
THE NYC BRANCH OF THE HELLFIRE CLUB IS DEFINITELY OWNED AND OPERATED BY THE PHOENIX CORP...
...AND QUENTIN QUIRE IS DEFINITELY ITS WHITE KING.
THE HELLFIRE CLUB PRESENTS
QUENTIN QUIR
17th BIRTHD
X-MEN COSPLAY REQUI

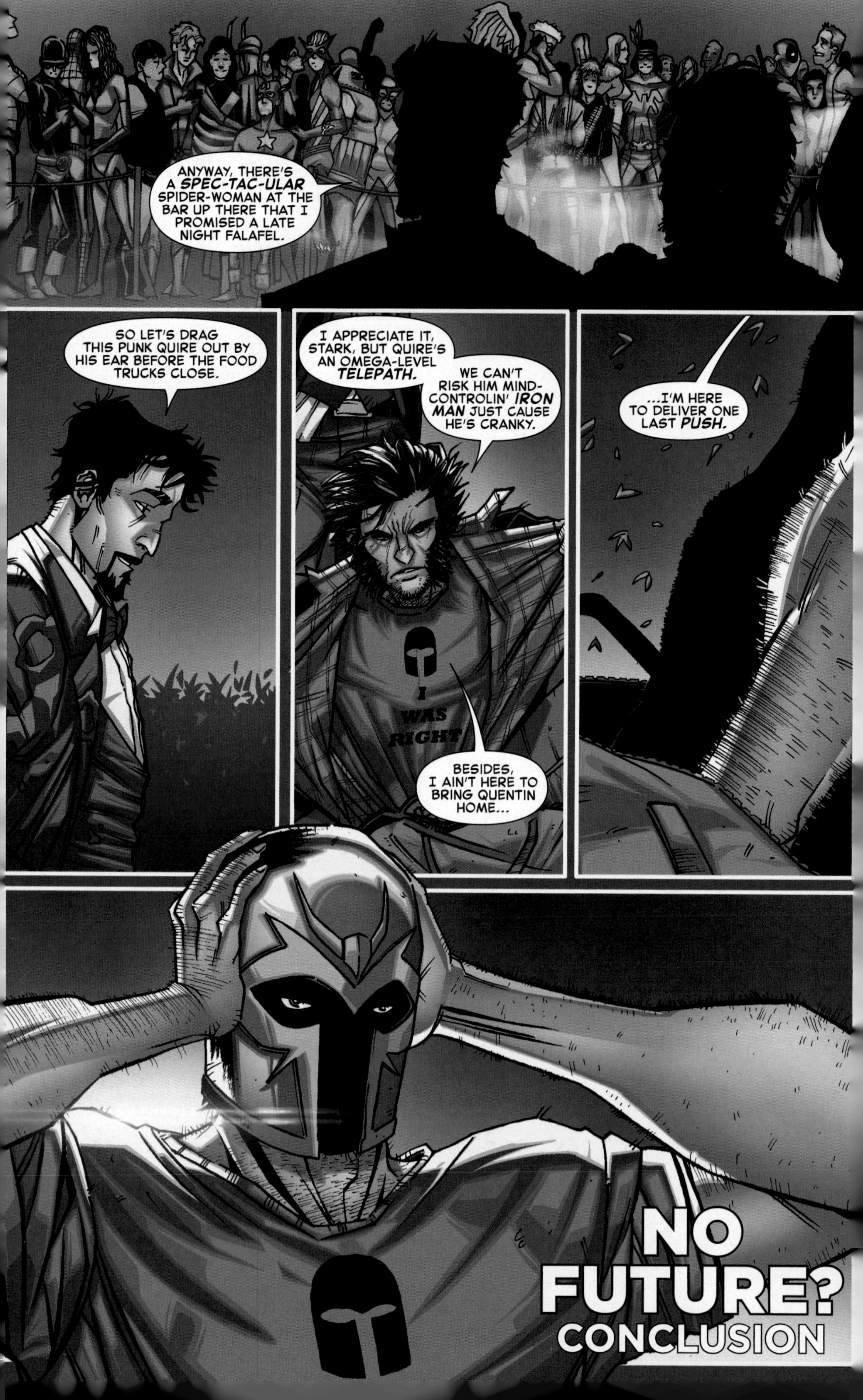
ANYWAY, THERE'S A SPEC-TAC-ULAR SPIDER-WOMAN AT THE BAR UP THERE THAT I PROMISED A LATE NIGHT FALAFEL.
SO LET'S DRAG THIS PUNK QUIRE OUT BY HIS EAR BEFORE THE FOOD TRUCKS CLOSE.
I APPRECIATE IT, STARK, BUT QUIRE'S AN OMEGA-LEVEL TELEPATH.
WE CAN'T RISK HIM MIND-CONTROLIN' IRON MAN JUST CAUSE HE'S CRANKY.
I WAS RIGHT
BESIDES, I AIN'T HERE TO BRING QUENTIN HOME...
...I'M HERE TO DELIVER ONE LAST PUSH.
NO FUTURE? CONCLUSION

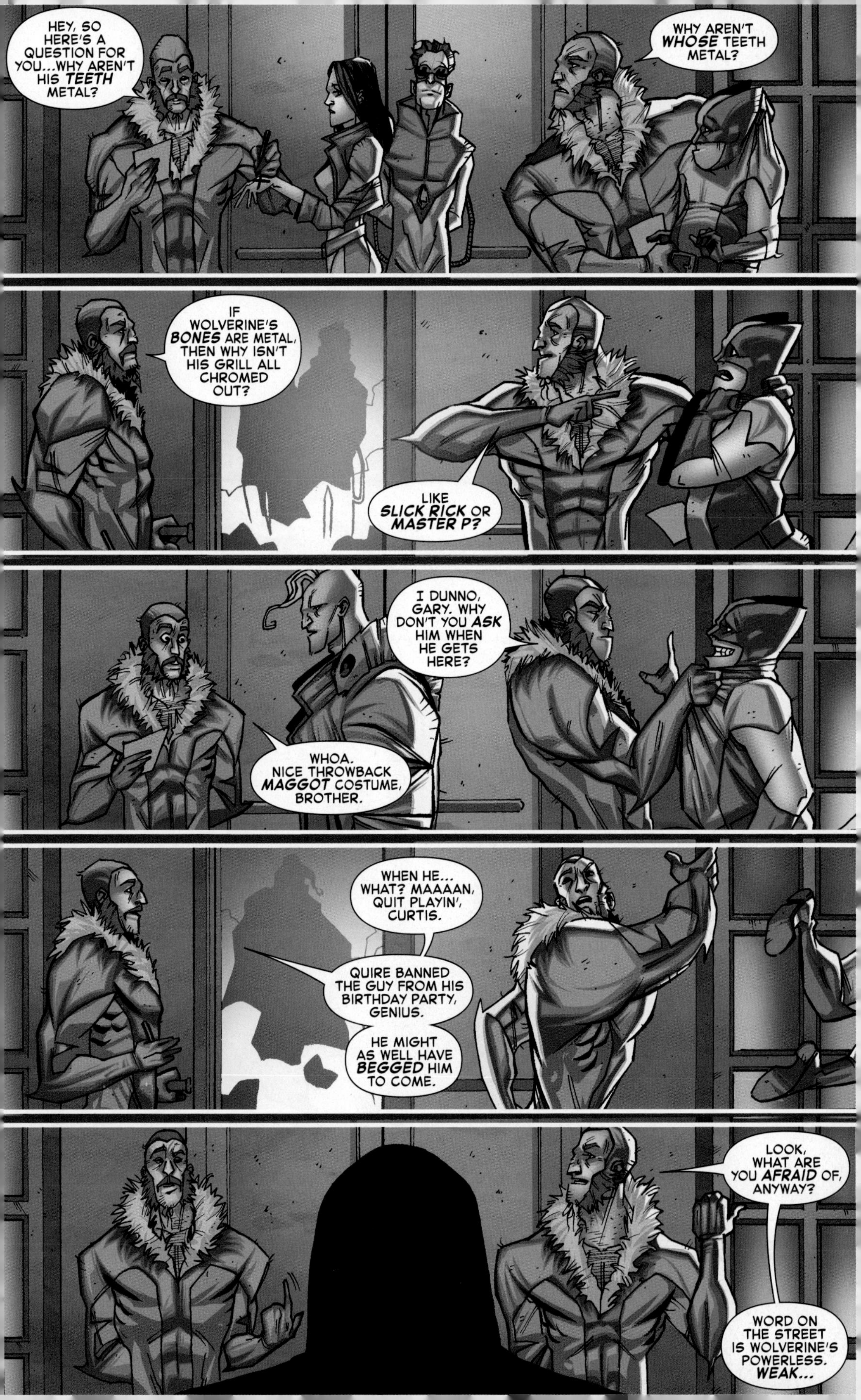
HEY, SO HERE'S A QUESTION FOR YOU...WHY AREN'T HIS TEETH METAL?
WHY AREN'T WHOSE TEETH METAL?
IF WOLVERINE'S BONES ARE METAL, THEN WHY ISN'T HIS GRILL ALL CHROMED OUT?
LIKE SLICK RICK OR MASTER P?
I DUNNO, GARY. WHY DON'T YOU ASK HIM WHEN HE GETS HERE?
WHOA. NICE THROWBACK MAGGOT COSTUME, BROTHER.
WHEN HE... WHAT? MAAAAN, QUIT PLAYIN', CURTIS.
QUIRE BANNED THE GUY FROM HIS BIRTHDAY PARTY, GENIUS.
HE MIGHT AS WELL HAVE BEGGED HIM TO COME.
LOOK, WHAT ARE YOU AFRAID OF, ANYWAY?
WORD ON THE STREET IS WOLVERINE'S POWERLESS. WEAK...

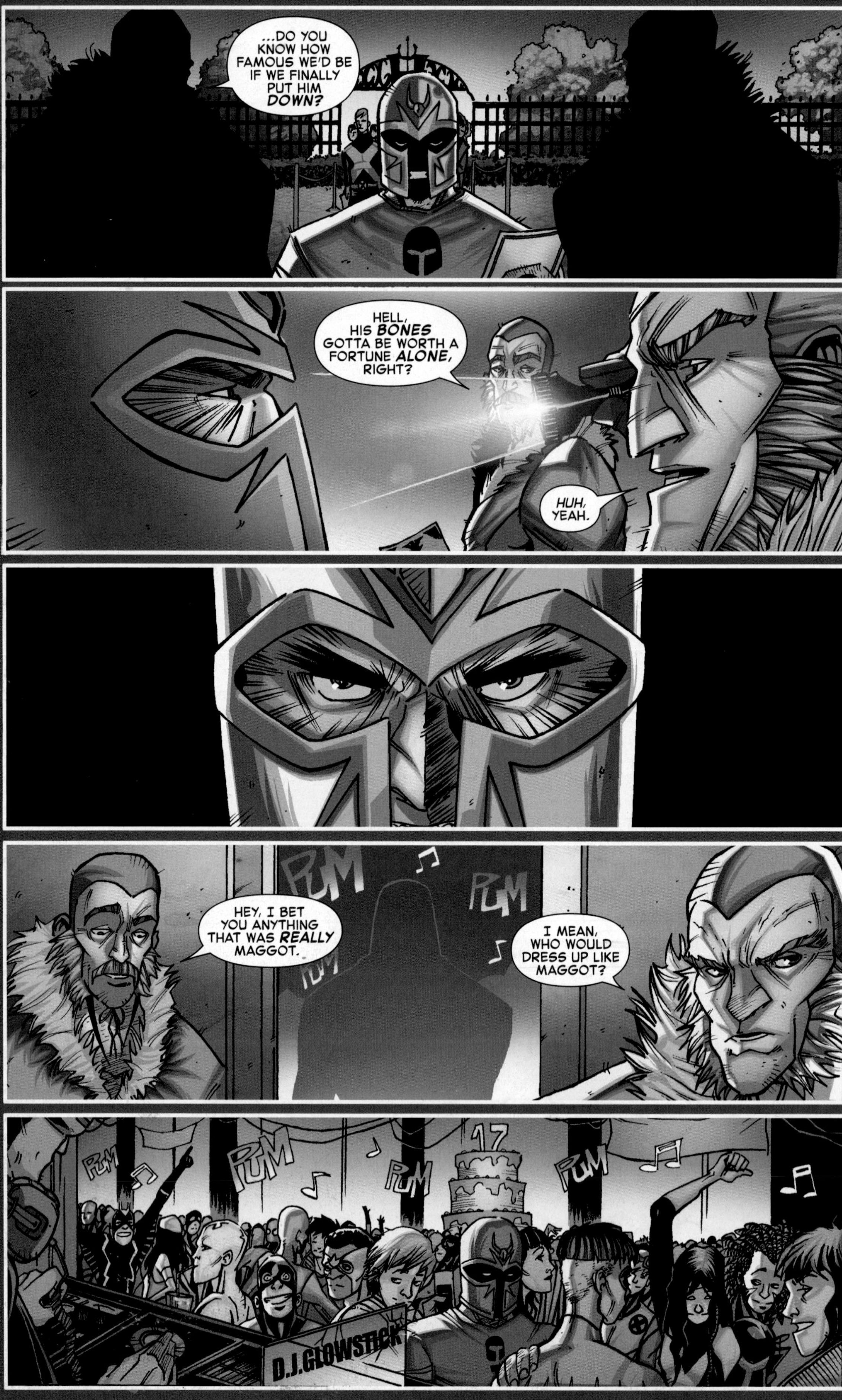
...DO YOU KNOW HOW FAMOUS WE'D BE IF WE FINALLY PUT HIM *DOWN?*
HELL, HIS *BONES* GOTTA BE WORTH A FORTUNE *ALONE,* RIGHT?
HUH, YEAH.
PUM
PUM
HEY, I BET YOU ANYTHING THAT WAS *REALLY* MAGGOT.
I MEAN, WHO WOULD DRESS UP LIKE MAGGOT?
PUM
PUM
PUM
PUM
17
D.J.GLOWSTICK

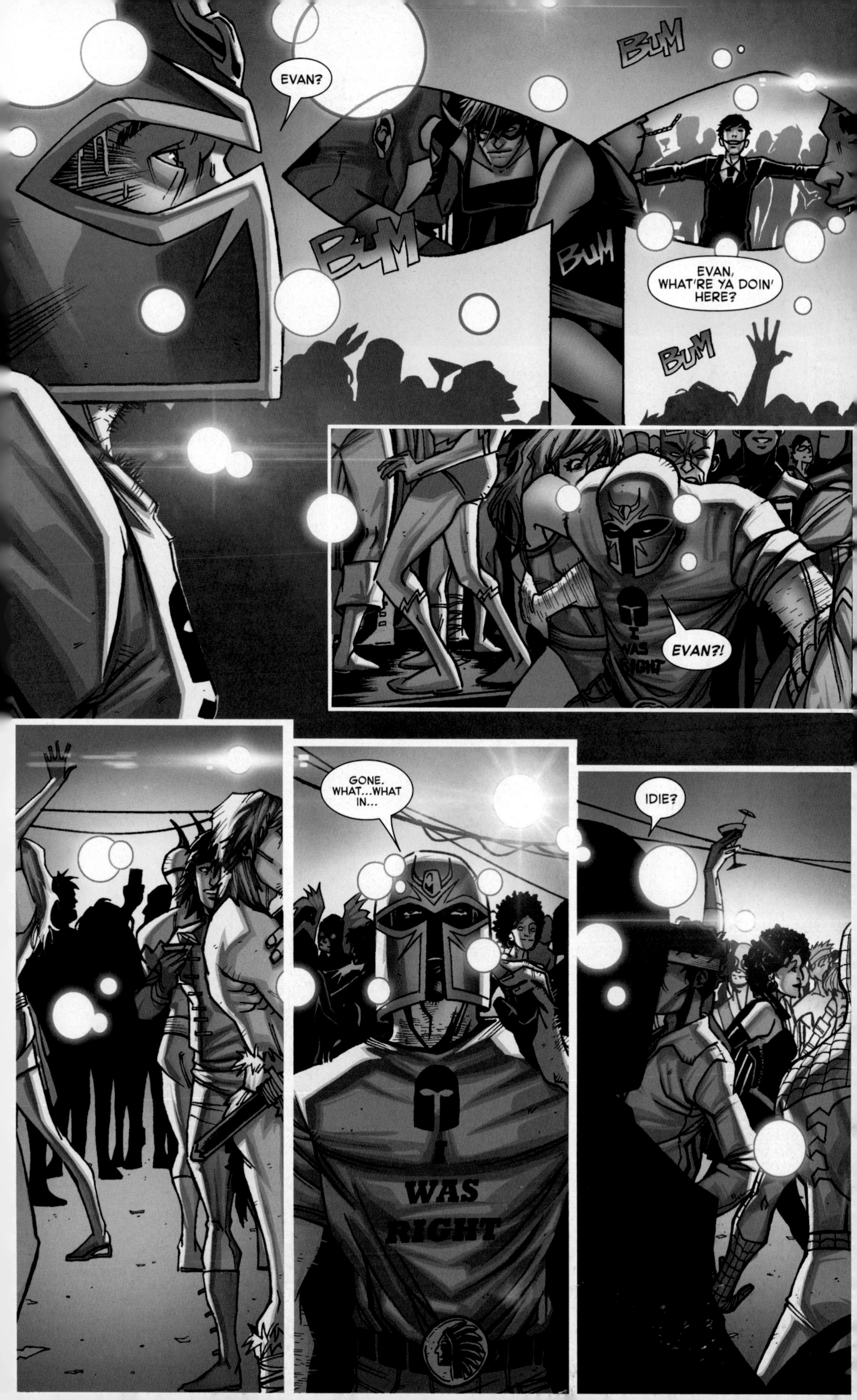

EVAN?
BUM
BUM
BUM
EVAN, WHAT'RE YA DOIN' HERE?
BUM
EVAN?!
I WAS RIGHT
GONE. WHAT...WHAT IN...
I WAS RIGHT
IDIE?

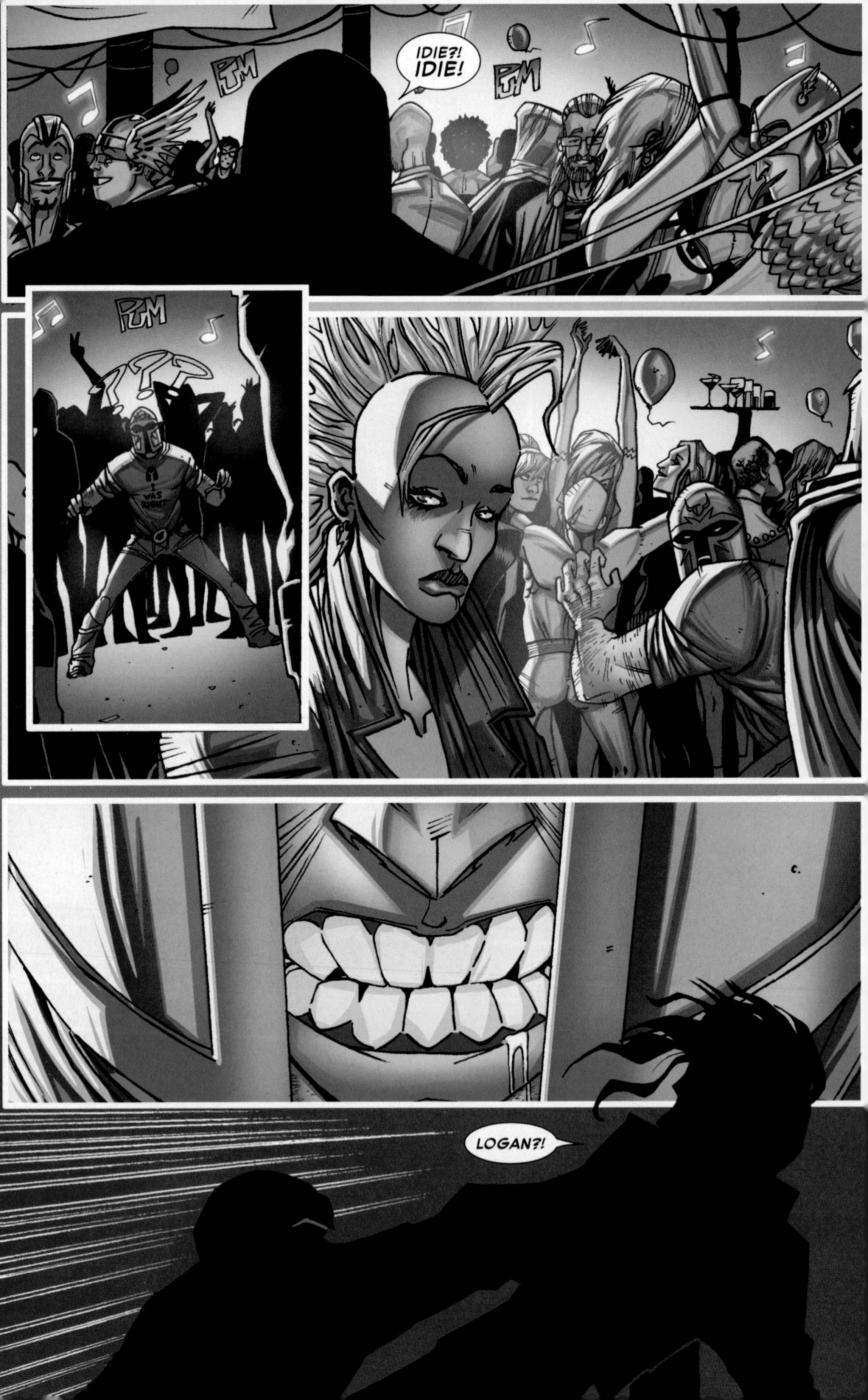
IDIE?! IDIE!
PUM
PUM
PUM
I WAS RIGHT
LOGAN?!

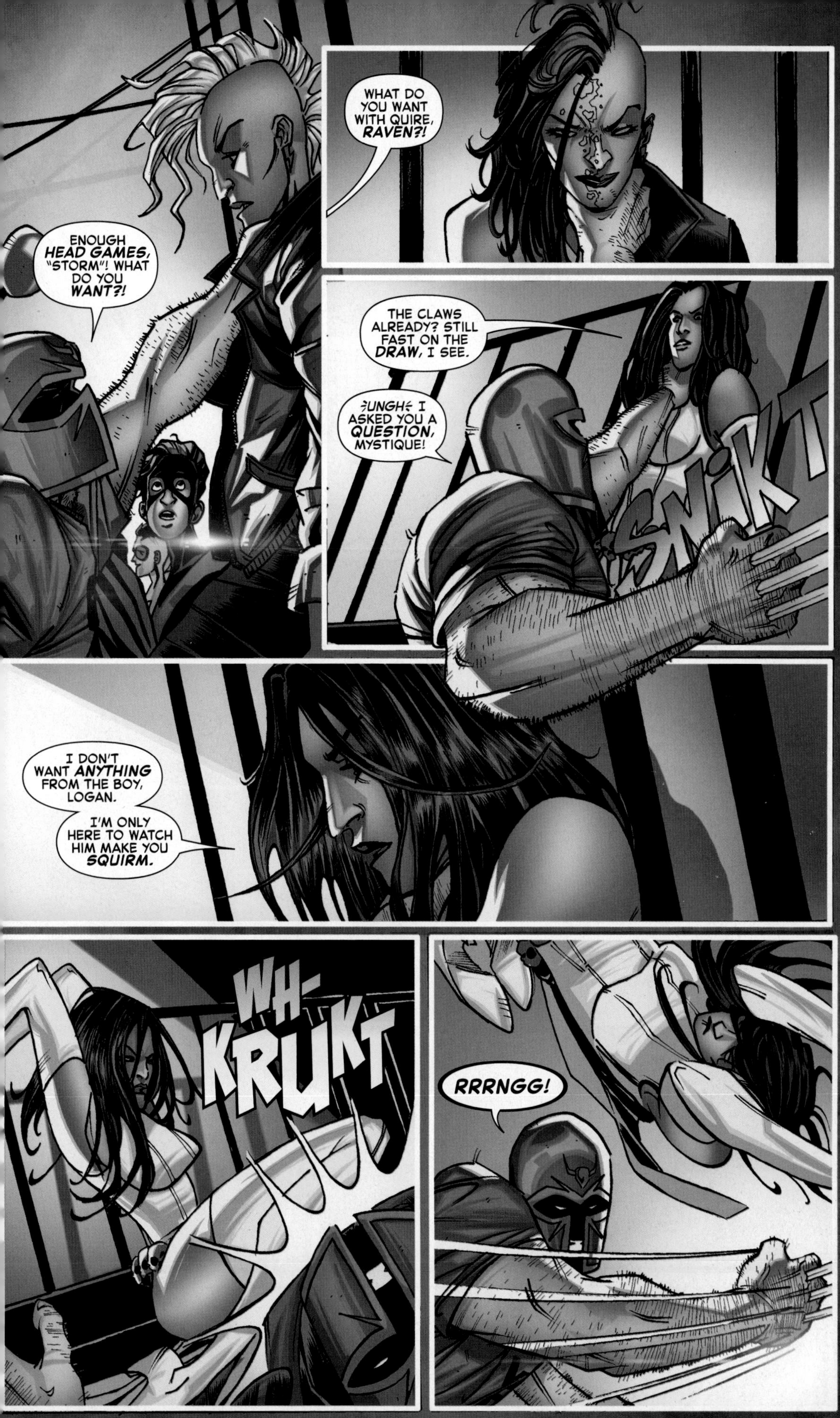
WHAT DO YOU WANT WITH QUIRE, RAVEN?!
ENOUGH HEAD GAMES, "STORM"! WHAT DO YOU WANT?!
THE CLAWS ALREADY? STILL FAST ON THE DRAW, I SEE.
UNGH I ASKED YOU A QUESTION, MYSTIQUE!
SNIKT
I DON'T WANT ANYTHING FROM THE BOY, LOGAN.
I'M ONLY HERE TO WATCH HIM MAKE YOU SQUIRM.
WH-KRUKT
RRRNGG!

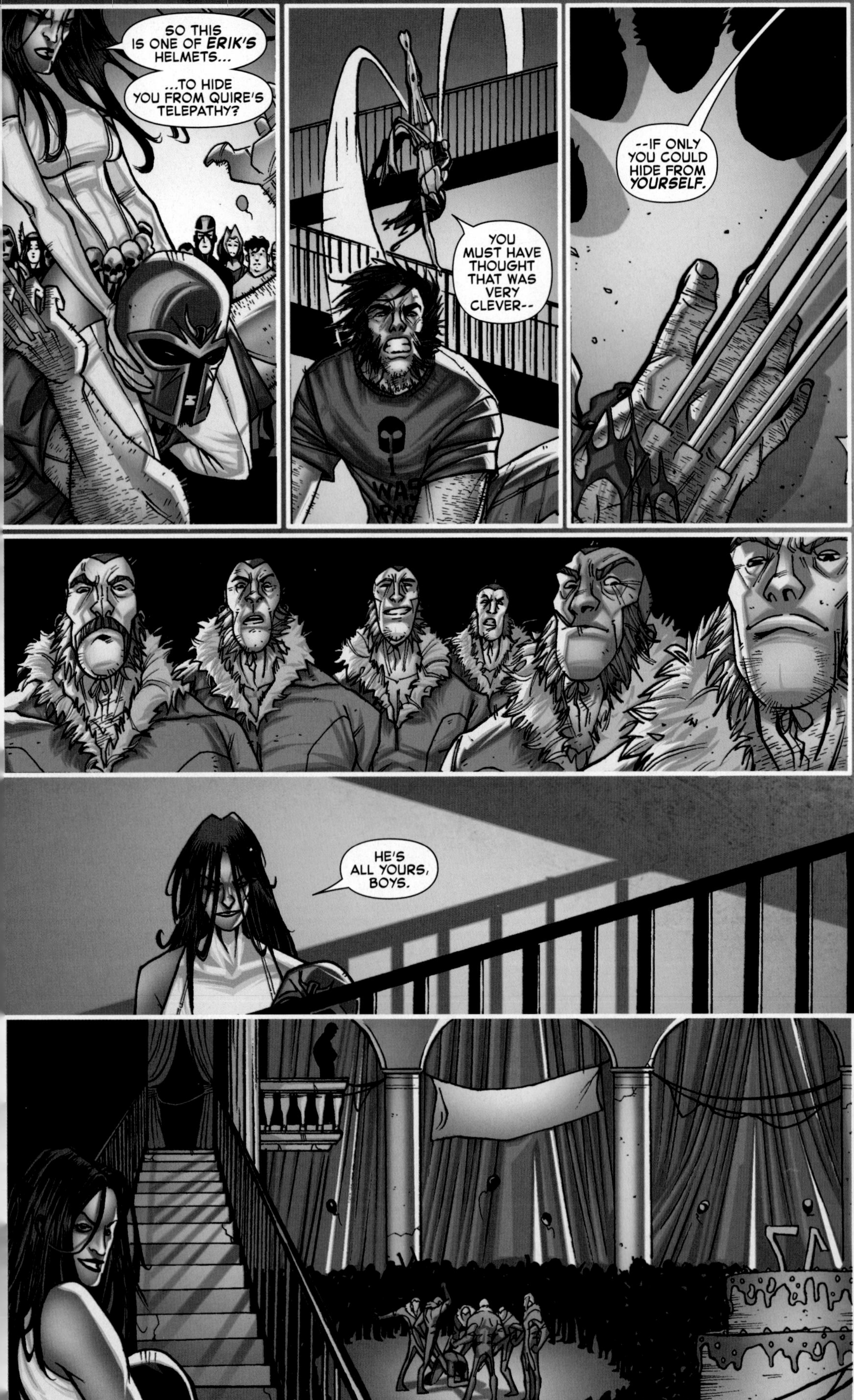
SO THIS IS ONE OF ERIK'S HELMETS...
...TO HIDE YOU FROM QUIRE'S TELEPATHY?
YOU MUST HAVE THOUGHT THAT WAS VERY CLEVER--
--IF ONLY YOU COULD HIDE FROM YOURSELF.
HE'S ALL YOURS, BOYS.

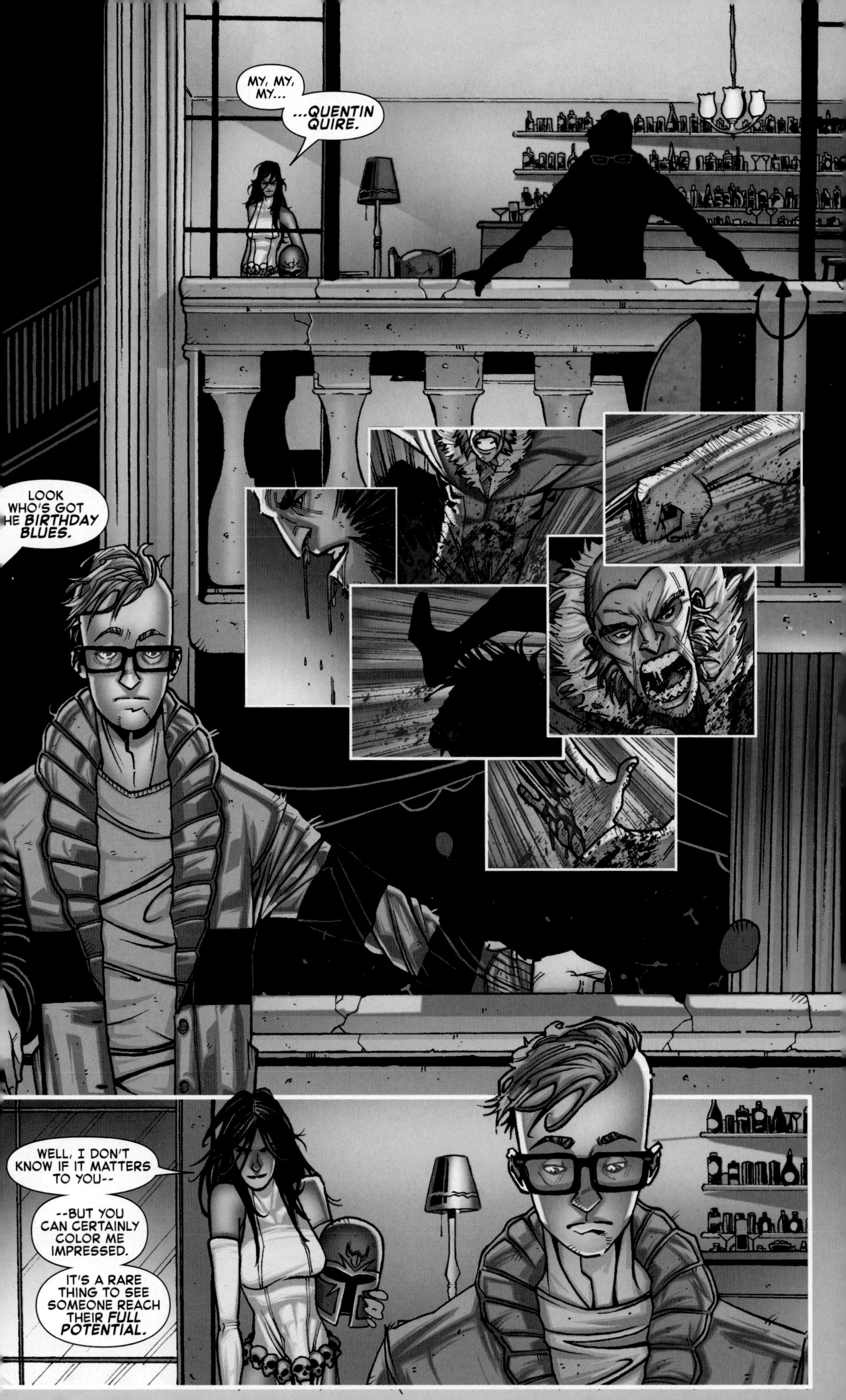

MY, MY, MY...
...QUENTIN QUIRE.
LOOK WHO'S GOT HE BIRTHDAY BLUES.
WELL, I DON'T KNOW IF IT MATTERS TO YOU--
--BUT YOU CAN CERTAINLY COLOR ME IMPRESSED.
IT'S A RARE THING TO SEE SOMEONE REACH THEIR FULL POTENTIAL.

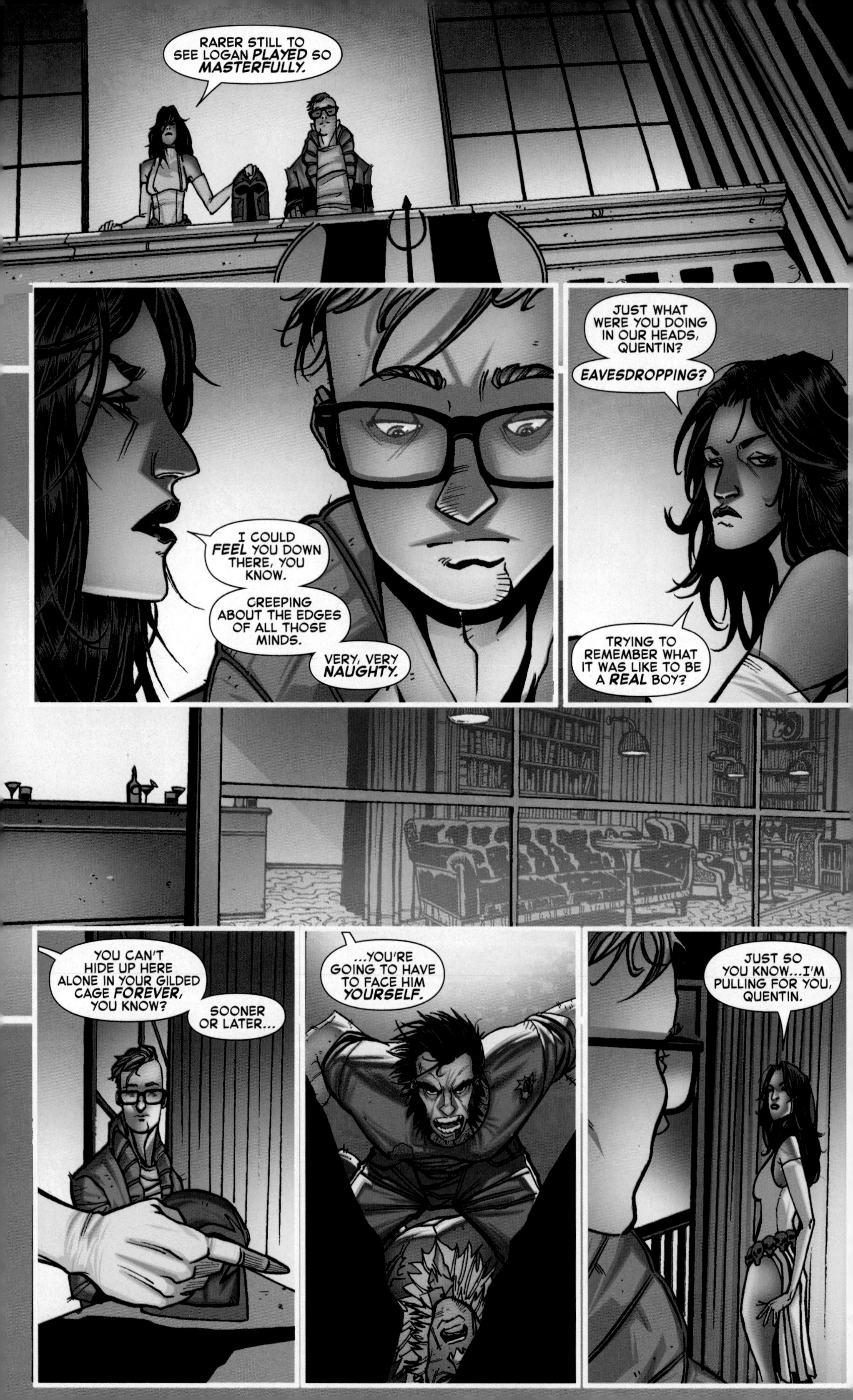

RARER STILL TO SEE LOGAN PLAYED SO MASTERFULLY.
I COULD FEEL YOU DOWN THERE, YOU KNOW.
CREEPING ABOUT THE EDGES OF ALL THOSE MINDS.
VERY, VERY NAUGHTY.
JUST WHAT WERE YOU DOING IN OUR HEADS, QUENTIN?
EAVESDROPPING?
TRYING TO REMEMBER WHAT IT WAS LIKE TO BE A REAL BOY?
YOU CAN'T HIDE UP HERE ALONE IN YOUR GILDED CAGE FOREVER, YOU KNOW?
SOONER OR LATER...
...YOU'RE GOING TO HAVE TO FACE HIM YOURSELF.
JUST SO YOU KNOW...I'M PULLING FOR YOU, QUENTIN.

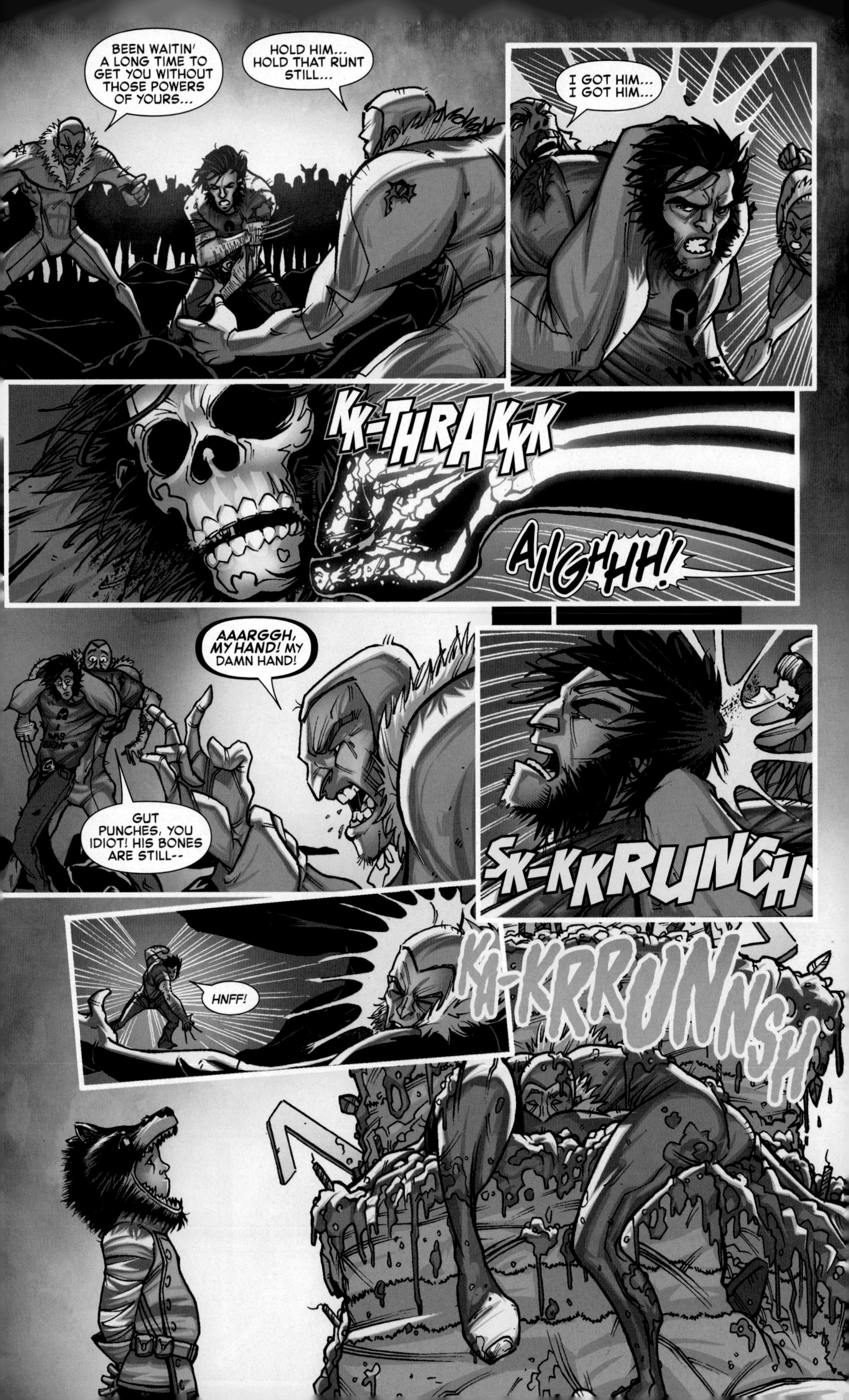
BEEN WAITIN' A LONG TIME TO GET YOU WITHOUT THOSE POWERS OF YOURS...
HOLD HIM... HOLD THAT RUNT STILL...
I GOT HIM... I GOT HIM...
KK-THRAKKK
AIGHHH!
AAARGGH, MY HAND! MY DAMN HAND!
GUT PUNCHES, YOU IDIOT! HIS BONES ARE STILL--
SK-KKRUNCH
HNFF!
KA-KRRUNNSH

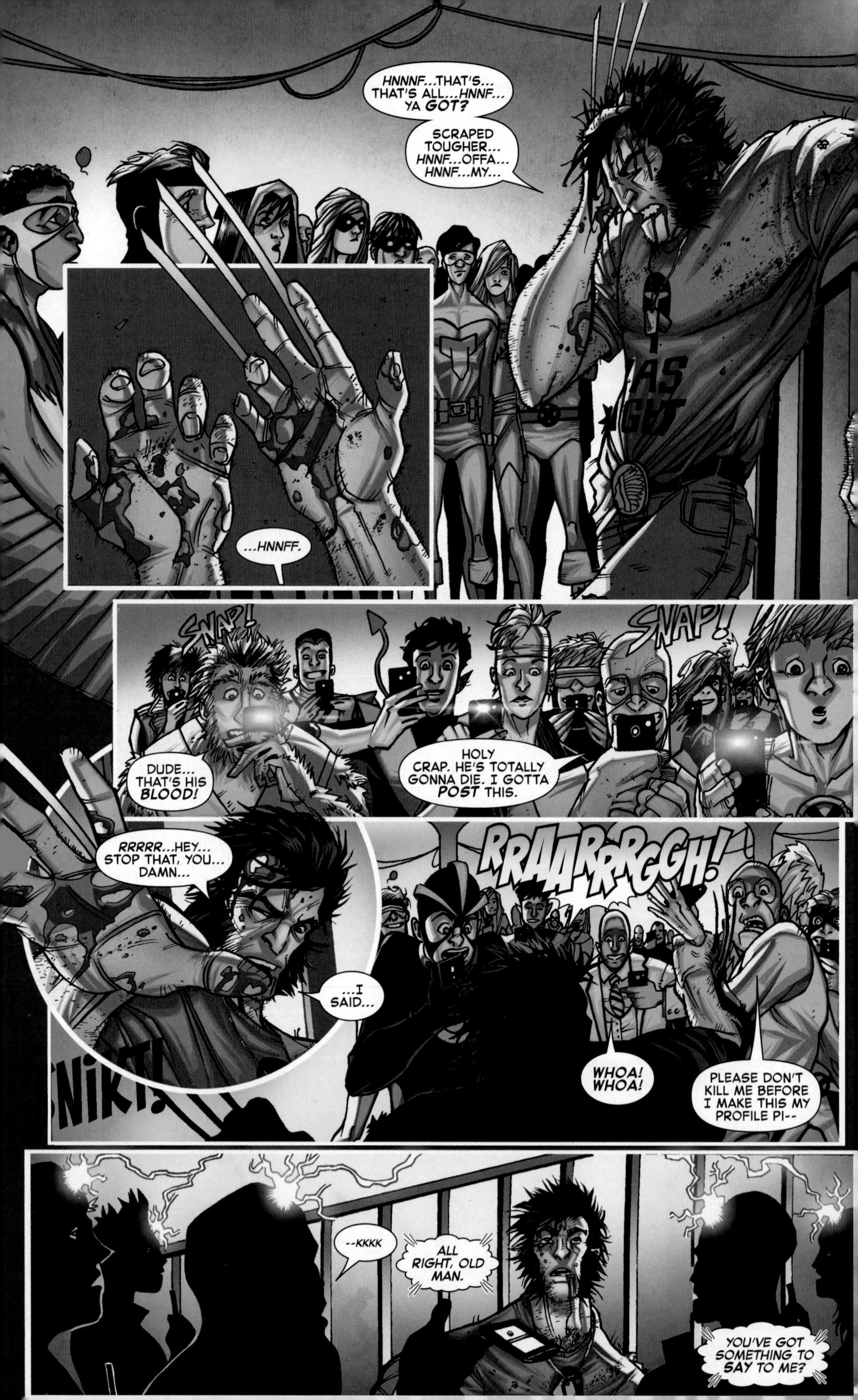
HNNNF...THAT'S... THAT'S ALL...HNNF... YA GOT?
SCRAPED TOUGHER... HNNF...OFFA... HNNF...MY...
...HNNFF.
SNAP!
SNAP!
DUDE... THAT'S HIS BLOOD!
HOLY CRAP. HE'S TOTALLY GONNA DIE. I GOTTA POST THIS.
RRRRR...HEY... STOP THAT, YOU... DAMN...
...I SAID...
SNIKT!
RRAARRRGGH!
WHOA! WHOA!
PLEASE DON'T KILL ME BEFORE I MAKE THIS MY PROFILE PI--
--KKKK
ALL RIGHT, OLD MAN.
YOU'VE GOT SOMETHING TO SAY TO ME?

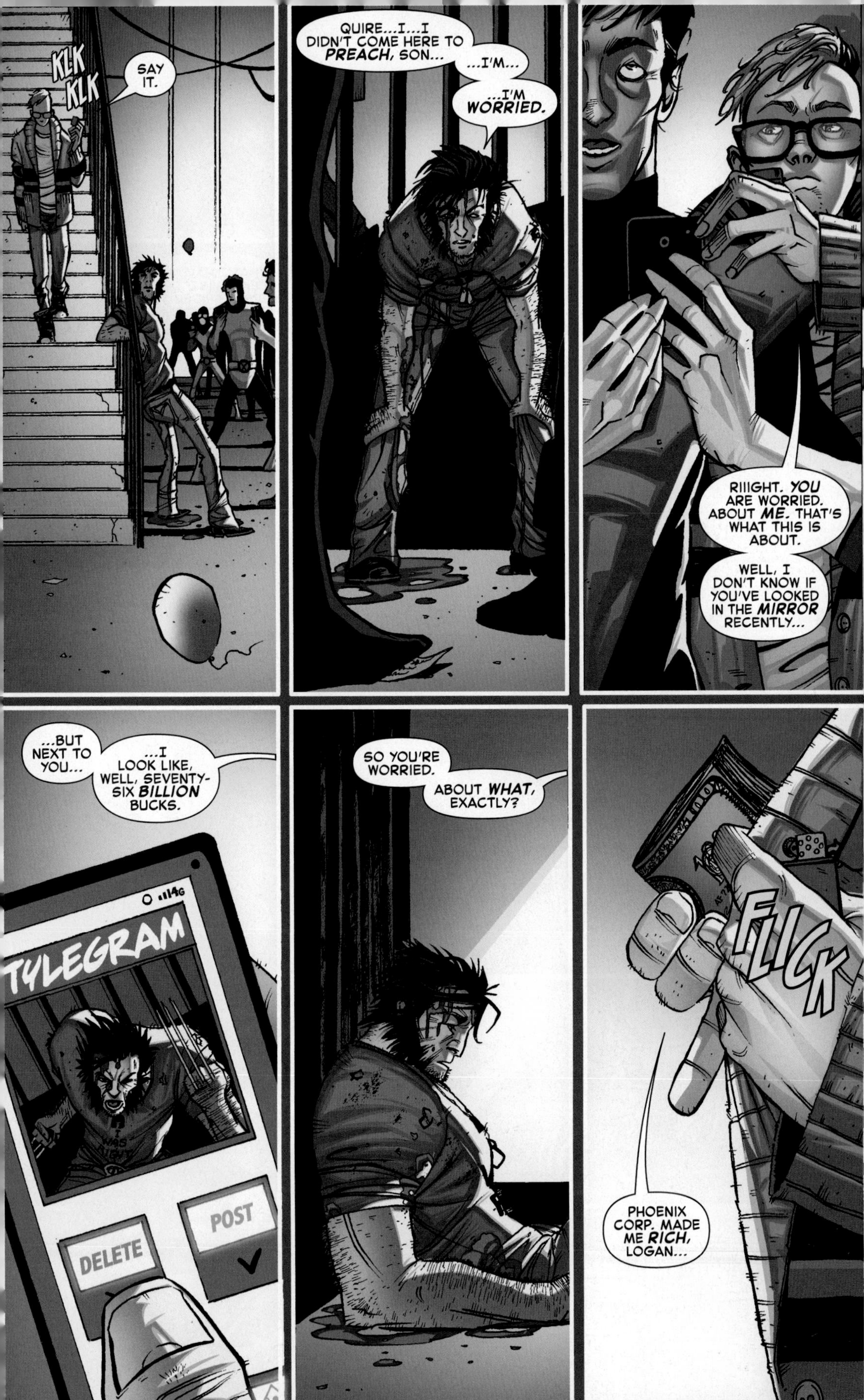
KLK KLK
SAY IT.
QUIRE...I...I DIDN'T COME HERE TO PREACH, SON...
...I'M...
...I'M WORRIED.
RIIIGHT. YOU ARE WORRIED. ABOUT ME. THAT'S WHAT THIS IS ABOUT.
WELL, I DON'T KNOW IF YOU'VE LOOKED IN THE MIRROR RECENTLY...
...BUT NEXT TO YOU...
...I LOOK LIKE, WELL, SEVENTY-SIX BILLION BUCKS.
TYLEGRAM
DELETE
POST
SO YOU'RE WORRIED.
ABOUT WHAT, EXACTLY?
FLICK
PHOENIX CORP. MADE ME RICH, LOGAN...

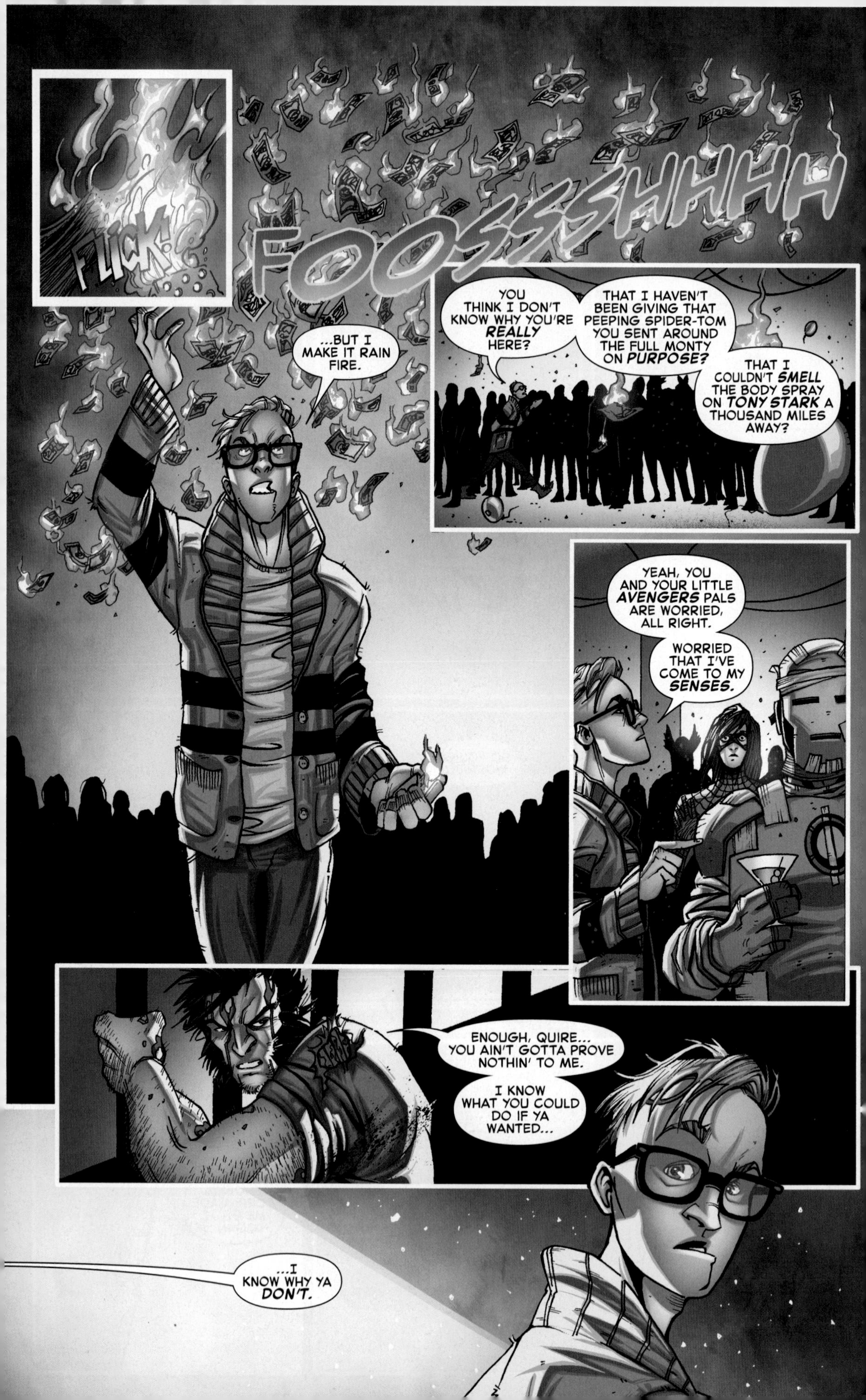
FLICK!
FOOSSSHHHH
...BUT I MAKE IT RAIN FIRE.
YOU THINK I DON'T KNOW WHY YOU'RE REALLY HERE?
THAT I HAVEN'T BEEN GIVING THAT PEEPING SPIDER-TOM YOU SENT AROUND THE FULL MONTY ON PURPOSE?
THAT I COULDN'T SMELL THE BODY SPRAY ON TONY STARK A THOUSAND MILES AWAY?
YEAH, YOU AND YOUR LITTLE AVENGERS PALS ARE WORRIED, ALL RIGHT.
WORRIED THAT I'VE COME TO MY SENSES.
ENOUGH, QUIRE... YOU AIN'T GOTTA PROVE NOTHIN' TO ME.
I KNOW WHAT YOU COULD DO IF YA WANTED...
...I KNOW WHY YA DON'T.

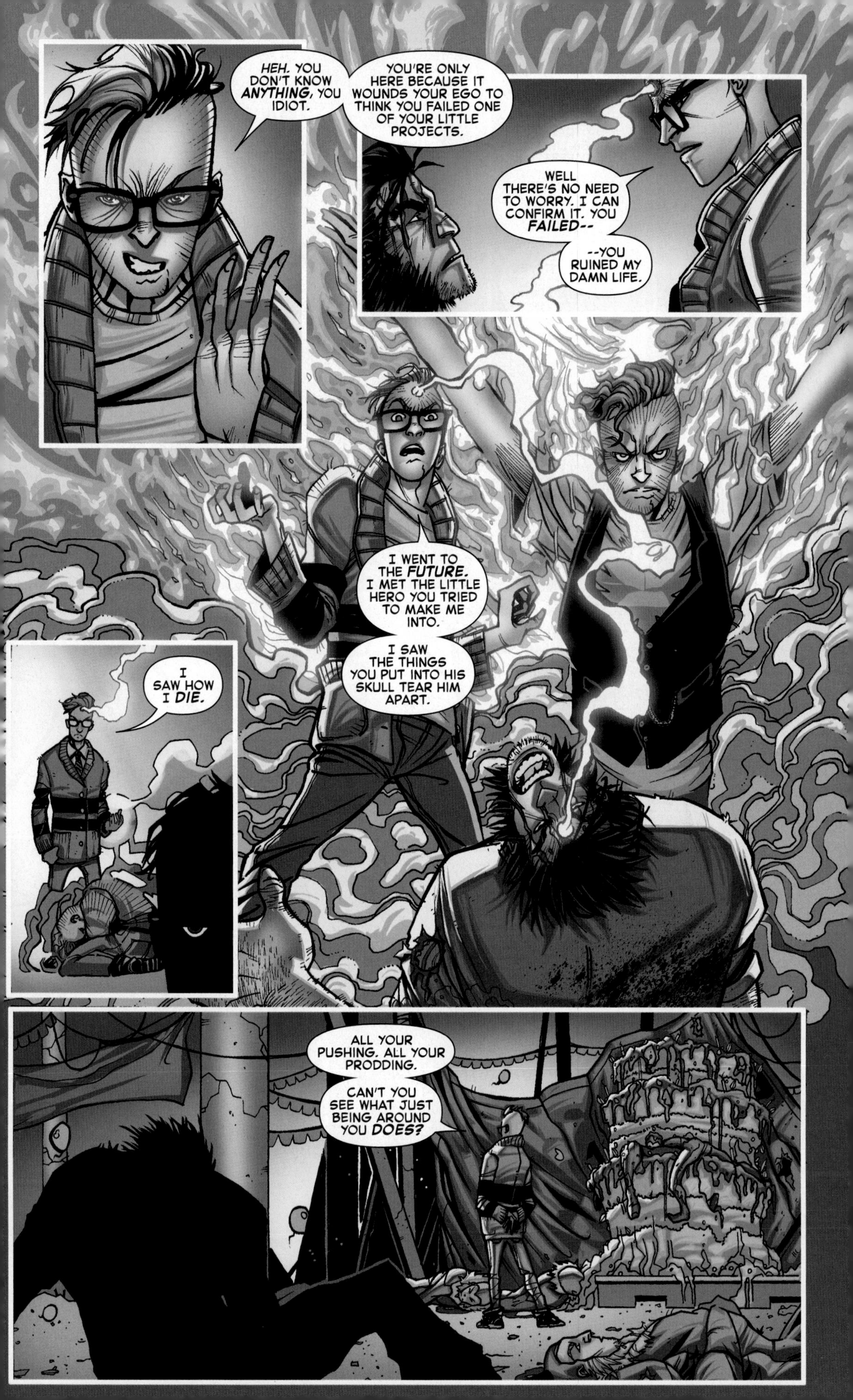

HEH. YOU DON'T KNOW *ANYTHING*, YOU IDIOT.
YOU'RE ONLY HERE BECAUSE IT WOUNDS YOUR EGO TO THINK YOU FAILED ONE OF YOUR LITTLE PROJECTS.
WELL THERE'S NO NEED TO WORRY. I CAN CONFIRM IT. YOU *FAILED*--
--YOU RUINED MY DAMN LIFE.
I WENT TO THE *FUTURE.* I MET THE LITTLE HERO YOU TRIED TO MAKE ME INTO.
I SAW THE THINGS YOU PUT INTO HIS SKULL TEAR HIM APART.
I SAW HOW I *DIE.*
ALL YOUR PUSHING. ALL YOUR PRODDING.
CAN'T YOU SEE WHAT JUST BEING AROUND YOU *DOES?*

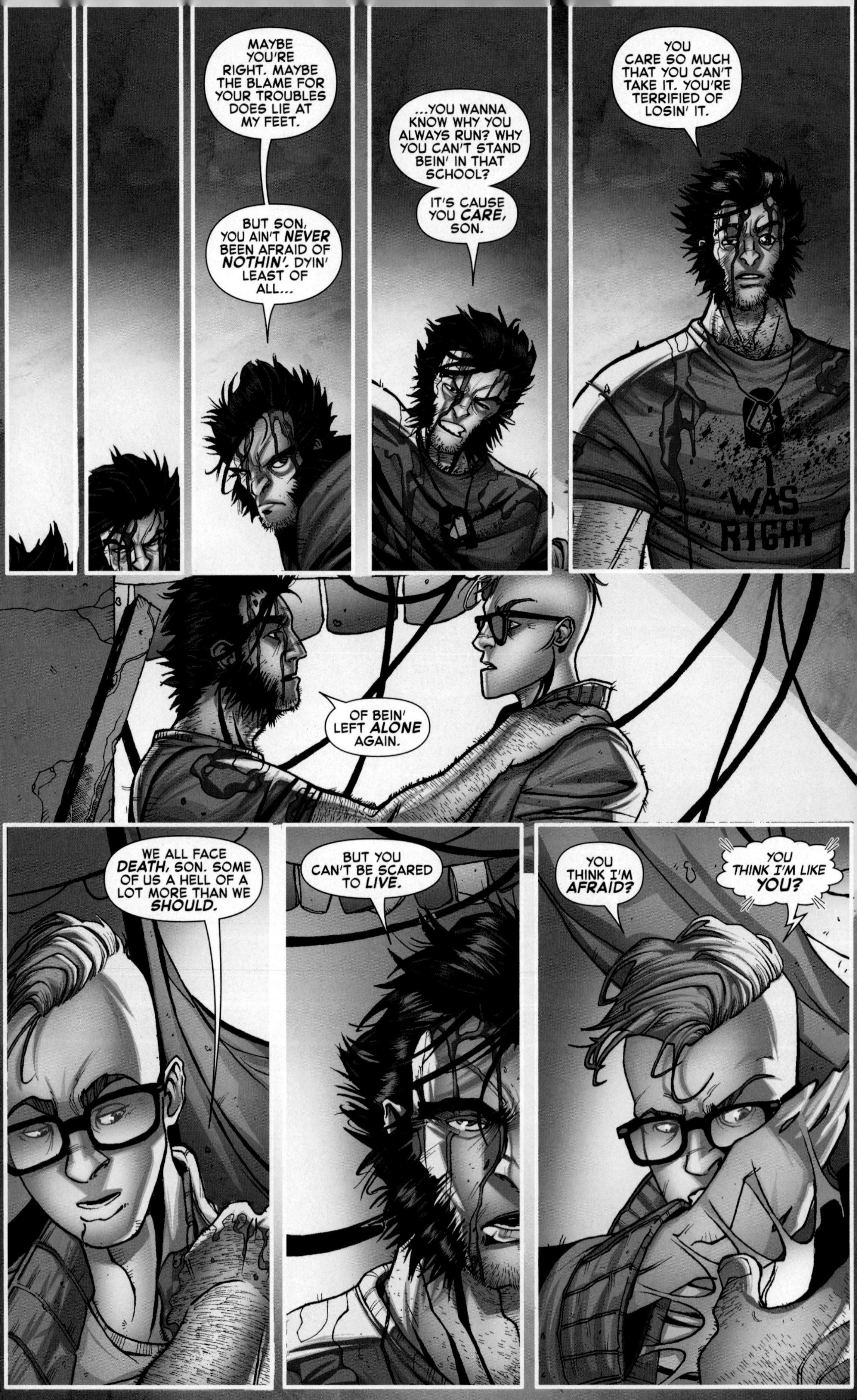
MAYBE YOU'RE RIGHT. MAYBE THE BLAME FOR YOUR TROUBLES DOES LIE AT MY FEET.
BUT SON, YOU AIN'T NEVER BEEN AFRAID OF NOTHIN'. DYIN' LEAST OF ALL...
...YOU WANNA KNOW WHY YOU ALWAYS RUN? WHY YOU CAN'T STAND BEIN' IN THAT SCHOOL?
IT'S CAUSE YOU CARE, SON.
YOU CARE SO MUCH THAT YOU CAN'T TAKE IT. YOU'RE TERRIFIED OF LOSIN' IT.
I WAS RIGHT
OF BEIN' LEFT ALONE AGAIN.
WE ALL FACE DEATH, SON. SOME OF US A HELL OF A LOT MORE THAN WE SHOULD.
BUT YOU CAN'T BE SCARED TO LIVE.
YOU THINK I'M AFRAID?
YOU THINK I'M LIKE YOU?

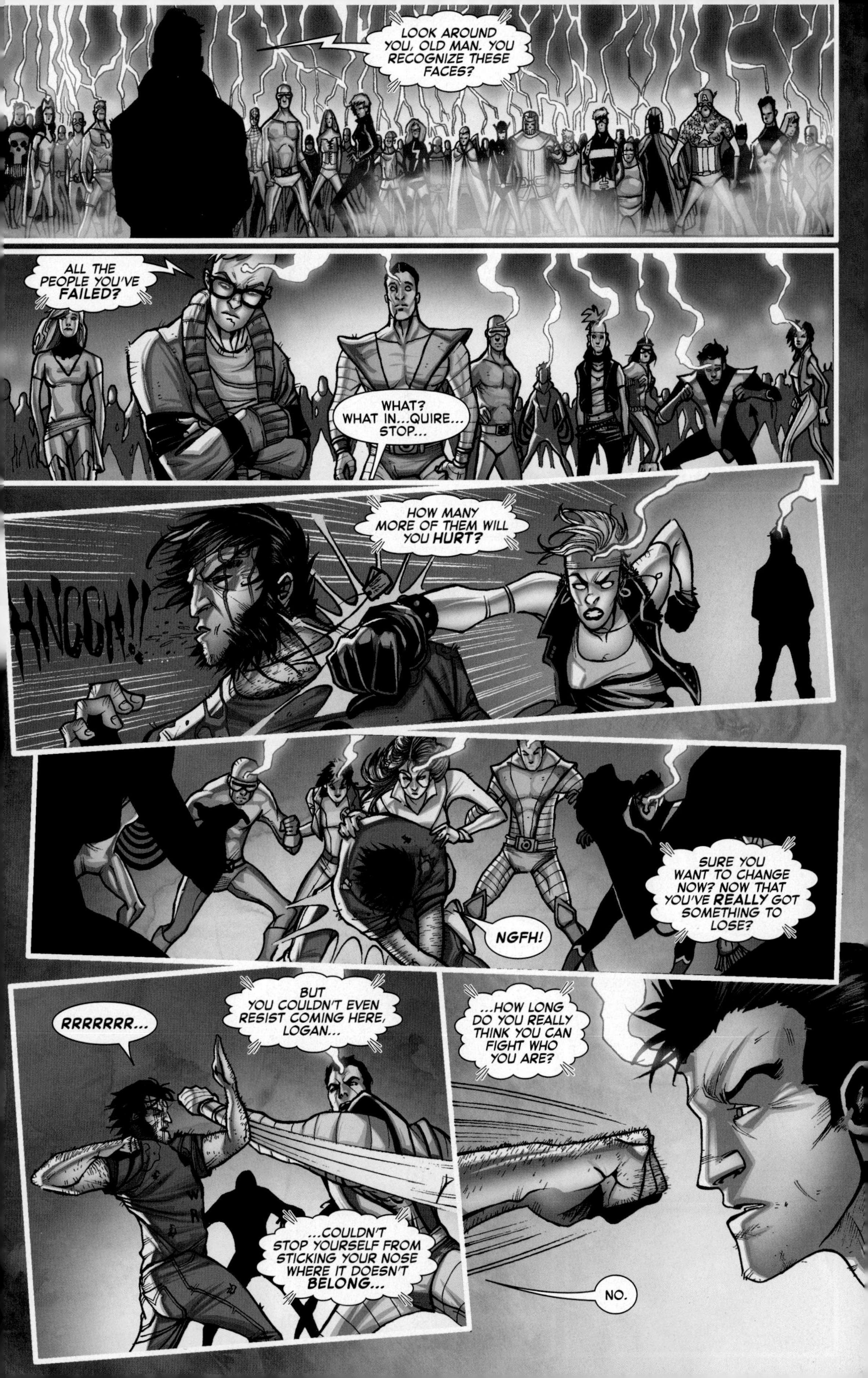
LOOK AROUND YOU, OLD MAN. YOU RECOGNIZE THESE FACES?
ALL THE PEOPLE YOU'VE FAILED?
WHAT? WHAT IN...QUIRE... STOP...
HOW MANY MORE OF THEM WILL YOU HURT?
HNGGH!!
SURE YOU WANT TO CHANGE NOW? NOW THAT YOU'VE REALLY GOT SOMETHING TO LOSE?
NGFH!
RRRRRRR...
BUT YOU COULDN'T EVEN RESIST COMING HERE, LOGAN...
...COULDN'T STOP YOURSELF FROM STICKING YOUR NOSE WHERE IT DOESN'T BELONG...
...HOW LONG DO YOU REALLY THINK YOU CAN FIGHT WHO YOU ARE?
NO.

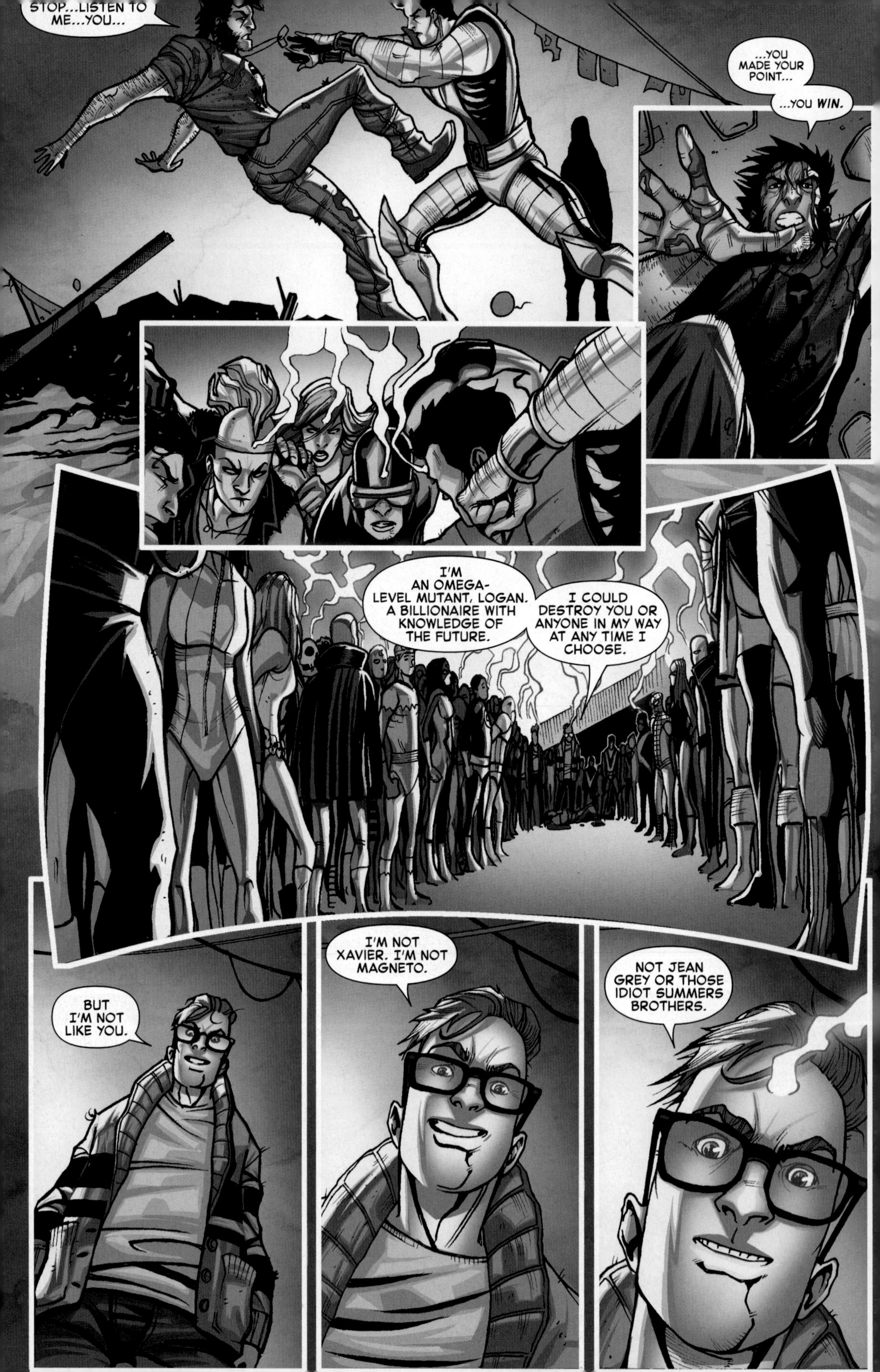
STOP...LISTEN TO ME...YOU...
...YOU MADE YOUR POINT...
...YOU WIN.
I'M AN OMEGA-LEVEL MUTANT, LOGAN. A BILLIONAIRE WITH KNOWLEDGE OF THE FUTURE.
I COULD DESTROY YOU OR ANYONE IN MY WAY AT ANY TIME I CHOOSE.
BUT I'M NOT LIKE YOU.
I'M NOT XAVIER. I'M NOT MAGNETO.
NOT JEAN GREY OR THOSE IDIOT SUMMERS BROTHERS.

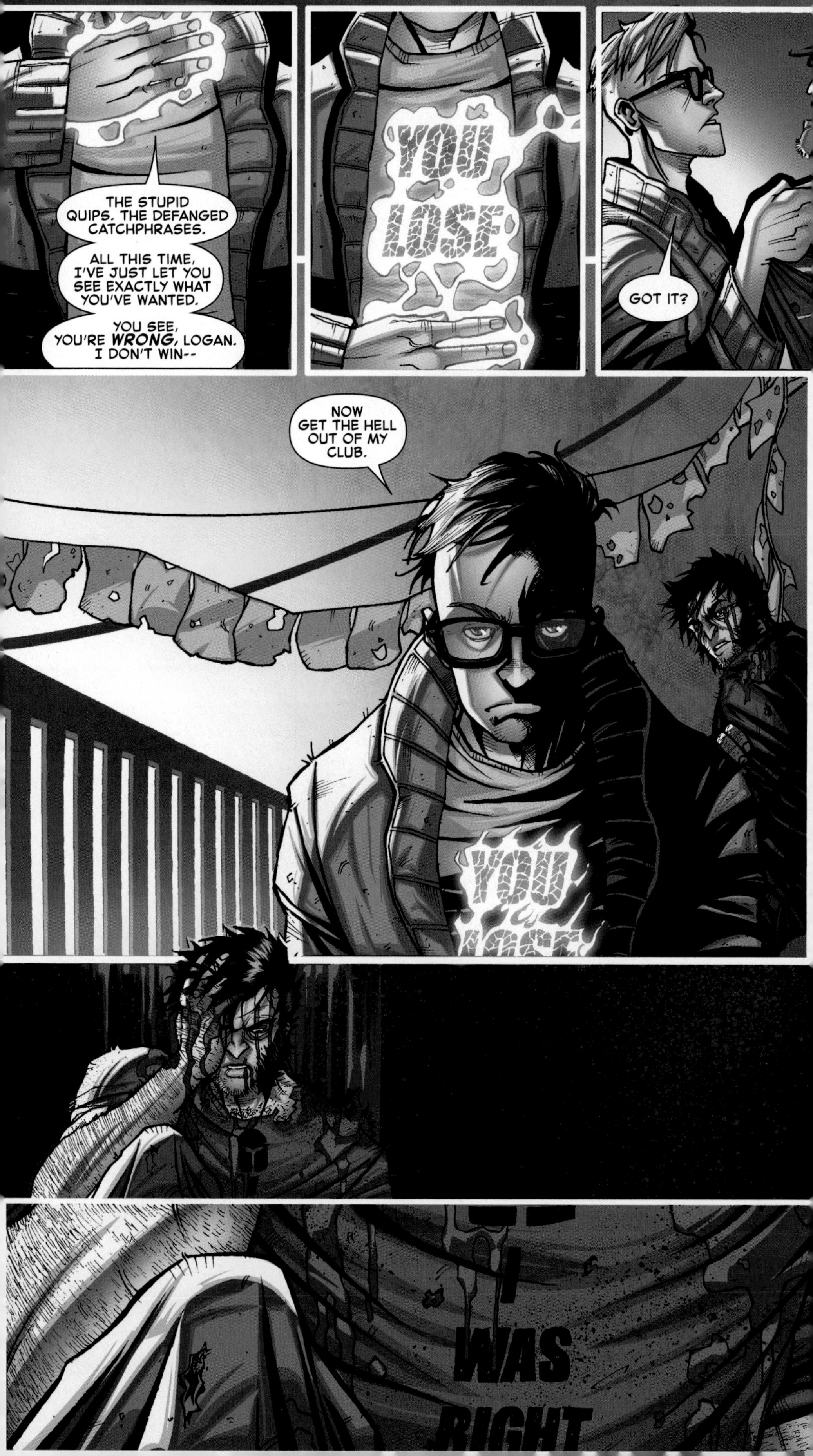
THE STUPID QUIPS. THE DEFANGED CATCHPHRASES.
ALL THIS TIME, I'VE JUST LET YOU SEE EXACTLY WHAT YOU'VE WANTED.
YOU SEE, YOU'RE WRONG, LOGAN. I DON'T WIN--
YOU LOSE
GOT IT?
NOW GET THE HELL OUT OF MY CLUB.
YOU
WAS

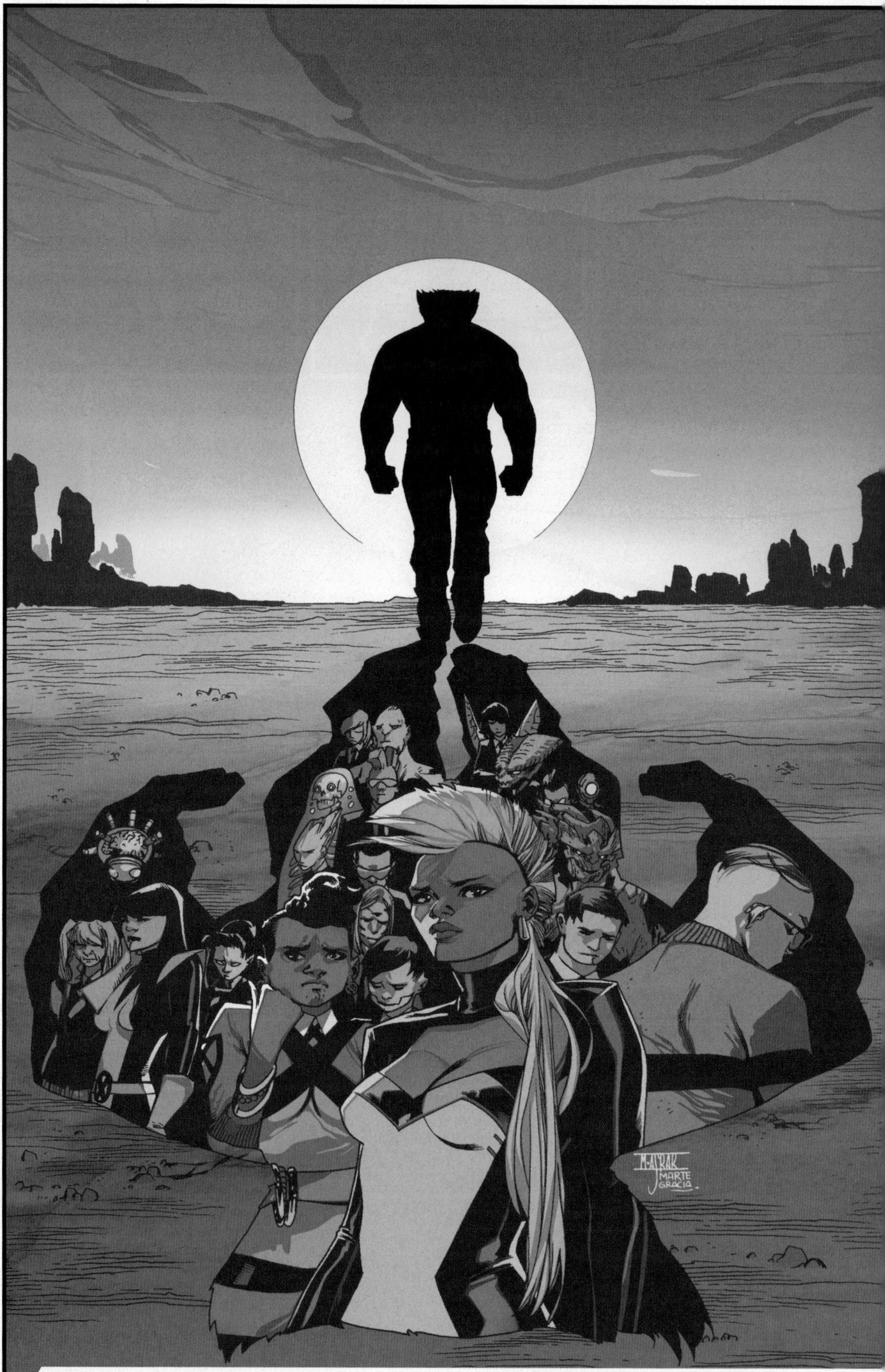
M·ALRAK
MARTE
GRACIA

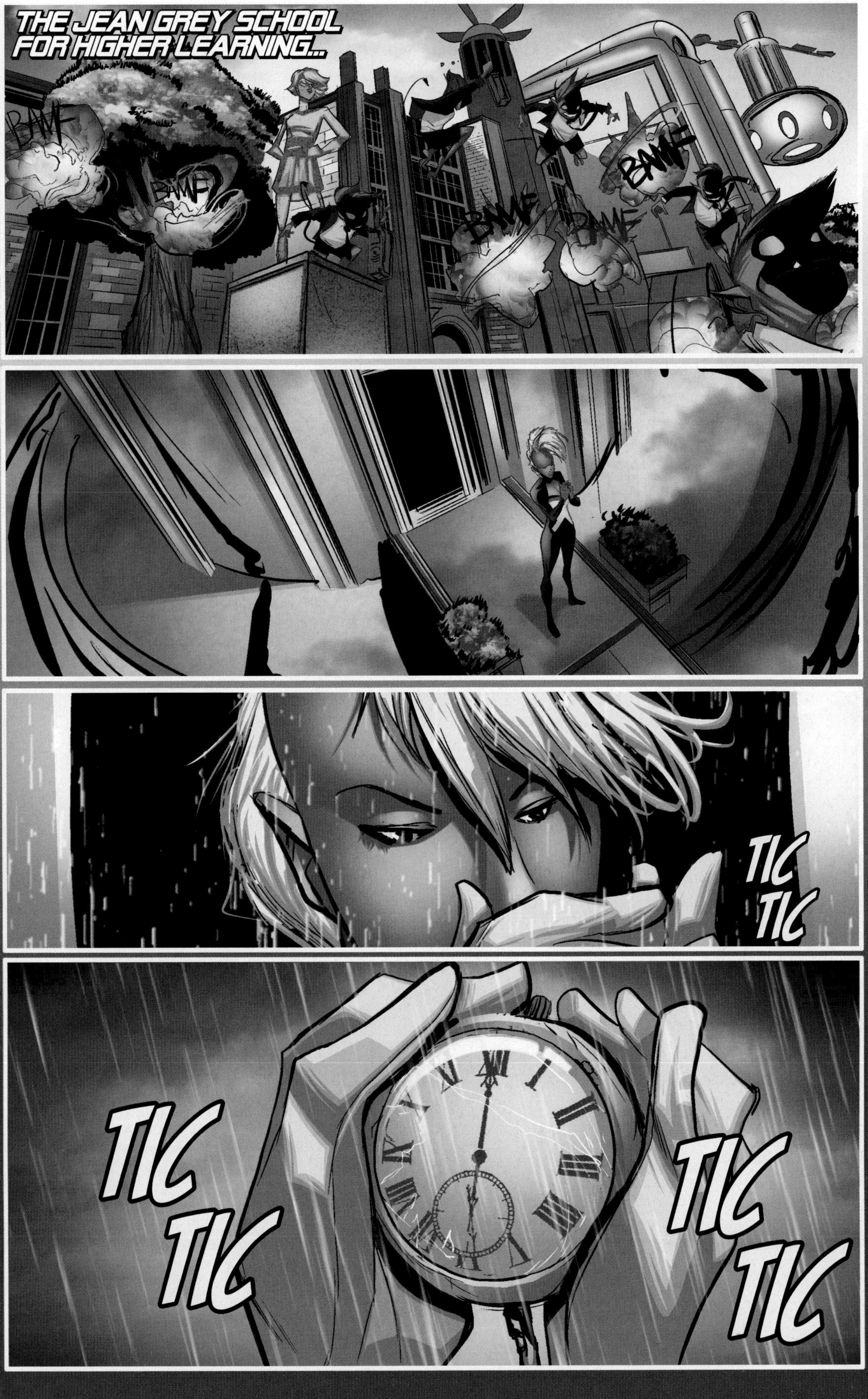
THE JEAN GREY SCHOOL FOR HIGHER LEARNING...
BAMF
BAMF
BAMF
BAMF
BAMF
TIC
TIC
TIC
TIC
TIC
TIC

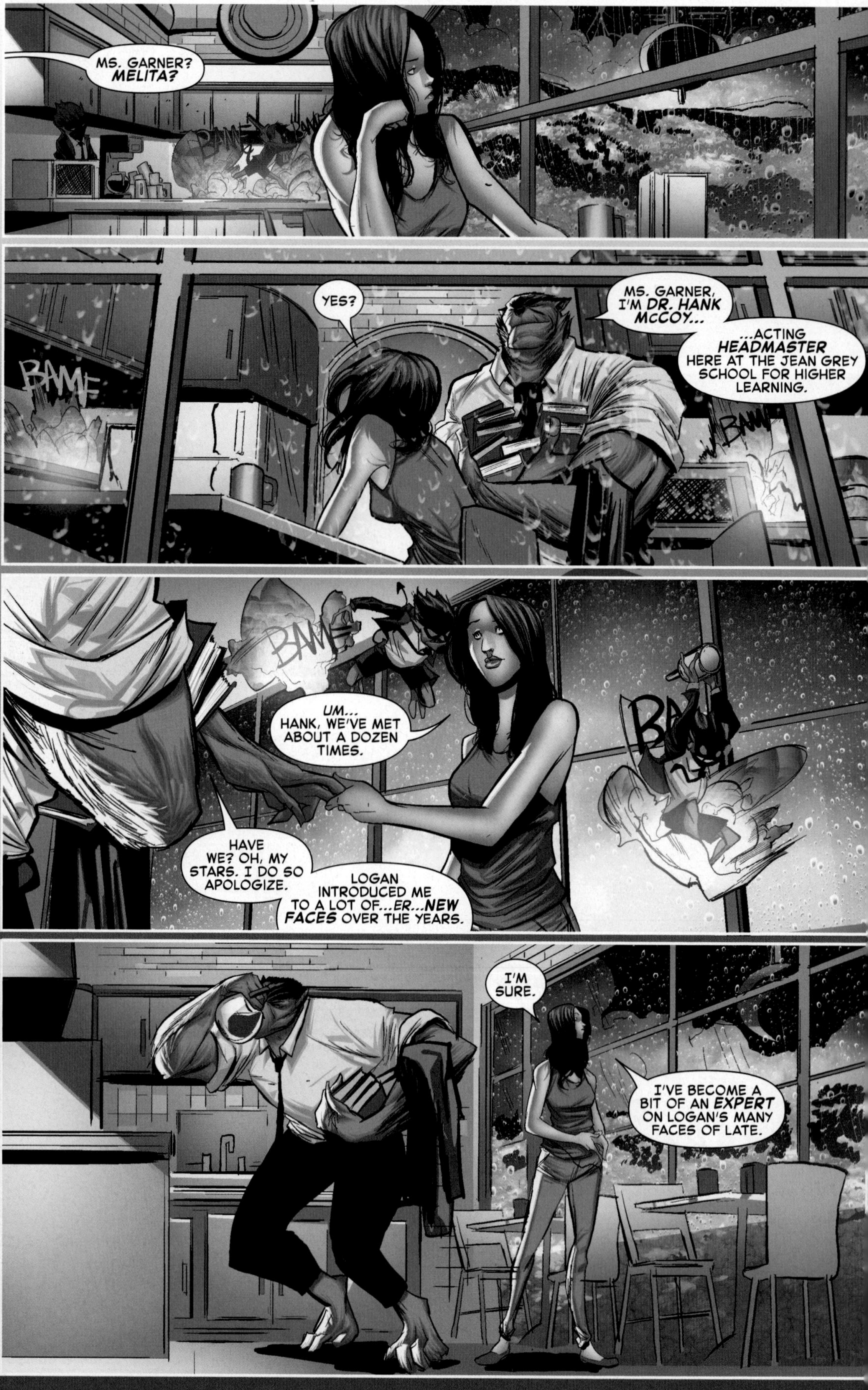

MS. GARNER? MELITA?
BAMF
BAMF
YES?
MS. GARNER, I'M DR. HANK McCOY...
...ACTING HEADMASTER HERE AT THE JEAN GREY SCHOOL FOR HIGHER LEARNING.
BAMF
BAMF
BAMF
UM... HANK, WE'VE MET ABOUT A DOZEN TIMES.
HAVE WE? OH, MY STARS. I DO SO APOLOGIZE.
LOGAN INTRODUCED ME TO A LOT OF...ER...NEW FACES OVER THE YEARS.
I'M SURE.
I'VE BECOME A BIT OF AN EXPERT ON LOGAN'S MANY FACES OF LATE.

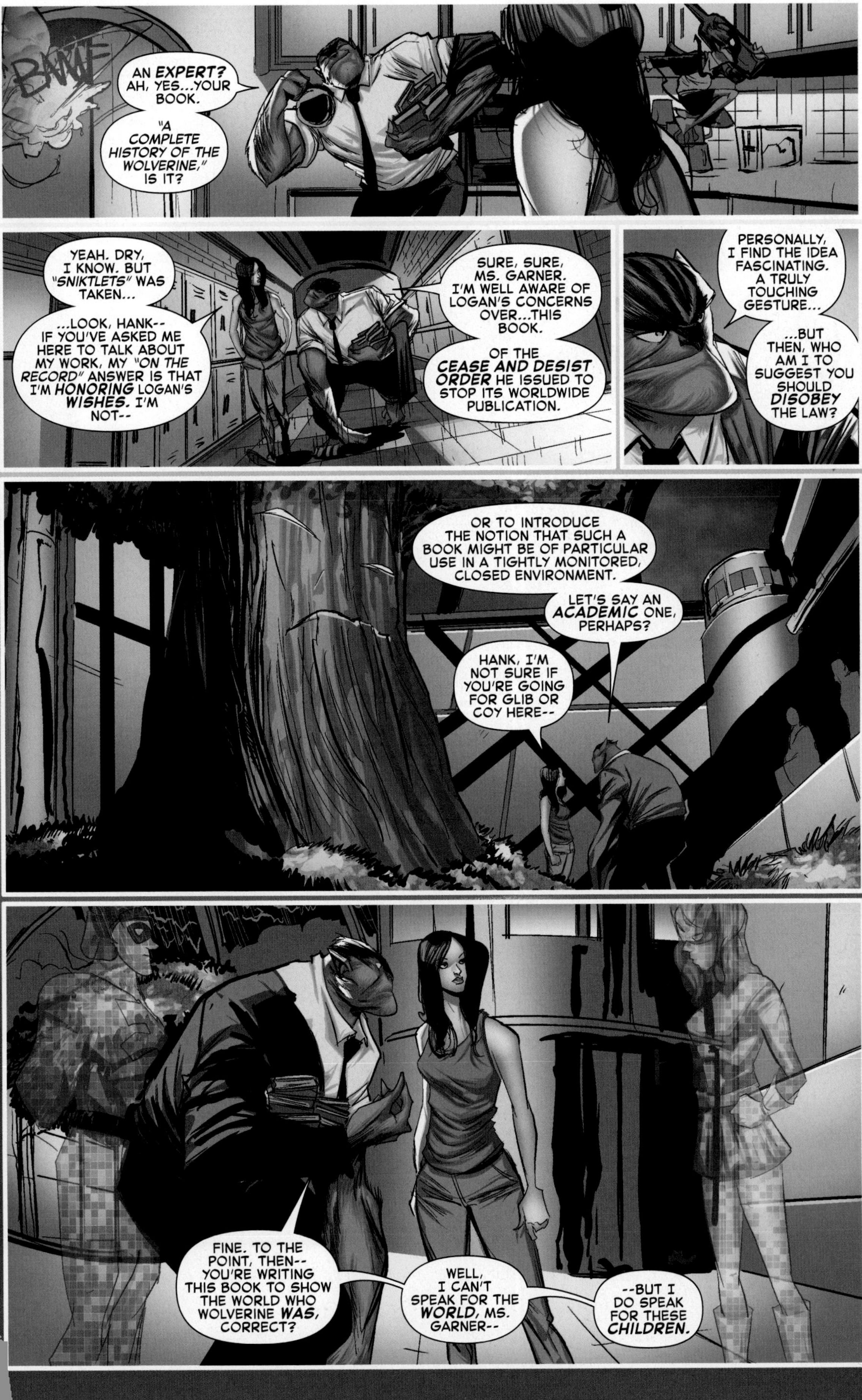
BAMF
AN EXPERT? AH, YES...YOUR BOOK.
"A COMPLETE HISTORY OF THE WOLVERINE," IS IT?
YEAH. DRY, I KNOW. BUT "SNIKTLETS" WAS TAKEN...
...LOOK, HANK-- IF YOU'VE ASKED ME HERE TO TALK ABOUT MY WORK, MY "ON THE RECORD" ANSWER IS THAT I'M HONORING LOGAN'S WISHES. I'M NOT--
SURE, SURE, MS. GARNER. I'M WELL AWARE OF LOGAN'S CONCERNS OVER...THIS BOOK.
OF THE CEASE AND DESIST ORDER HE ISSUED TO STOP ITS WORLDWIDE PUBLICATION.
PERSONALLY, I FIND THE IDEA FASCINATING. A TRULY TOUCHING GESTURE...
...BUT THEN, WHO AM I TO SUGGEST YOU SHOULD DISOBEY THE LAW?
OR TO INTRODUCE THE NOTION THAT SUCH A BOOK MIGHT BE OF PARTICULAR USE IN A TIGHTLY MONITORED, CLOSED ENVIRONMENT.
LET'S SAY AN ACADEMIC ONE, PERHAPS?
HANK, I'M NOT SURE IF YOU'RE GOING FOR GLIB OR COY HERE--
FINE. TO THE POINT, THEN-- YOU'RE WRITING THIS BOOK TO SHOW THE WORLD WHO WOLVERINE WAS, CORRECT?
WELL, I CAN'T SPEAK FOR THE WORLD, MS. GARNER--
--BUT I DO SPEAK FOR THESE CHILDREN.

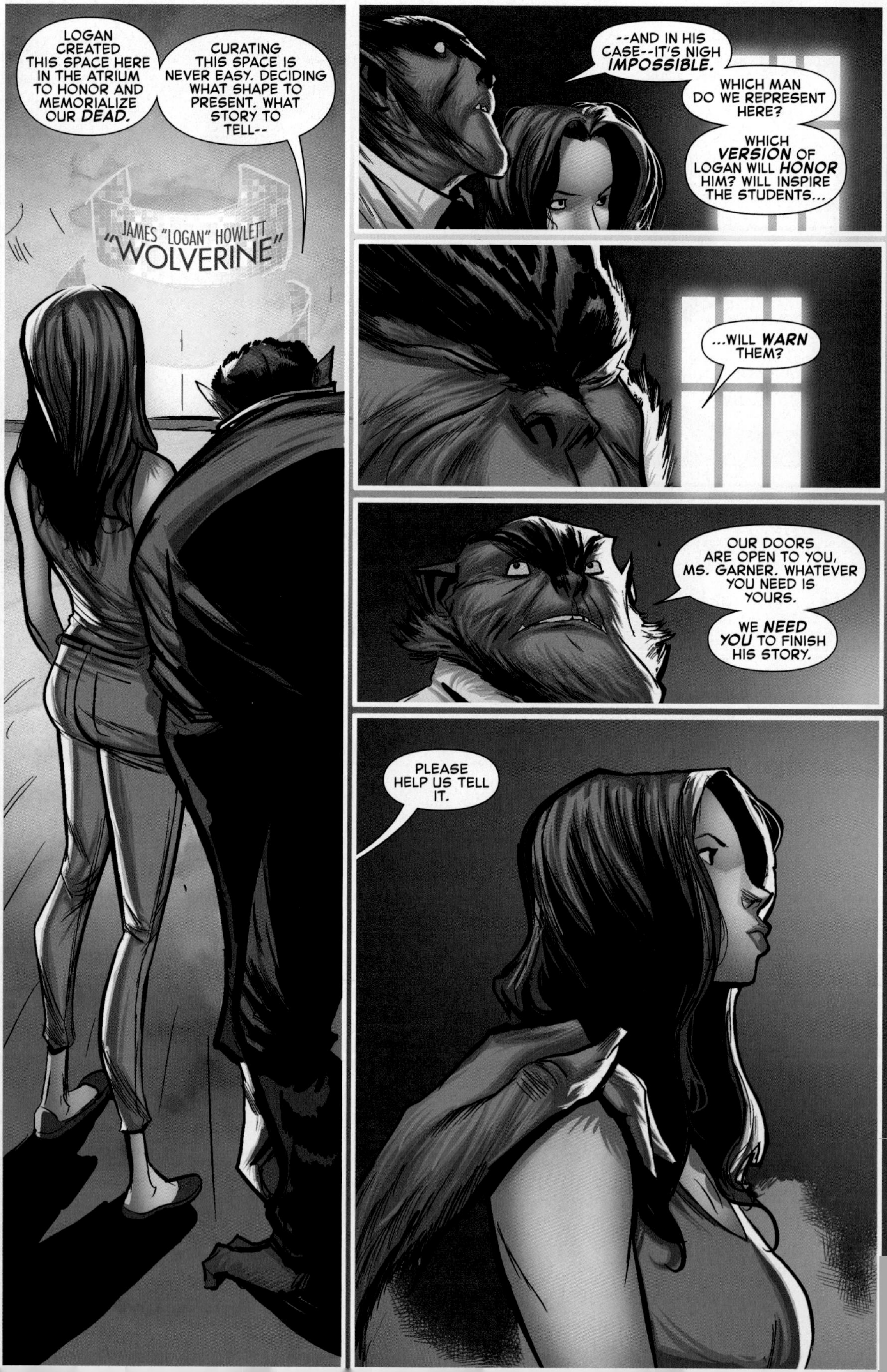
LOGAN CREATED THIS SPACE HERE IN THE ATRIUM TO HONOR AND MEMORIALIZE OUR DEAD.
CURATING THIS SPACE IS NEVER EASY. DECIDING WHAT SHAPE TO PRESENT. WHAT STORY TO TELL--
JAMES "LOGAN" HOWLETT
"WOLVERINE"
--AND IN HIS CASE--IT'S NIGH IMPOSSIBLE.
WHICH MAN DO WE REPRESENT HERE?
WHICH VERSION OF LOGAN WILL HONOR HIM? WILL INSPIRE THE STUDENTS...
...WILL WARN THEM?
OUR DOORS ARE OPEN TO YOU, MS. GARNER. WHATEVER YOU NEED IS YOURS.
WE NEED YOU TO FINISH HIS STORY.
PLEASE HELP US TELL IT.

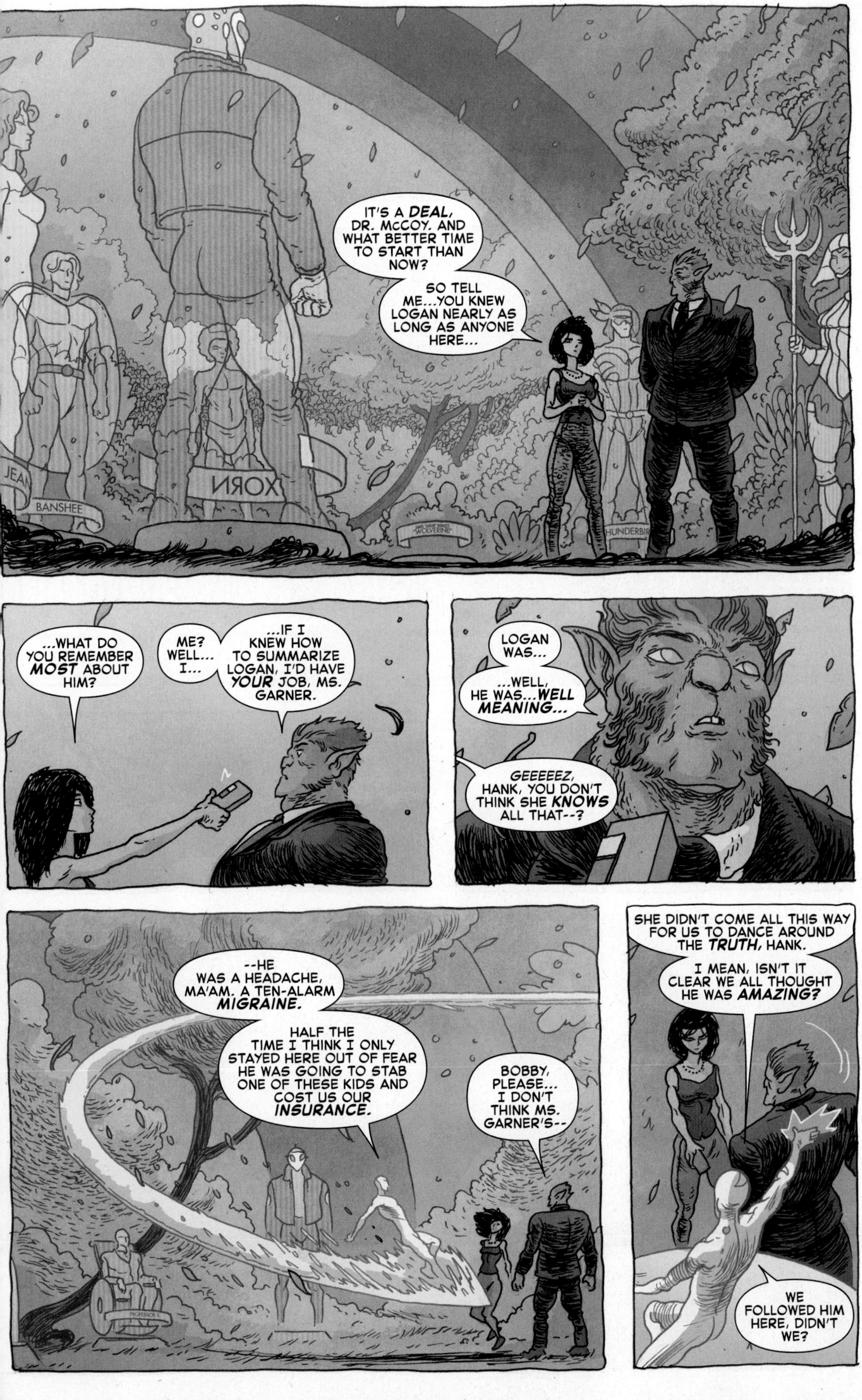
JEAN
BANSHEE
XORN
IT'S A DEAL, DR. McCOY. AND WHAT BETTER TIME TO START THAN NOW?
SO TELL ME...YOU KNEW LOGAN NEARLY AS LONG AS ANYONE HERE...
...WHAT DO YOU REMEMBER MOST ABOUT HIM?
ME? WELL... I...
...IF I KNEW HOW TO SUMMARIZE LOGAN, I'D HAVE YOUR JOB, MS. GARNER.
LOGAN WAS...
...WELL, HE WAS...WELL MEANING...
GEEEEEZ, HANK, YOU DON'T THINK SHE KNOWS ALL THAT--?
--HE WAS A HEADACHE, MA'AM. A TEN-ALARM MIGRAINE.
HALF THE TIME I THINK I ONLY STAYED HERE OUT OF FEAR HE WAS GOING TO STAB ONE OF THESE KIDS AND COST US OUR INSURANCE.
BOBBY, PLEASE... I DON'T THINK MS. GARNER'S--
SHE DIDN'T COME ALL THIS WAY FOR US TO DANCE AROUND THE TRUTH, HANK.
I MEAN, ISN'T IT CLEAR WE ALL THOUGHT HE WAS AMAZING?
WE FOLLOWED HIM HERE, DIDN'T WE?

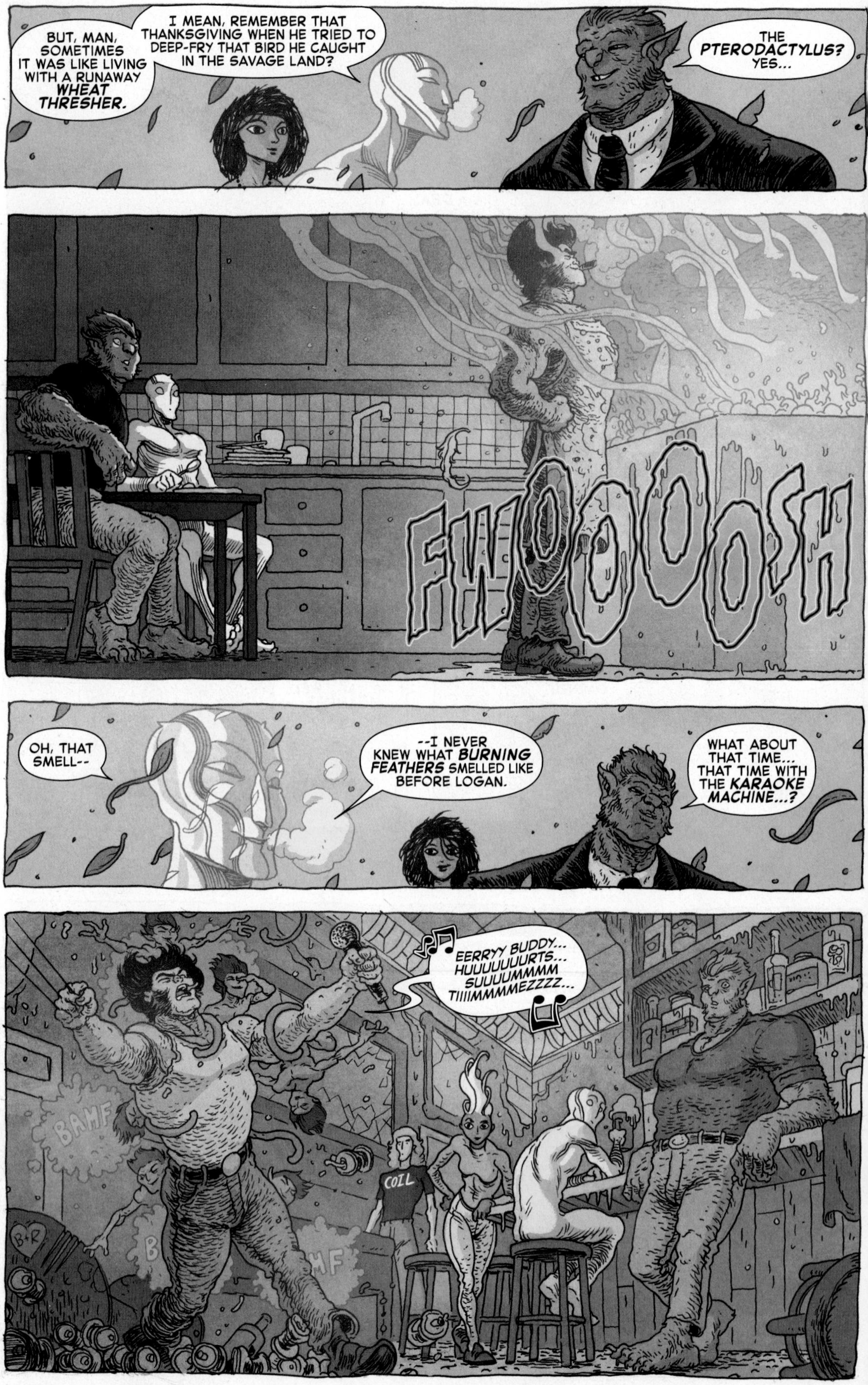
BUT, MAN, SOMETIMES IT WAS LIKE LIVING WITH A RUNAWAY WHEAT THRESHER.
I MEAN, REMEMBER THAT THANKSGIVING WHEN HE TRIED TO DEEP-FRY THAT BIRD HE CAUGHT IN THE SAVAGE LAND?
THE PTERODACTYLUS? YES...
FWOOOOSH
OH, THAT SMELL--
--I NEVER KNEW WHAT BURNING FEATHERS SMELLED LIKE BEFORE LOGAN.
WHAT ABOUT THAT TIME... THAT TIME WITH THE KARAOKE MACHINE...?
EERRYY BUDDY... HUUUUUUURTS... SUUUUMMMM TIIIIMMMMMEZZZZ...
BAMF
COIL
B+R

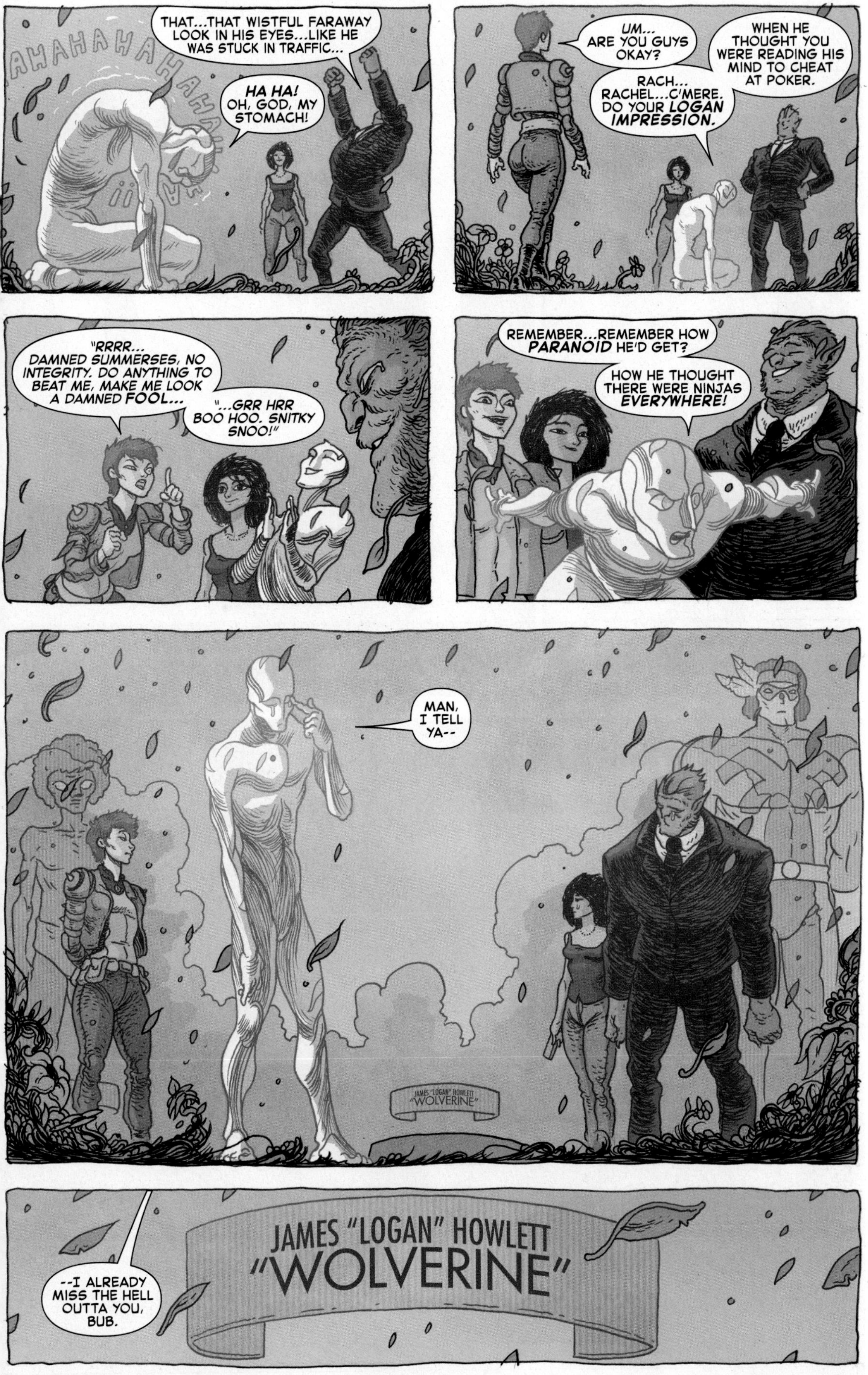
THAT...THAT WISTFUL FARAWAY LOOK IN HIS EYES...LIKE HE WAS STUCK IN TRAFFIC...
HAHAHAHAHAHAHAHA
HA HA! OH, GOD, MY STOMACH!
UM... ARE YOU GUYS OKAY?
WHEN HE THOUGHT YOU WERE READING HIS MIND TO CHEAT AT POKER.
RACH... RACHEL...C'MERE. DO YOUR LOGAN IMPRESSION.
"RRRR... DAMNED SUMMERSES, NO INTEGRITY. DO ANYTHING TO BEAT ME, MAKE ME LOOK A DAMNED FOOL...
"...GRR HRR BOO HOO. SNITKY SNOO!"
REMEMBER...REMEMBER HOW PARANOID HE'D GET?
HOW HE THOUGHT THERE WERE NINJAS EVERYWHERE!
MAN, I TELL YA--
JAMES "LOGAN" HOWLETT "WOLVERINE"
--I ALREADY MISS THE HELL OUTTA YOU, BUB.
JAMES "LOGAN" HOWLETT "WOLVERINE"

WWWWWWNNZZ
WWWWWWNNZZZZ
WWWNNNZZZ

I'M SORRY, MS. GARNER, I DON'T MEAN TO BE *RUDE.*

I JUST--

ADAMANTIUM DRILL-BITS

--I JUST *NEED* TO FINISH THIS.

IT'S OKAY, *HISAKO.* I UNDERSTAND.

WE CAN TALK WHENEVER YOU'RE READY.

BRONG
BRONG
BRONG

WAIT.

LOGAN REALLY DID *BELIEVE* IN THIS PLACE, YOU KNOW.

SOME OF THE OTHERS MIGHT TELL YOU IT'S A *JOKE*, OR THAT HE BUILT IT OUT OF *GUILT.*

BUT THAT'S NOT TRUE.

HE KNEW THAT MUTANTKIND NEEDED HIM TO BE MORE THAN OUR SWORD--

--WE NEEDED A *SHIELD.*

WWWWWWWWWNNNZ
WWWWWNNNNN

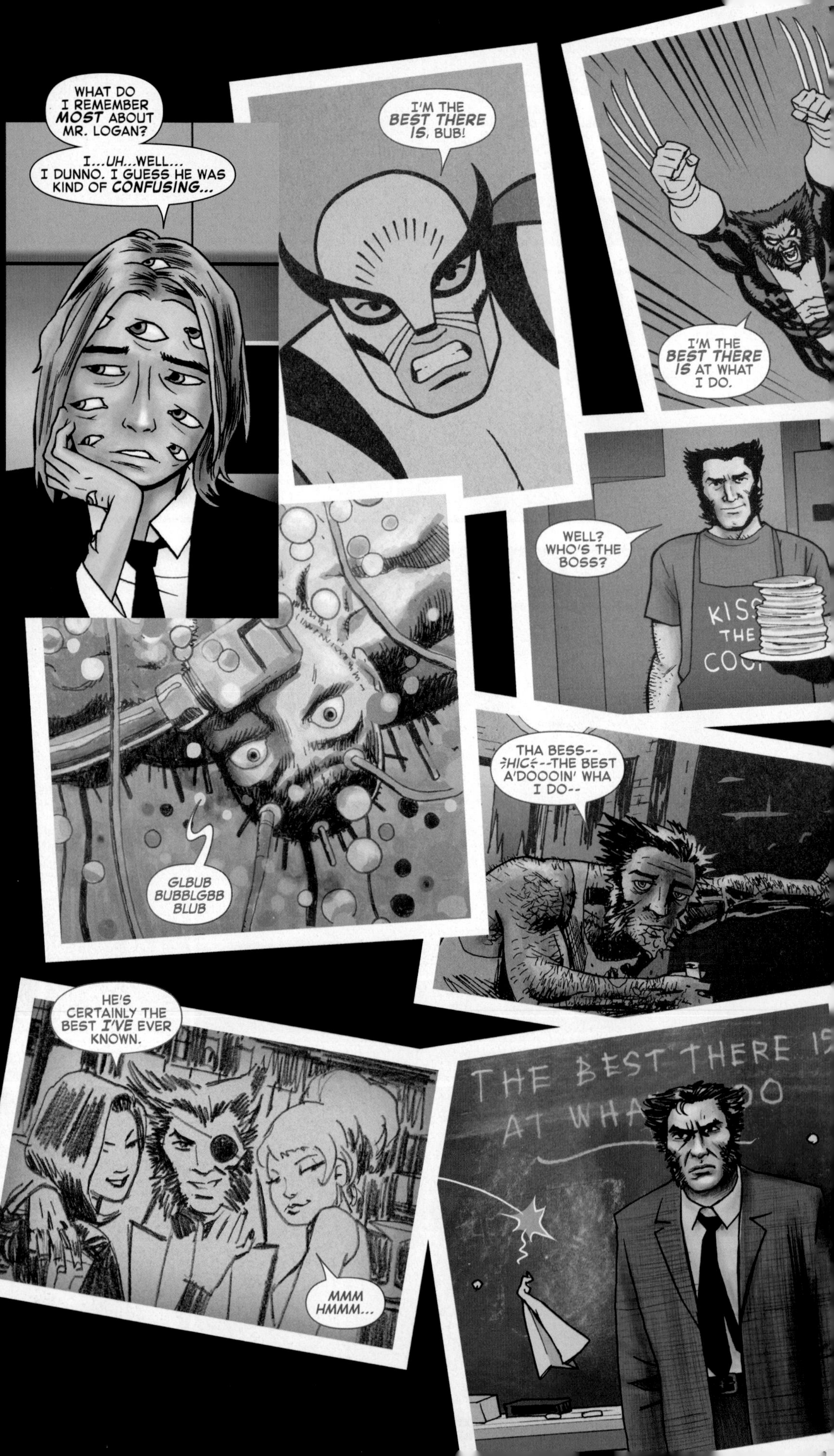
WHAT DO I REMEMBER MOST ABOUT MR. LOGAN?
I...UH...WELL... I DUNNO. I GUESS HE WAS KIND OF CONFUSING...
I'M THE BEST THERE IS, BUB!
I'M THE BEST THERE IS AT WHAT I DO.
WELL? WHO'S THE BOSS?
KISS THE COO
GLBUB BUBBLGBB BLUB
THA BESS-- HIC --THE BEST A'DOOOIN' WHA I DO--
HE'S CERTAINLY THE BEST I'VE EVER KNOWN.
MMM HMMM...
THE BEST THERE IS AT WHA DO

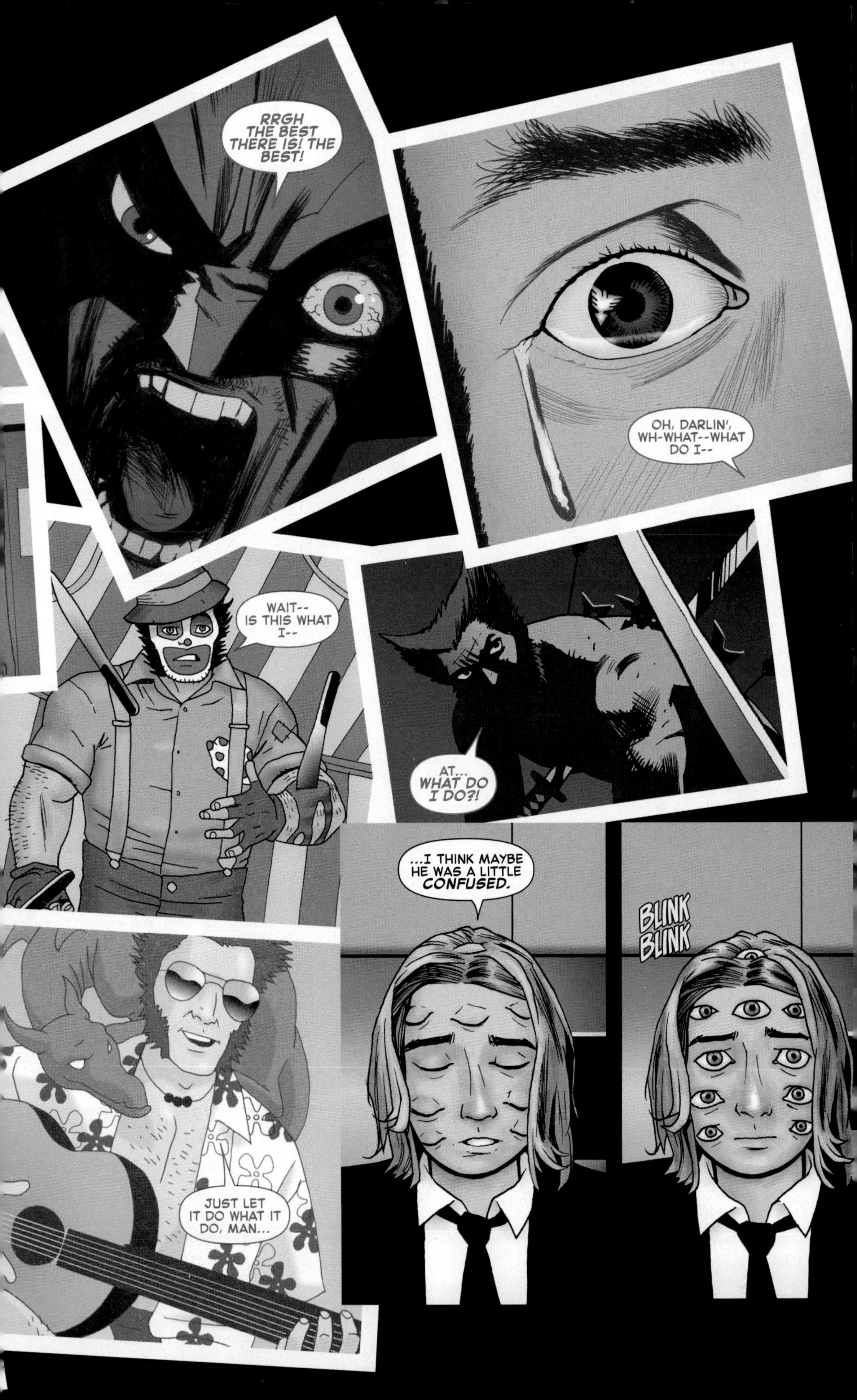
RRGH THE BEST THERE IS! THE BEST!
OH, DARLIN', WH-WHAT--WHAT DO I--
WAIT-- IS THIS WHAT I--
AT... WHAT DO I DO?!
JUST LET IT DO WHAT IT DO, MAN...
...I THINK MAYBE HE WAS A LITTLE CONFUSED.
BLINK BLINK

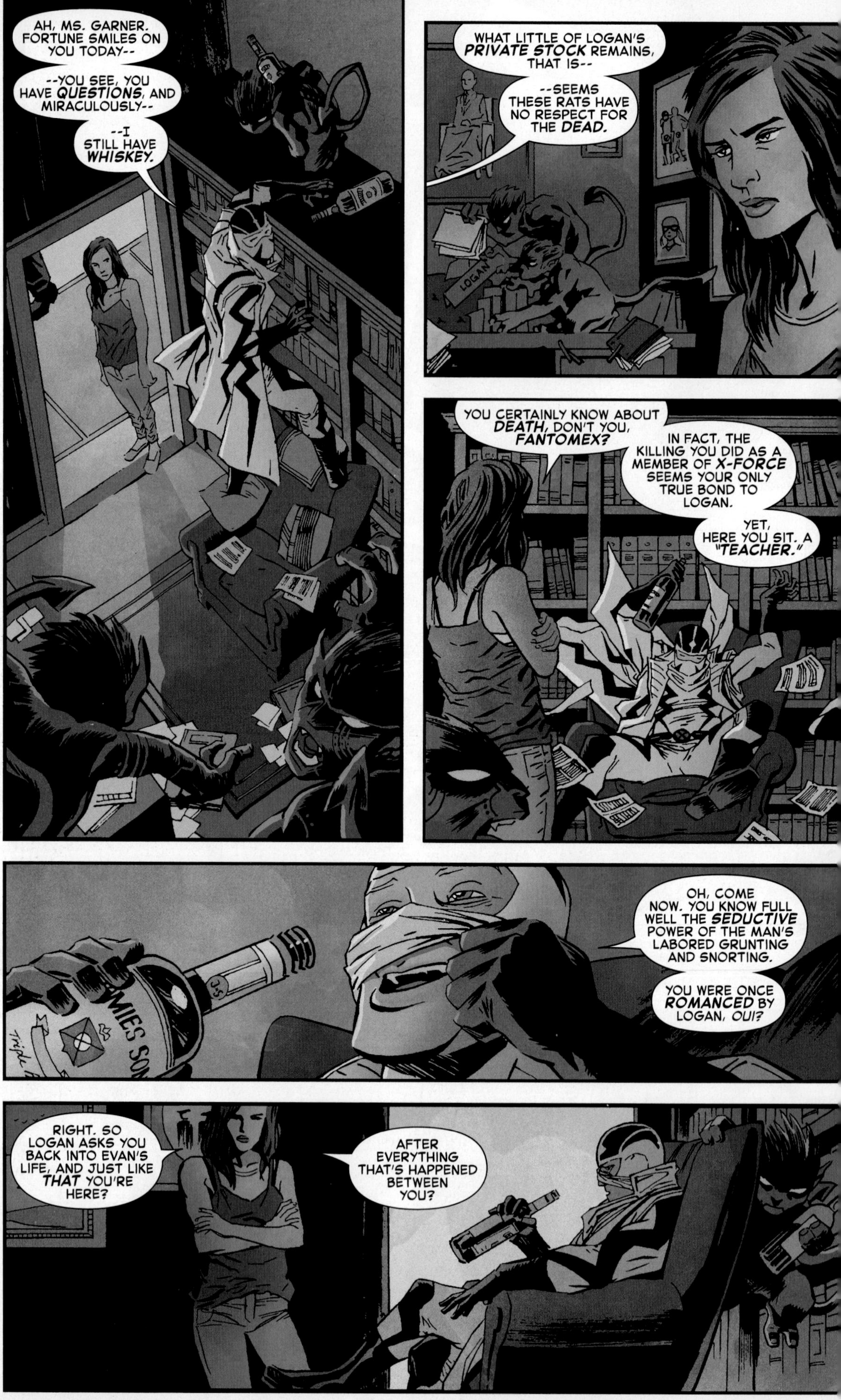
AH, MS. GARNER. FORTUNE SMILES ON YOU TODAY--
--YOU SEE, YOU HAVE QUESTIONS, AND MIRACULOUSLY--
--I STILL HAVE WHISKEY.
WHAT LITTLE OF LOGAN'S PRIVATE STOCK REMAINS, THAT IS--
--SEEMS THESE RATS HAVE NO RESPECT FOR THE DEAD.
LOGAN
YOU CERTAINLY KNOW ABOUT DEATH, DON'T YOU, FANTOMEX?
IN FACT, THE KILLING YOU DID AS A MEMBER OF X-FORCE SEEMS YOUR ONLY TRUE BOND TO LOGAN.
YET, HERE YOU SIT. A "TEACHER."
OH, COME NOW. YOU KNOW FULL WELL THE SEDUCTIVE POWER OF THE MAN'S LABORED GRUNTING AND SNORTING.
YOU WERE ONCE ROMANCED BY LOGAN, OUI?
RIGHT. SO LOGAN ASKS YOU BACK INTO EVAN'S LIFE, AND JUST LIKE THAT YOU'RE HERE?
AFTER EVERYTHING THAT'S HAPPENED BETWEEN YOU?

TELL ME--YOU KNOW LOSS WELL, DO YOU, CHÉRI?

IN YOUR LINE OF WORK, YOU HAVE EXPERIENCED IT BEFORE, OUI?

BUT WHAT DO YOU KNOW OF THEFT?

AS YOU KNOW, I AM QUITE THE EXPERT ON THE SUBJECT.

IN HIS OWN WAY, SO, TOO, WAS YOUR BELOVED LOGAN.

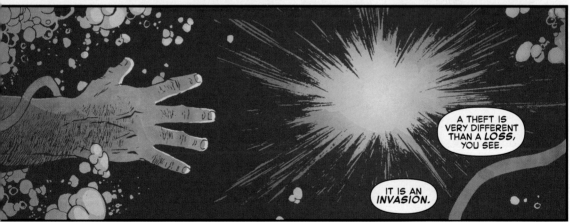

A THEFT IS VERY DIFFERENT THAN A LOSS, YOU SEE.

IT IS AN INVASION.

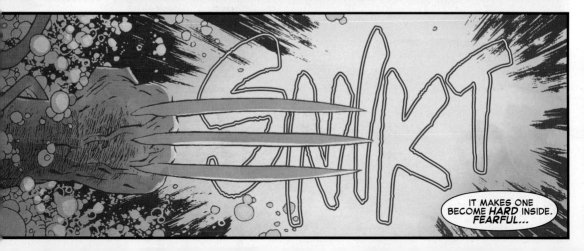

SNIKT

IT MAKES ONE BECOME HARD INSIDE. FEARFUL...

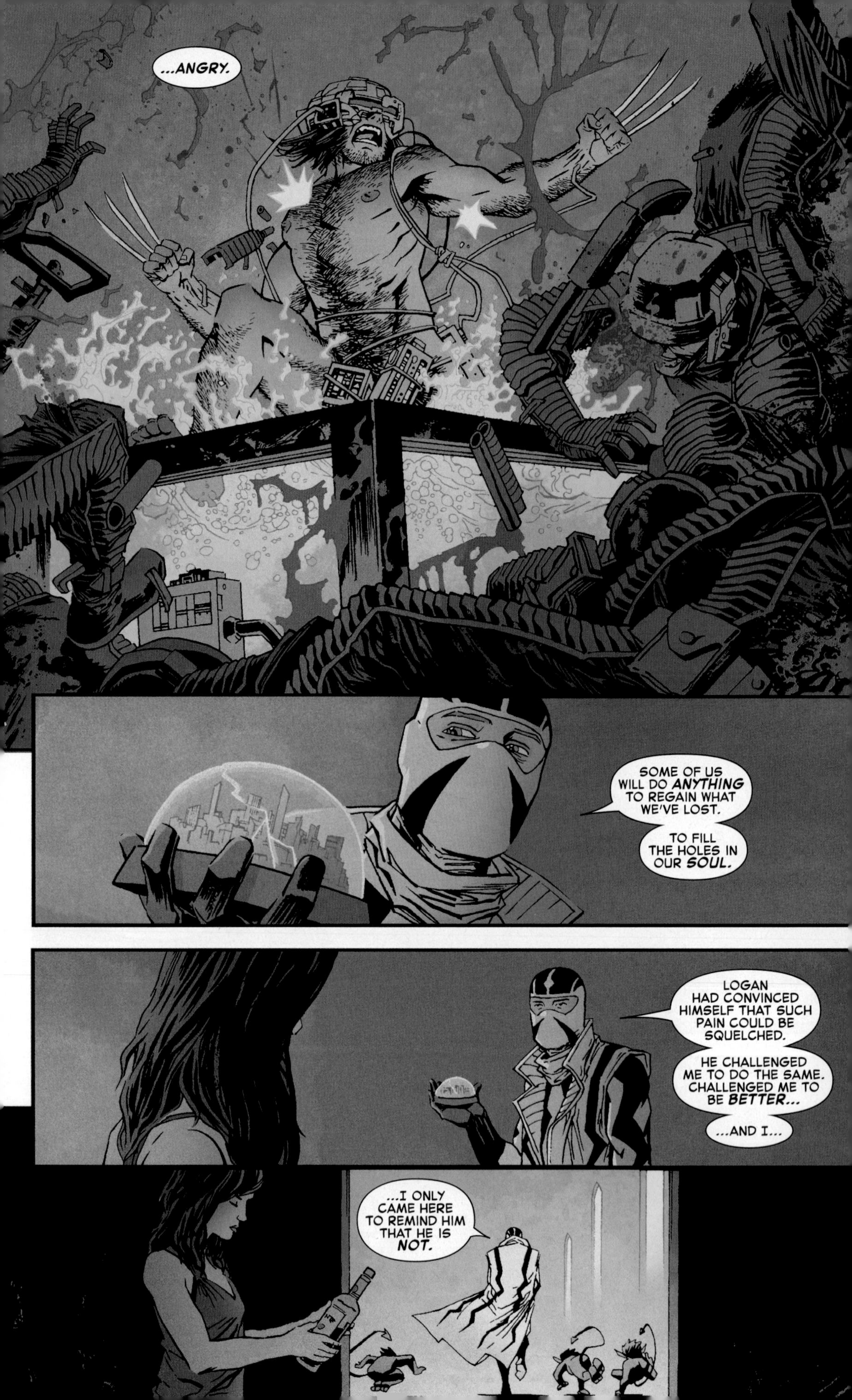
...ANGRY.
SOME OF US WILL DO ANYTHING TO REGAIN WHAT WE'VE LOST.
TO FILL THE HOLES IN OUR SOUL.
LOGAN HAD CONVINCED HIMSELF THAT SUCH PAIN COULD BE SQUELCHED.
HE CHALLENGED ME TO DO THE SAME. CHALLENGED ME TO BE BETTER...
...AND I...
...I ONLY CAME HERE TO REMIND HIM THAT HE IS NOT.

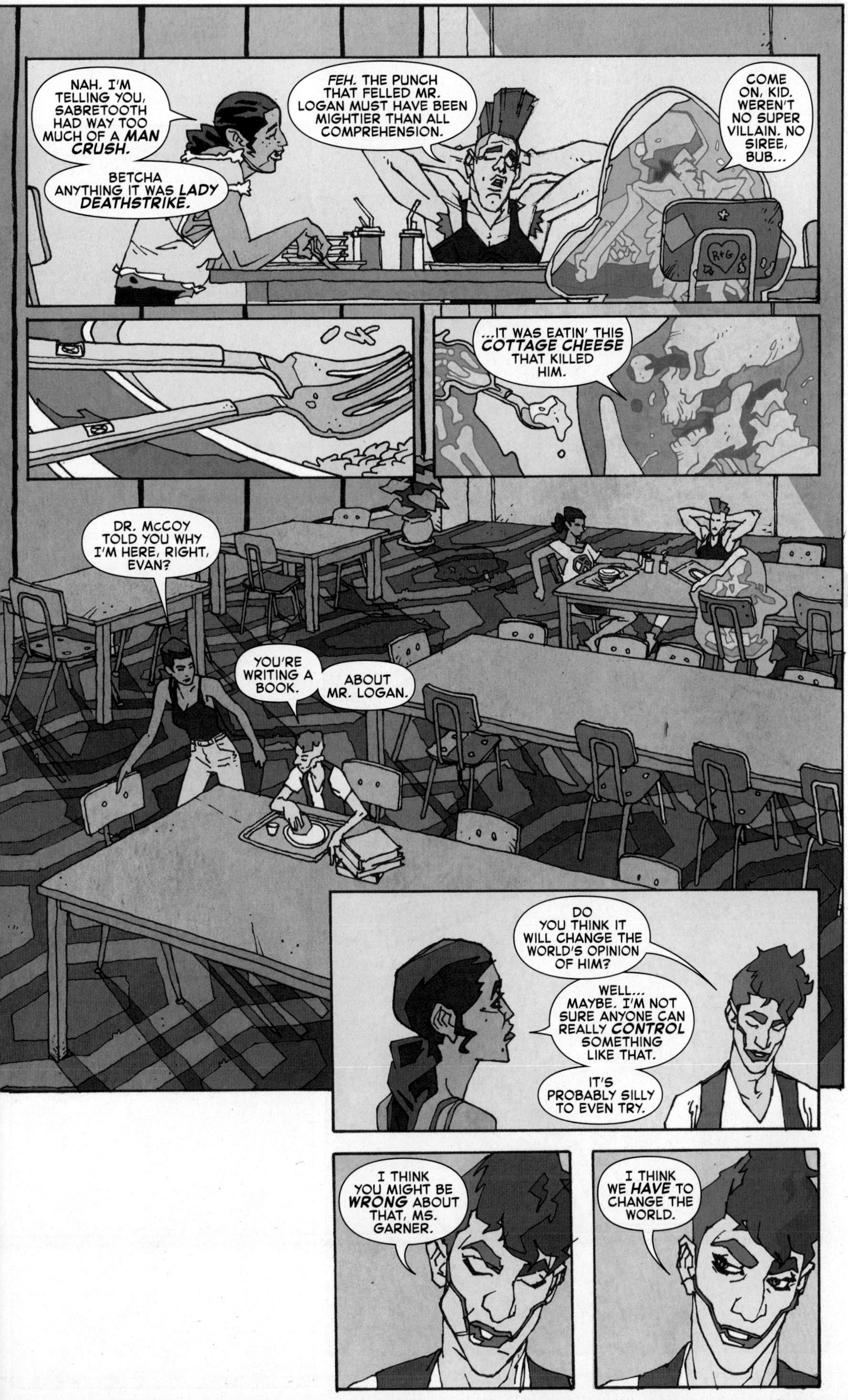
NAH. I'M TELLING YOU, SABRETOOTH HAD WAY TOO MUCH OF A MAN CRUSH.
BETCHA ANYTHING IT WAS LADY DEATHSTRIKE.
FEH. THE PUNCH THAT FELLED MR. LOGAN MUST HAVE BEEN MIGHTIER THAN ALL COMPREHENSION.
COME ON, KID. WEREN'T NO SUPER VILLAIN. NO SIREE, BUB...
...IT WAS EATIN' THIS COTTAGE CHEESE THAT KILLED HIM.
DR. McCOY TOLD YOU WHY I'M HERE, RIGHT, EVAN?
YOU'RE WRITING A BOOK.
ABOUT MR. LOGAN.
DO YOU THINK IT WILL CHANGE THE WORLD'S OPINION OF HIM?
WELL... MAYBE. I'M NOT SURE ANYONE CAN REALLY CONTROL SOMETHING LIKE THAT.
IT'S PROBABLY SILLY TO EVEN TRY.
I THINK YOU MIGHT BE WRONG ABOUT THAT, MS. GARNER.
I THINK WE HAVE TO CHANGE THE WORLD.

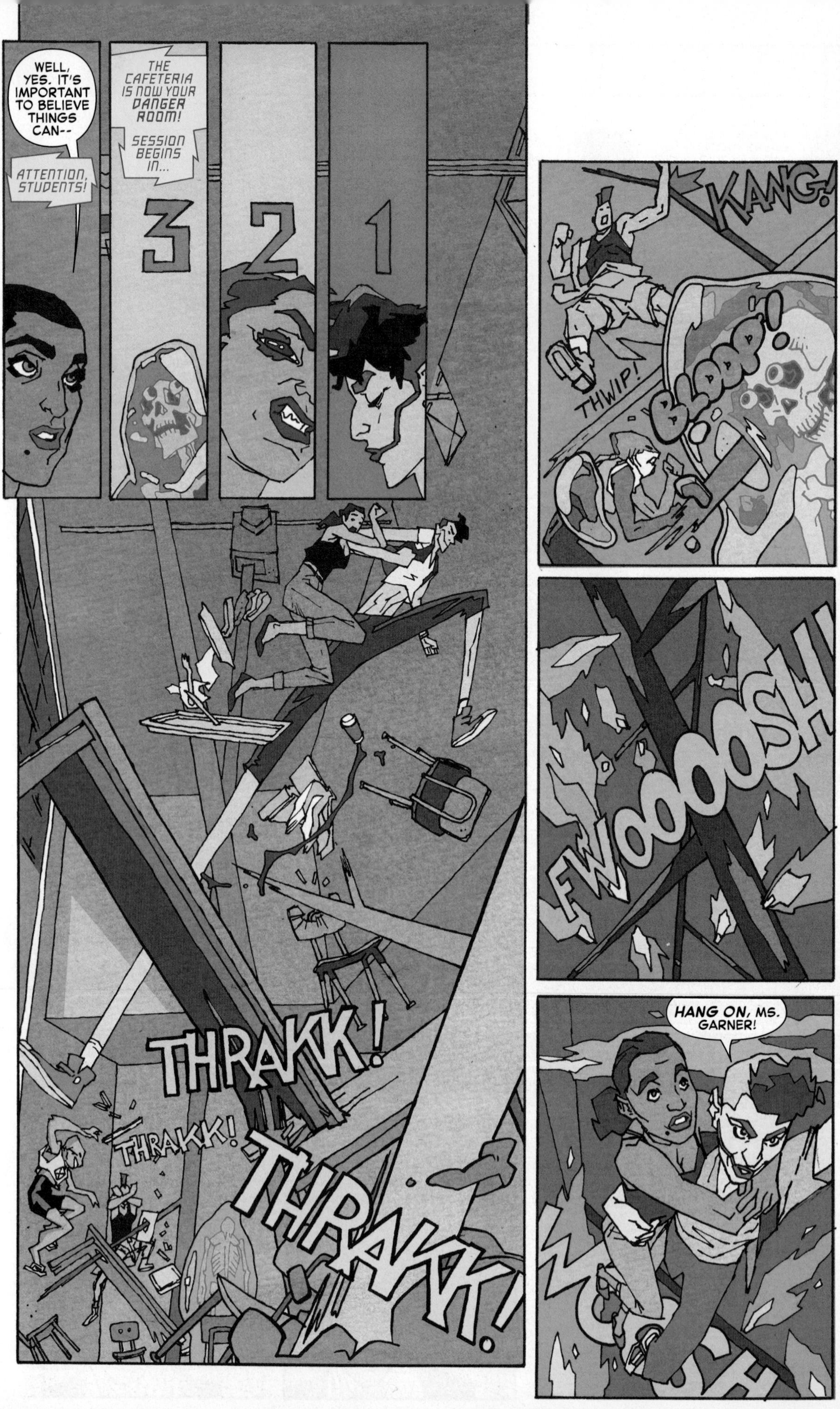
WELL, YES. IT'S IMPORTANT TO BELIEVE THINGS CAN--
ATTENTION, STUDENTS!
THE CAFETERIA IS NOW YOUR DANGER ROOM!
SESSION BEGINS IN...
3
2
1
THRAKK!
THRAKK!
THRAKK!
KANG!
THWIP!
BLOOP!
FWOOOOSH!
HANG ON, MS. GARNER!

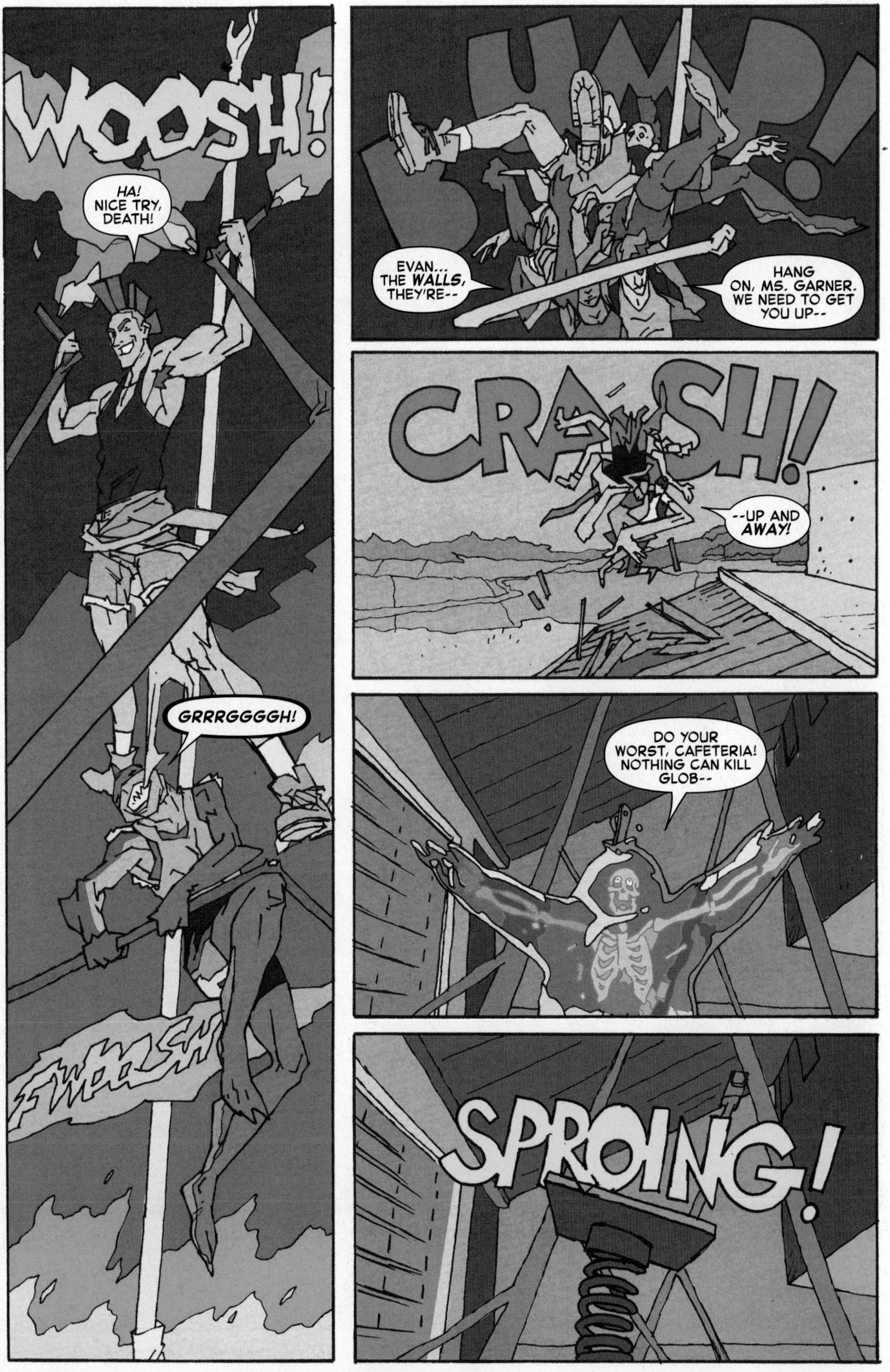
WOOSH!
HA! NICE TRY, DEATH!
GRRRGGGGH!
FWOOSH
THUMP!
EVAN... THE WALLS, THEY'RE--
HANG ON, MS. GARNER. WE NEED TO GET YOU UP--
CRASH!
--UP AND AWAY!
DO YOUR WORST, CAFETERIA! NOTHING CAN KILL GLOB--
SPROING!

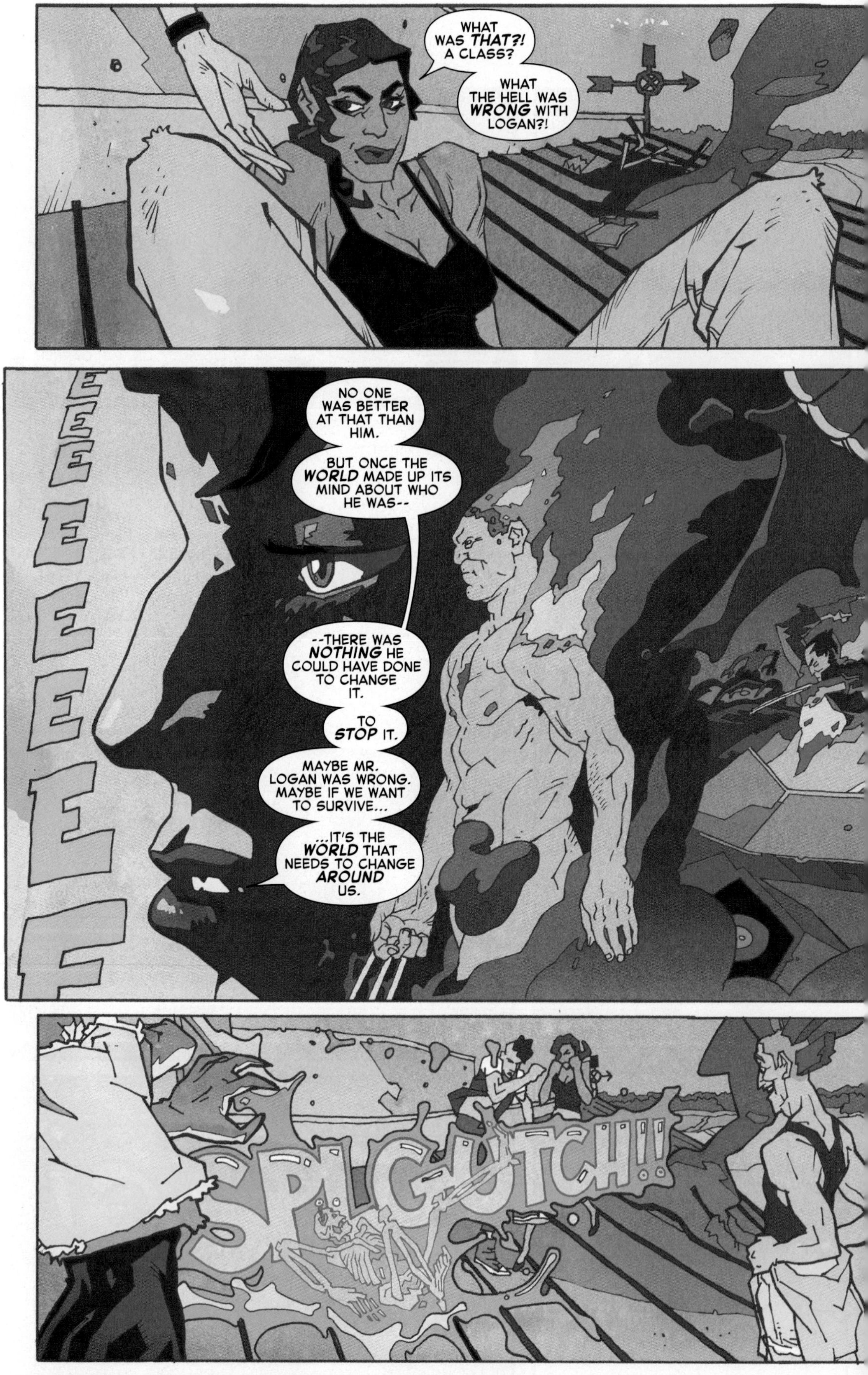

WHAT WAS THAT?! A CLASS?
WHAT THE HELL WAS WRONG WITH LOGAN?!
EEEEEEEF
NO ONE WAS BETTER AT THAT THAN HIM.
BUT ONCE THE WORLD MADE UP ITS MIND ABOUT WHO HE WAS--
--THERE WAS NOTHING HE COULD HAVE DONE TO CHANGE IT.
TO STOP IT.
MAYBE MR. LOGAN WAS WRONG. MAYBE IF WE WANT TO SURVIVE...
...IT'S THE WORLD THAT NEEDS TO CHANGE AROUND US.
SPLGUTCH!!

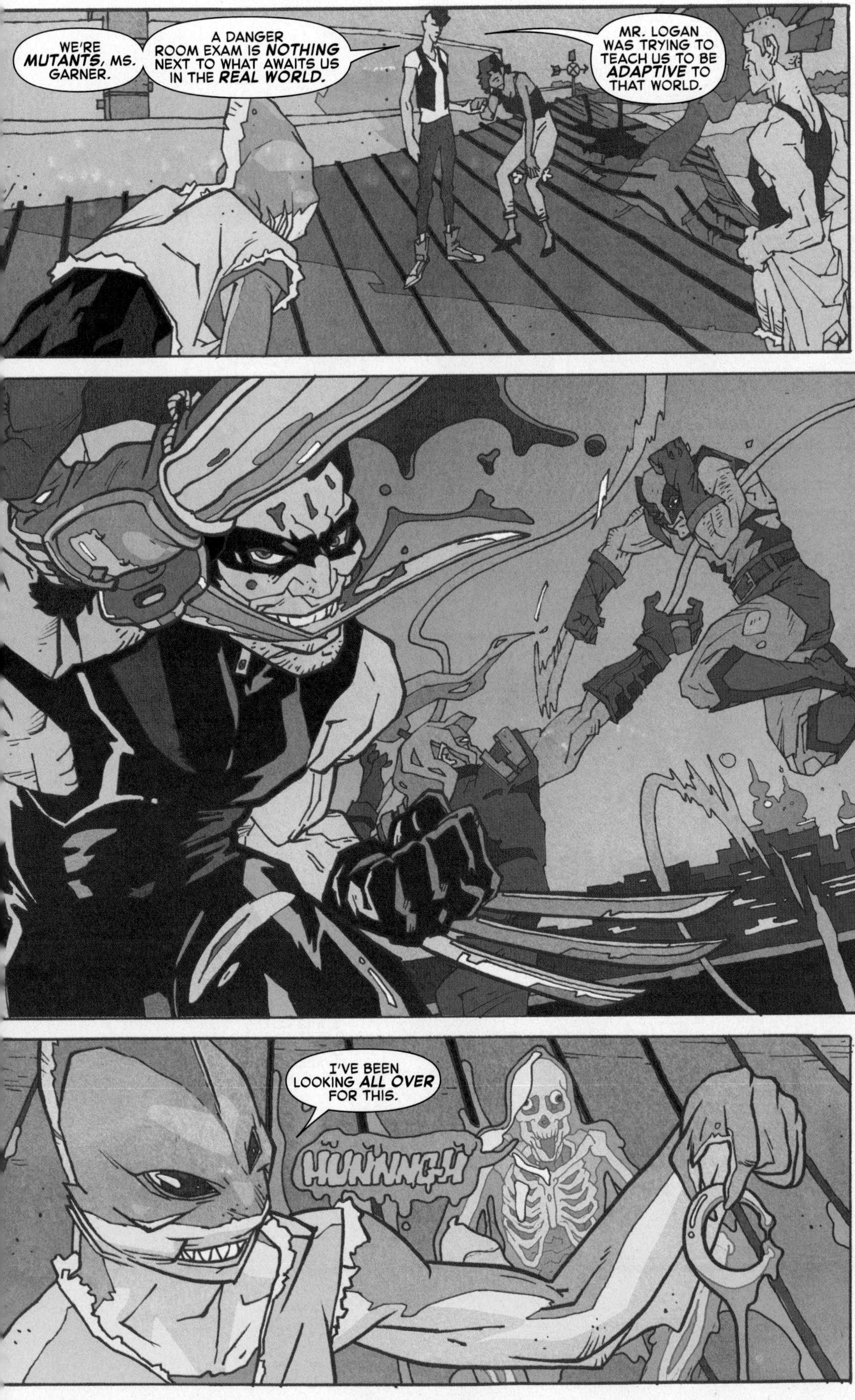
WE'RE MUTANTS, MS. GARNER.
A DANGER ROOM EXAM IS NOTHING NEXT TO WHAT AWAITS US IN THE REAL WORLD.
MR. LOGAN WAS TRYING TO TEACH US TO BE ADAPTIVE TO THAT WORLD.
I'VE BEEN LOOKING ALL OVER FOR THIS.
HUNNNGH

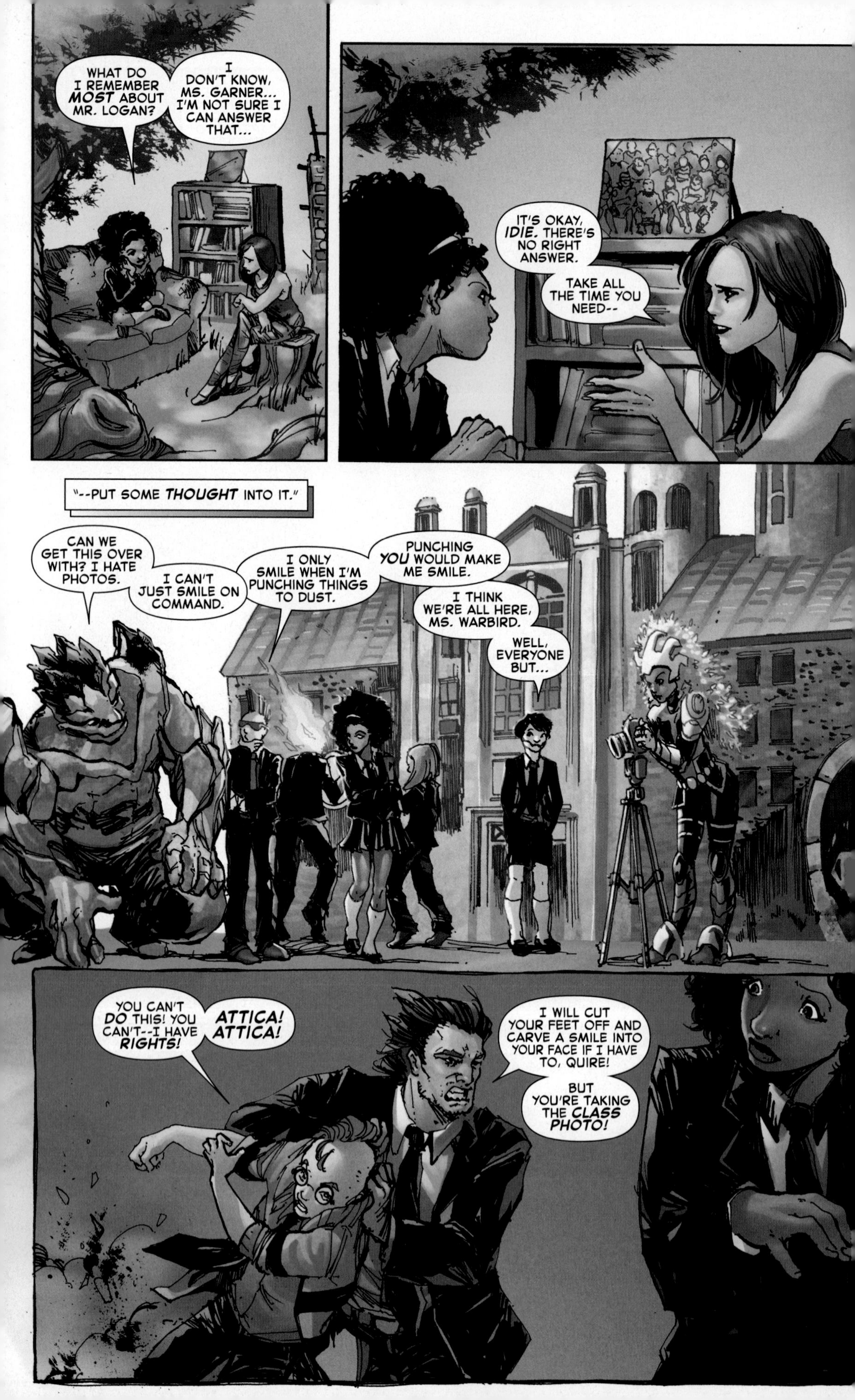
WHAT DO I REMEMBER MOST ABOUT MR. LOGAN?
I DON'T KNOW, MS. GARNER... I'M NOT SURE I CAN ANSWER THAT...
IT'S OKAY, IDIE. THERE'S NO RIGHT ANSWER.
TAKE ALL THE TIME YOU NEED--
"--PUT SOME THOUGHT INTO IT."
CAN WE GET THIS OVER WITH? I HATE PHOTOS.
I CAN'T JUST SMILE ON COMMAND.
I ONLY SMILE WHEN I'M PUNCHING THINGS TO DUST.
PUNCHING YOU WOULD MAKE ME SMILE.
I THINK WE'RE ALL HERE, MS. WARBIRD.
WELL, EVERYONE BUT...
YOU CAN'T DO THIS! YOU CAN'T--I HAVE RIGHTS!
ATTICA! ATTICA!
I WILL CUT YOUR FEET OFF AND CARVE A SMILE INTO YOUR FACE IF I HAVE TO, QUIRE!
BUT YOU'RE TAKING THE CLASS PHOTO!

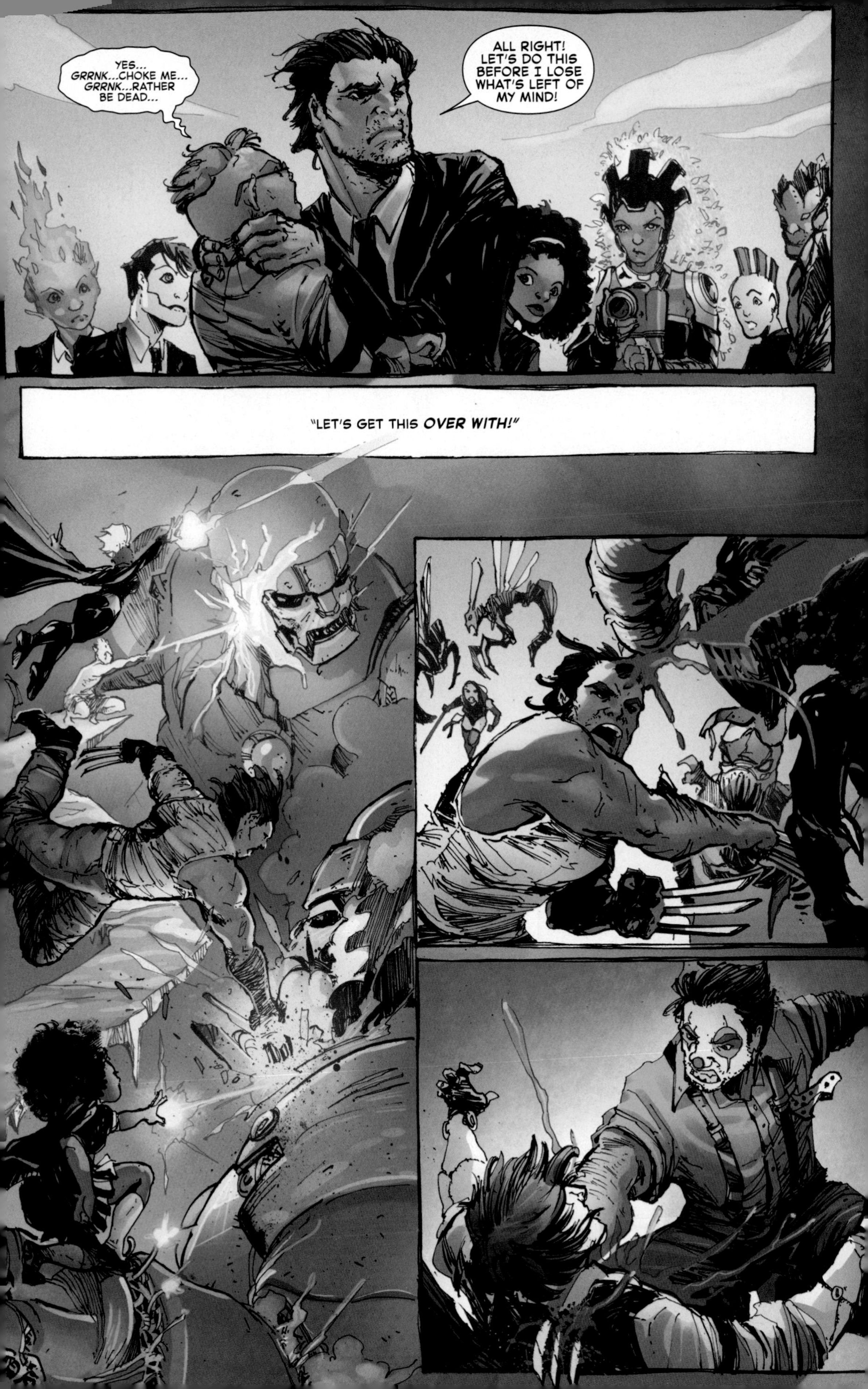
YES... GRRNK...CHOKE ME... GRRNK...RATHER BE DEAD...
ALL RIGHT! LET'S DO THIS BEFORE I LOSE WHAT'S LEFT OF MY MIND!
"LET'S GET THIS OVER WITH!"

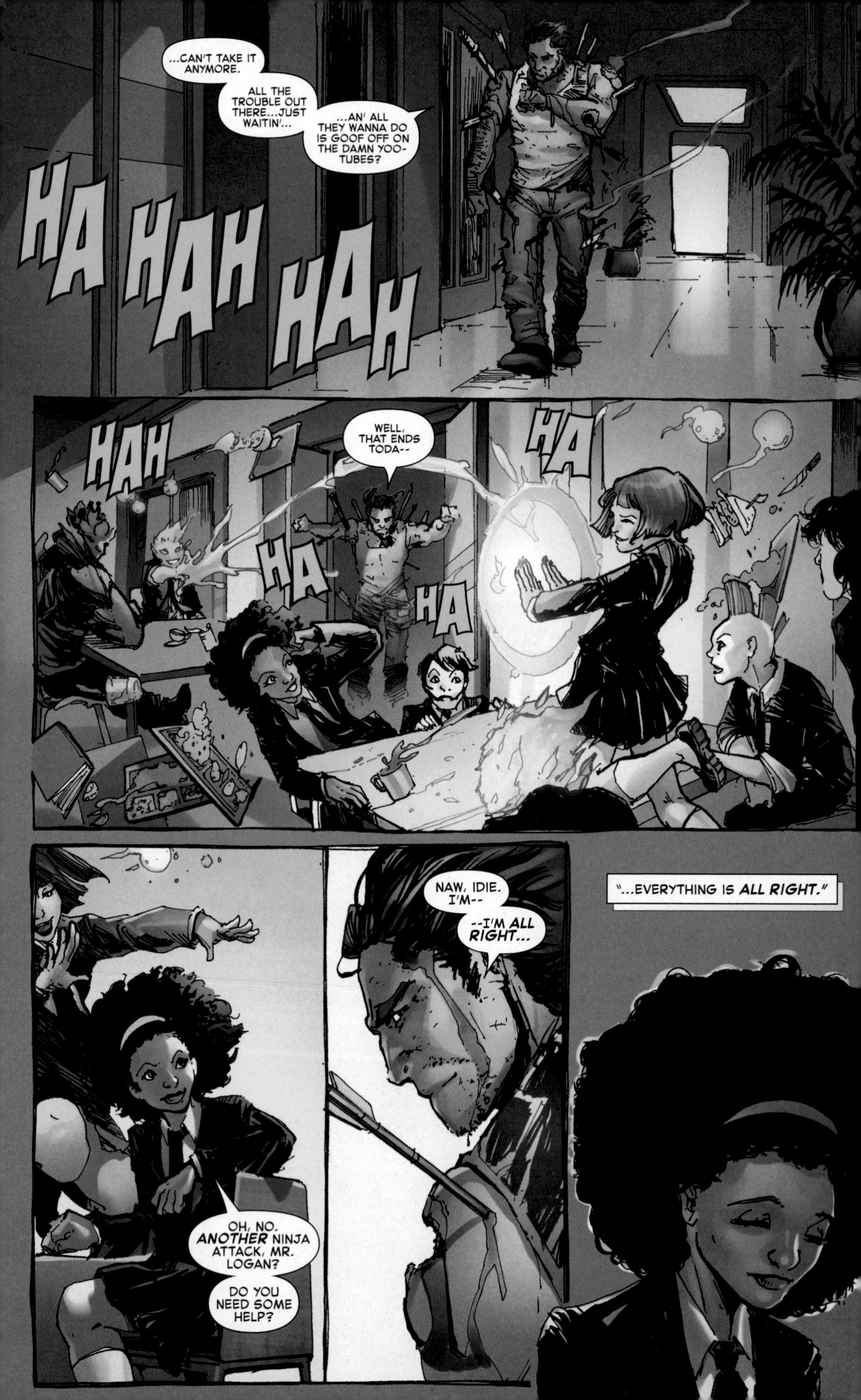
...CAN'T TAKE IT ANYMORE.
ALL THE TROUBLE OUT THERE...JUST WAITIN'...
...AN' ALL THEY WANNA DO IS GOOF OFF ON THE DAMN YOO-TUBES?
HA HAH HAH
HAH
WELL, THAT ENDS TODA--
HA
HA
HA
NAW, IDIE. I'M--
--I'M ALL RIGHT...
"...EVERYTHING IS ALL RIGHT."
OH, NO. ANOTHER NINJA ATTACK, MR. LOGAN?
DO YOU NEED SOME HELP?

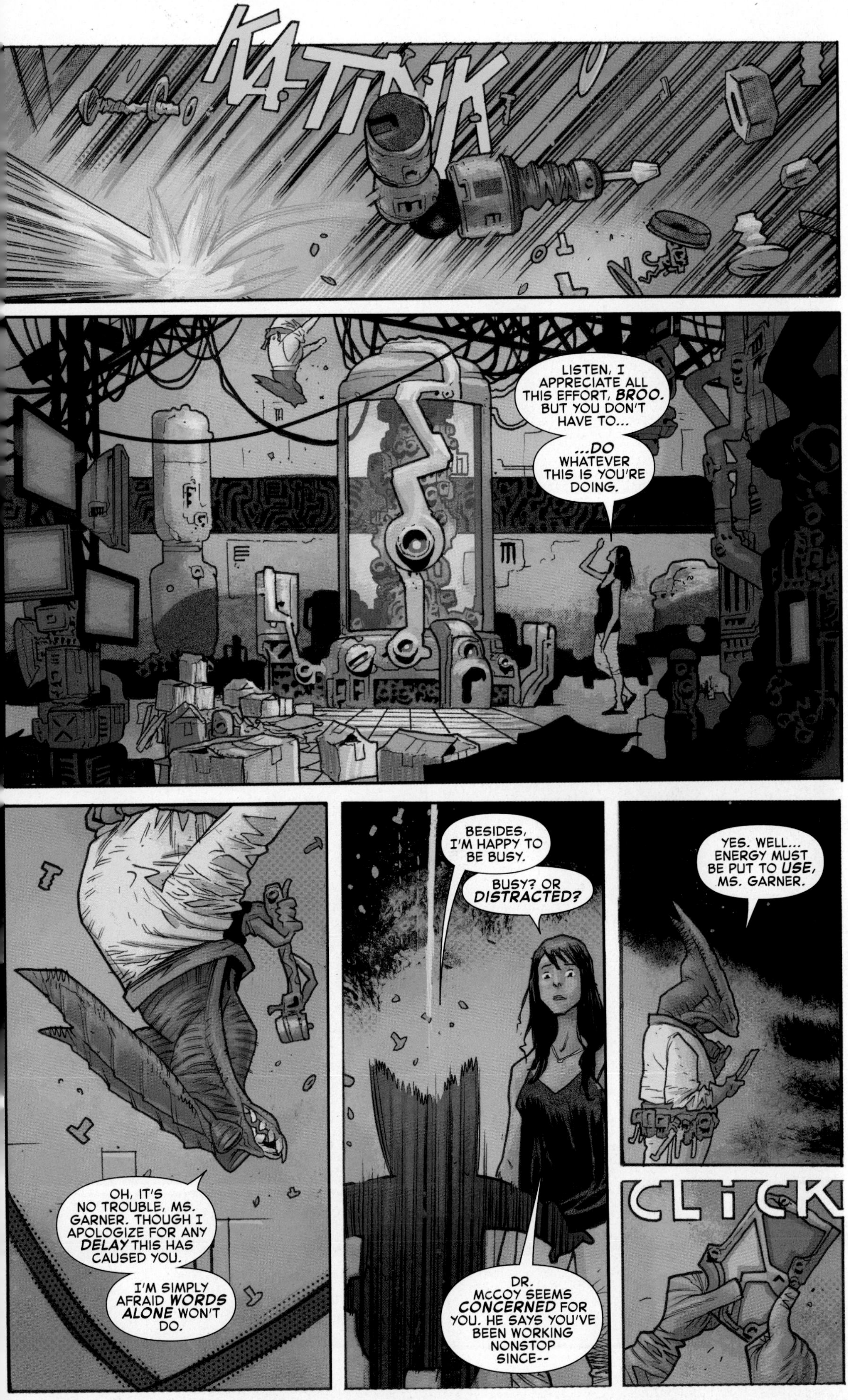
KA-TINK
LISTEN, I APPRECIATE ALL THIS EFFORT, BROO. BUT YOU DON'T HAVE TO...
...DO WHATEVER THIS IS YOU'RE DOING.
OH, IT'S NO TROUBLE, MS. GARNER. THOUGH I APOLOGIZE FOR ANY DELAY THIS HAS CAUSED YOU.
I'M SIMPLY AFRAID WORDS ALONE WON'T DO.
BESIDES, I'M HAPPY TO BE BUSY.
BUSY? OR DISTRACTED?
DR. McCOY SEEMS CONCERNED FOR YOU. HE SAYS YOU'VE BEEN WORKING NONSTOP SINCE--
YES. WELL... ENERGY MUST BE PUT TO USE, MS. GARNER.
CLICK

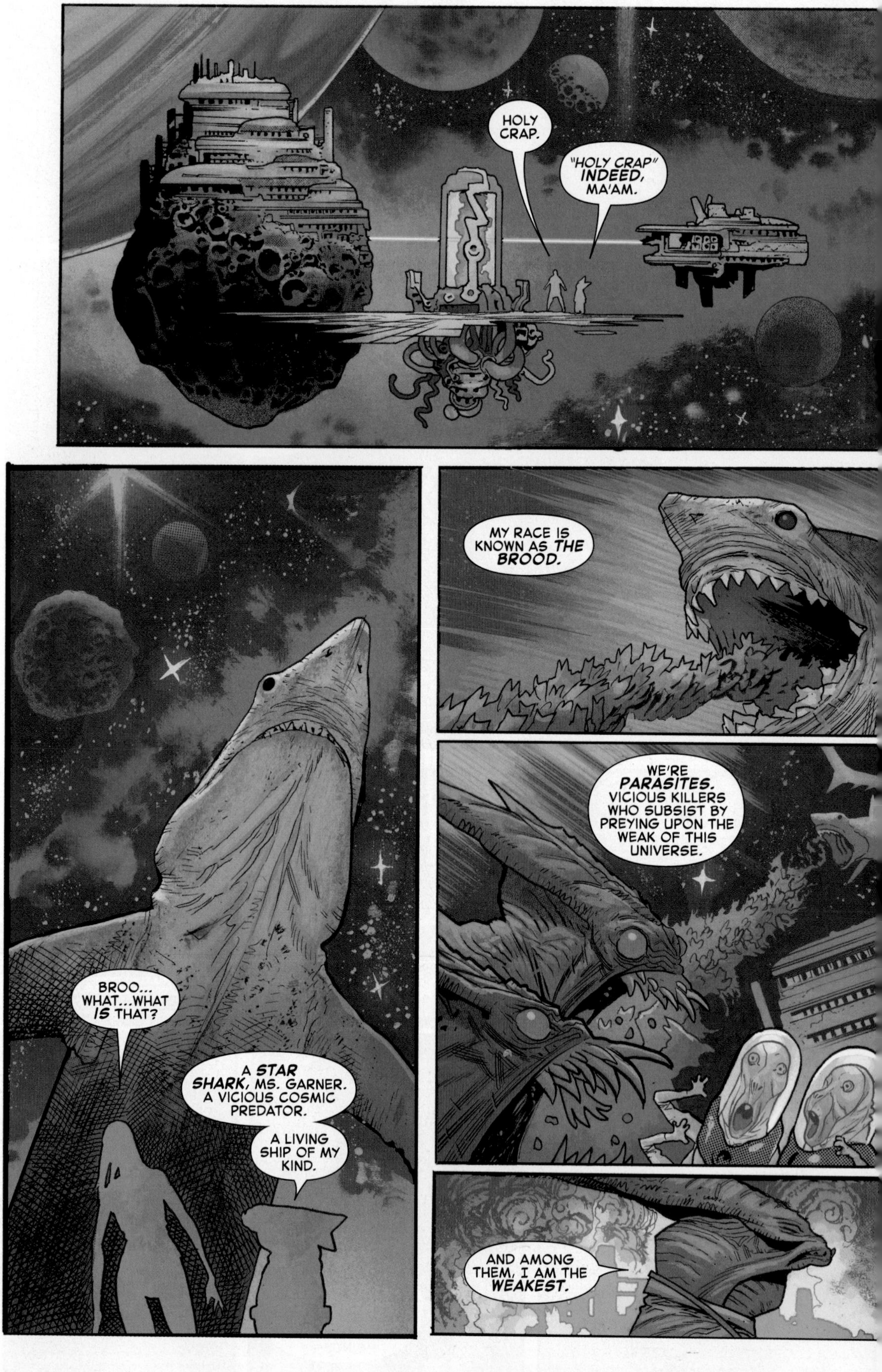
HOLY CRAP.
"HOLY CRAP" INDEED, MA'AM.
BROO... WHAT...WHAT IS THAT?
A STAR SHARK, MS. GARNER. A VICIOUS COSMIC PREDATOR.
A LIVING SHIP OF MY KIND.
MY RACE IS KNOWN AS THE BROOD.
WE'RE PARASITES. VICIOUS KILLERS WHO SUBSIST BY PREYING UPON THE WEAK OF THIS UNIVERSE.
AND AMONG THEM, I AM THE WEAKEST.

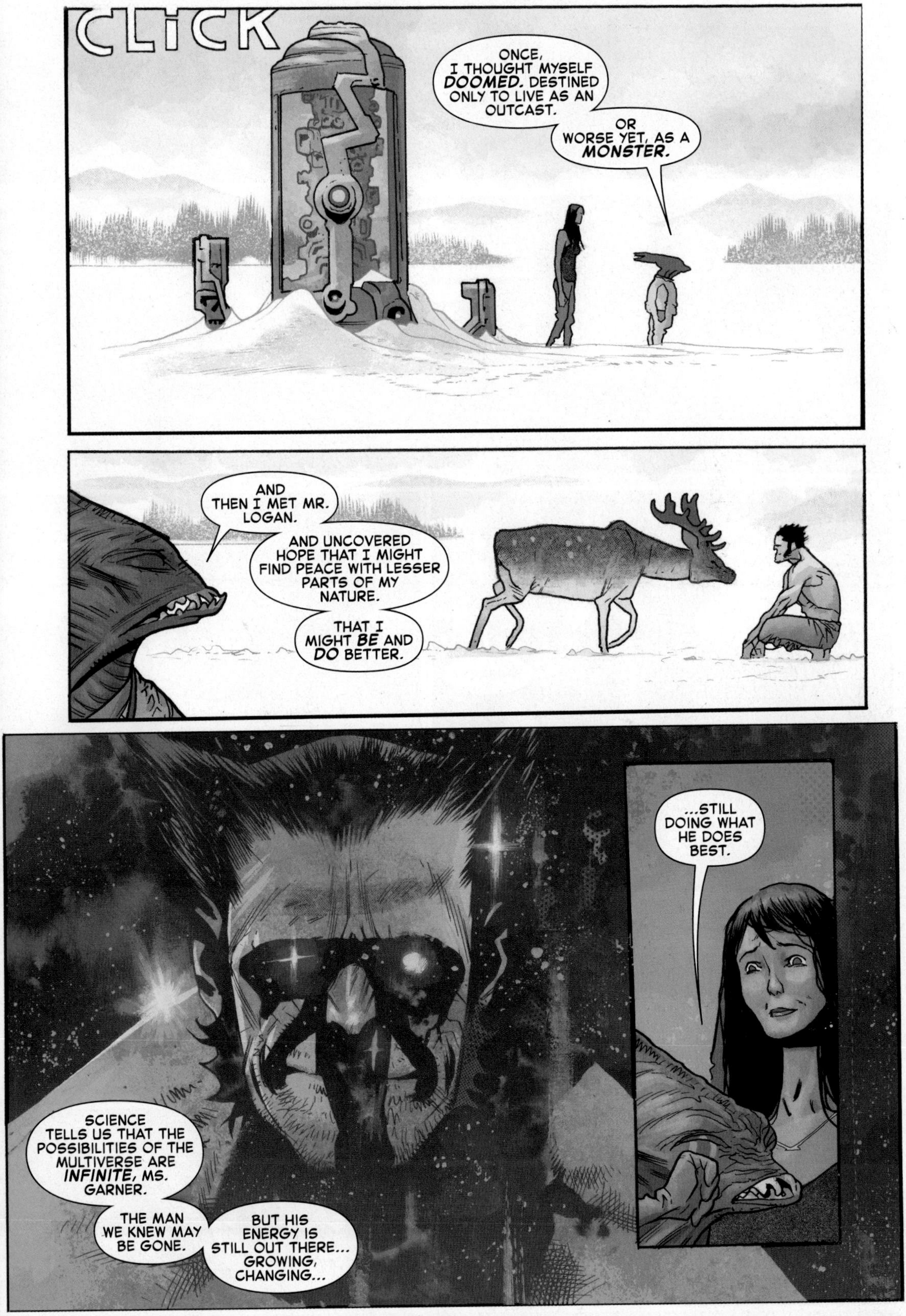
CLICK
ONCE, I THOUGHT MYSELF DOOMED. DESTINED ONLY TO LIVE AS AN OUTCAST.
OR WORSE YET, AS A MONSTER.
AND THEN I MET MR. LOGAN.
AND UNCOVERED HOPE THAT I MIGHT FIND PEACE WITH LESSER PARTS OF MY NATURE.
THAT I MIGHT BE AND DO BETTER.
SCIENCE TELLS US THAT THE POSSIBILITIES OF THE MULTIVERSE ARE INFINITE, MS. GARNER.
THE MAN WE KNEW MAY BE GONE.
BUT HIS ENERGY IS STILL OUT THERE... GROWING, CHANGING...
...STILL DOING WHAT HE DOES BEST.

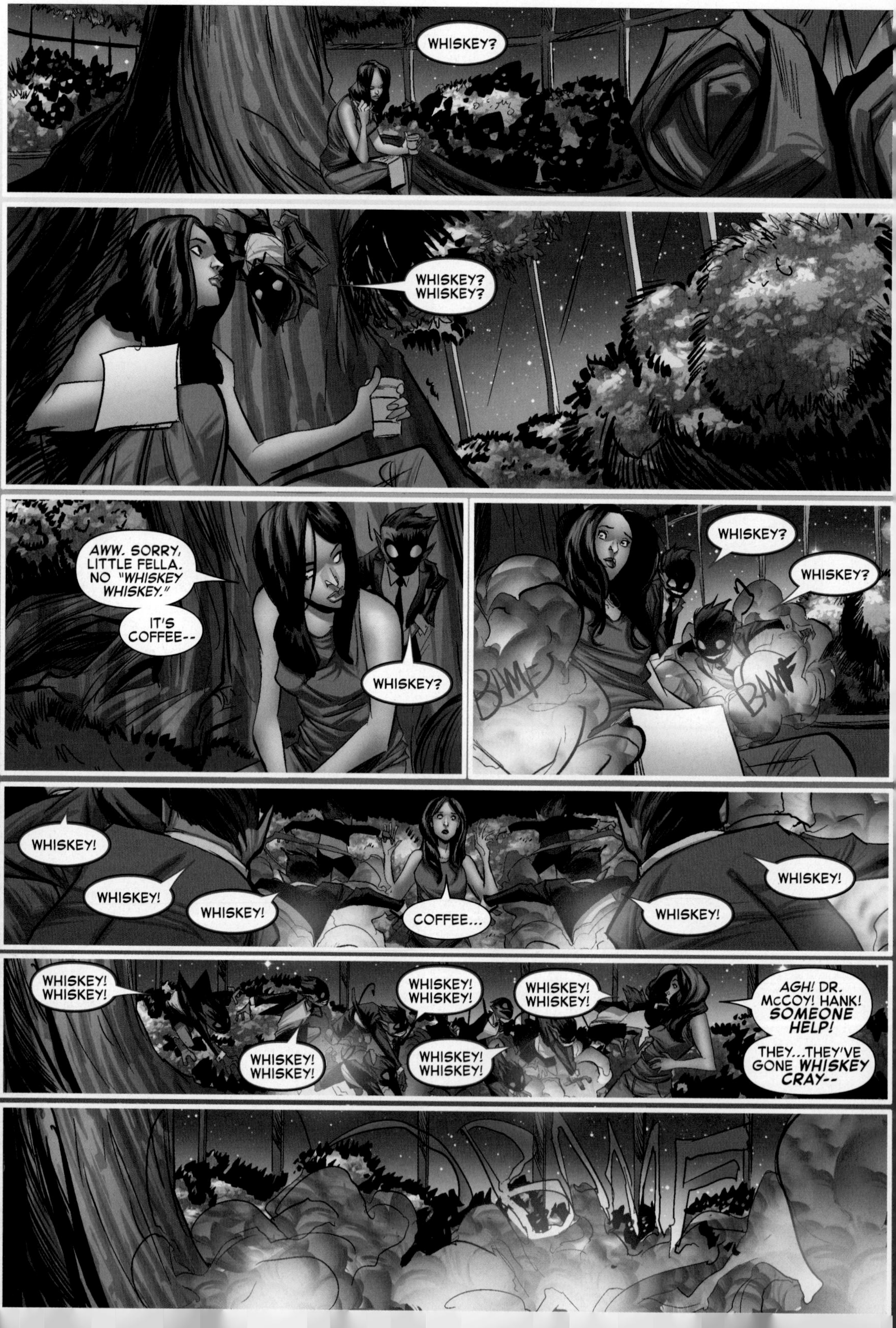
WHISKEY?
WHISKEY? WHISKEY?
AWW. SORRY, LITTLE FELLA. NO "WHISKEY WHISKEY."
IT'S COFFEE--
WHISKEY?
WHISKEY?
WHISKEY?
BAMF
BAMF
WHISKEY!
WHISKEY!
WHISKEY!
COFFEE...
WHISKEY!
WHISKEY!
WHISKEY! WHISKEY!
WHISKEY! WHISKEY!
WHISKEY! WHISKEY!
WHISKEY! WHISKEY!
WHISKEY! WHISKEY!
AGH! DR. McCOY! HANK! SOMEONE HELP!
THEY...THEY'VE GONE WHISKEY CRAY--
BAMF

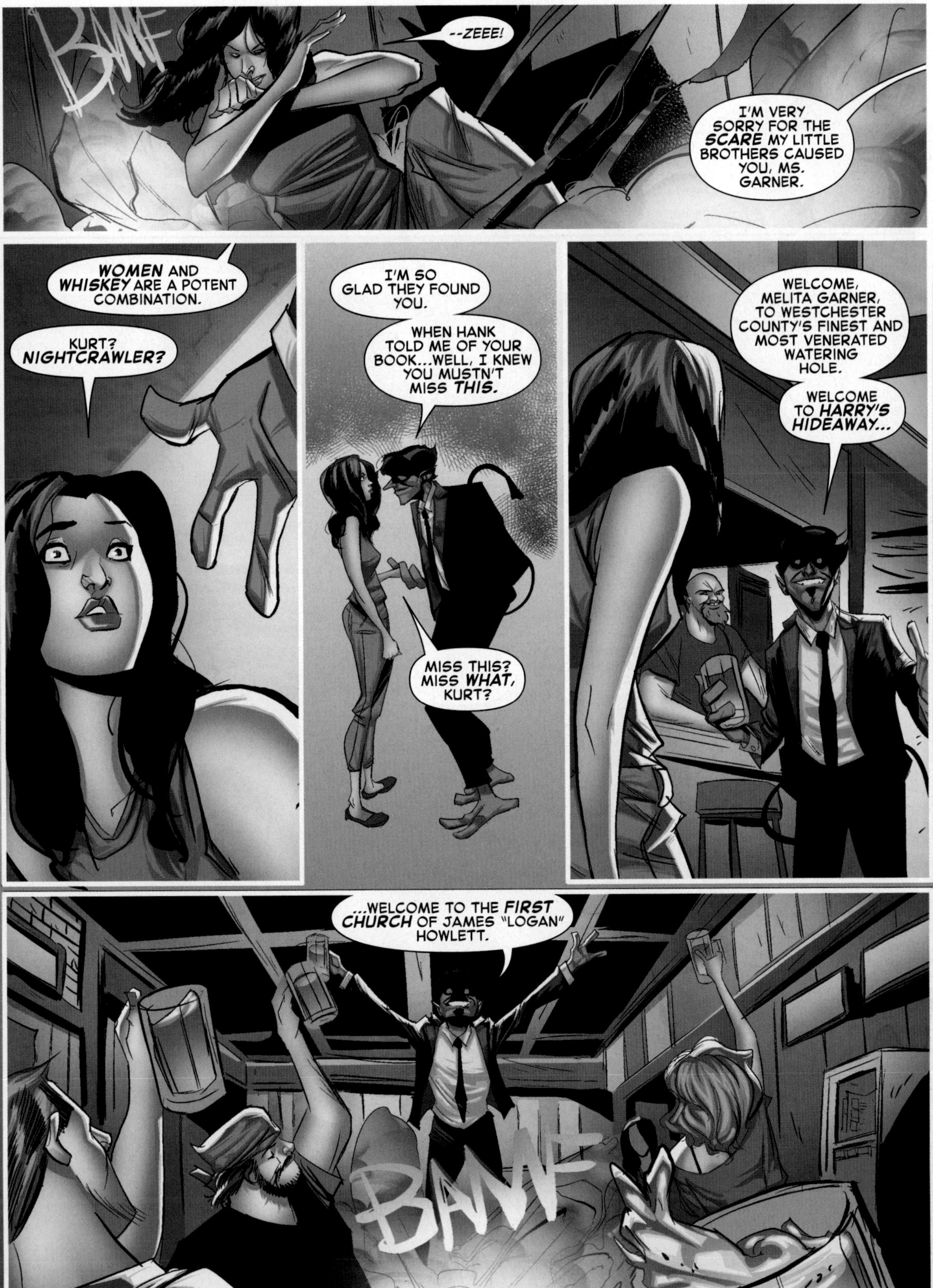
BAMF
--ZEEE!
I'M VERY SORRY FOR THE SCARE MY LITTLE BROTHERS CAUSED YOU, MS. GARNER.
WOMEN AND WHISKEY ARE A POTENT COMBINATION.
KURT? NIGHTCRAWLER?
I'M SO GLAD THEY FOUND YOU.
WHEN HANK TOLD ME OF YOUR BOOK...WELL, I KNEW YOU MUSTN'T MISS THIS.
MISS THIS? MISS WHAT, KURT?
WELCOME, MELITA GARNER, TO WESTCHESTER COUNTY'S FINEST AND MOST VENERATED WATERING HOLE.
WELCOME TO HARRY'S HIDEAWAY...
...WELCOME TO THE FIRST CHURCH OF JAMES "LOGAN" HOWLETT.
BAMF

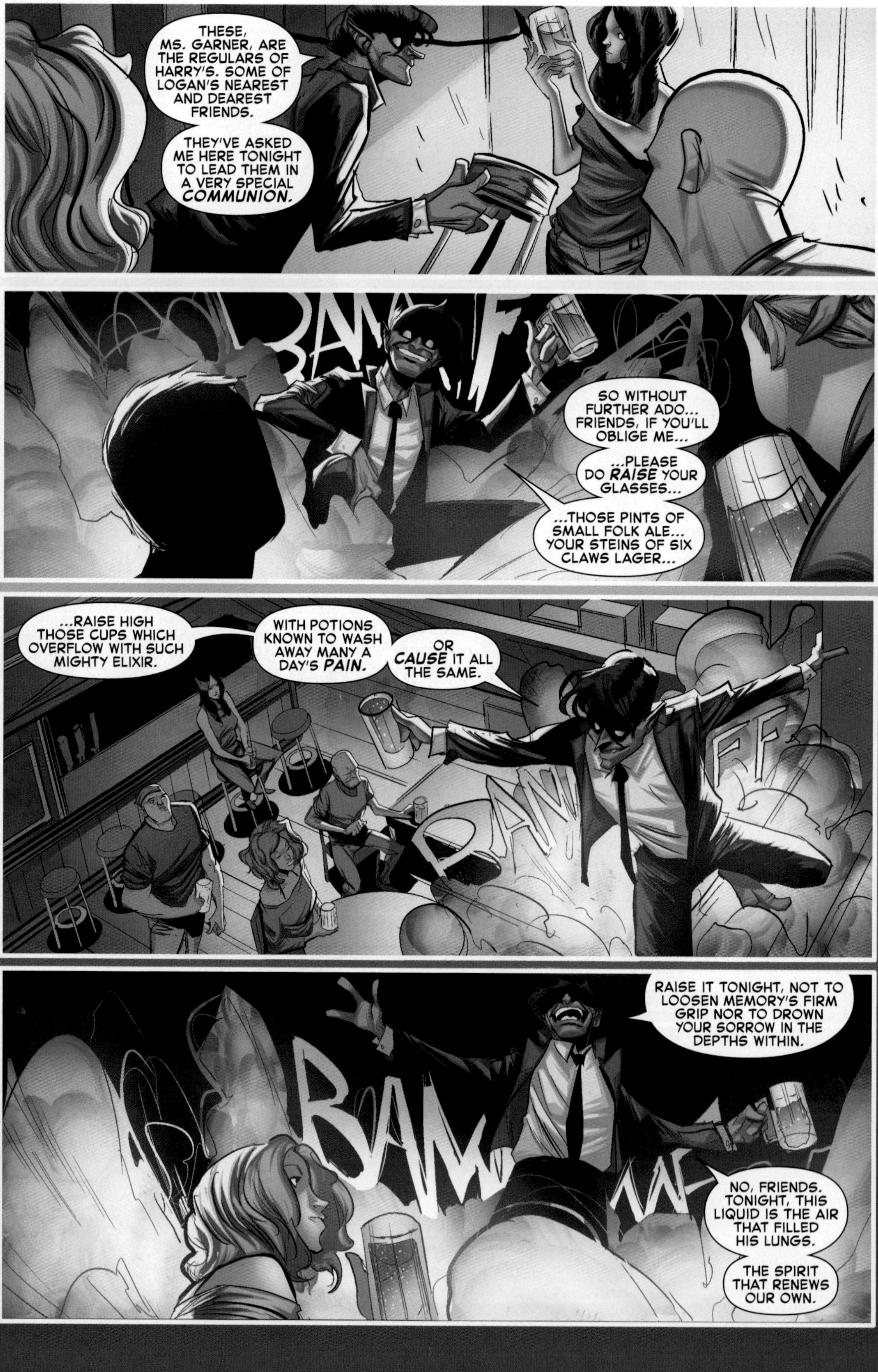
THESE, MS. GARNER, ARE THE REGULARS OF HARRY'S. SOME OF LOGAN'S NEAREST AND DEAREST FRIENDS.
THEY'VE ASKED ME HERE TONIGHT TO LEAD THEM IN A VERY SPECIAL ***COMMUNION.***
SO WITHOUT FURTHER ADO... FRIENDS, IF YOU'LL OBLIGE ME...
...PLEASE DO ***RAISE*** YOUR GLASSES...
...THOSE PINTS OF SMALL FOLK ALE... YOUR STEINS OF SIX CLAWS LAGER...
...RAISE HIGH THOSE CUPS WHICH OVERFLOW WITH SUCH MIGHTY ELIXIR.
WITH POTIONS KNOWN TO WASH AWAY MANY A DAY'S ***PAIN.***
OR ***CAUSE*** IT ALL THE SAME.
RAISE IT TONIGHT, NOT TO LOOSEN MEMORY'S FIRM GRIP NOR TO DROWN YOUR SORROW IN THE DEPTHS WITHIN.
NO, FRIENDS. TONIGHT, THIS LIQUID IS THE AIR THAT FILLED HIS LUNGS.
THE SPIRIT THAT RENEWS OUR OWN.

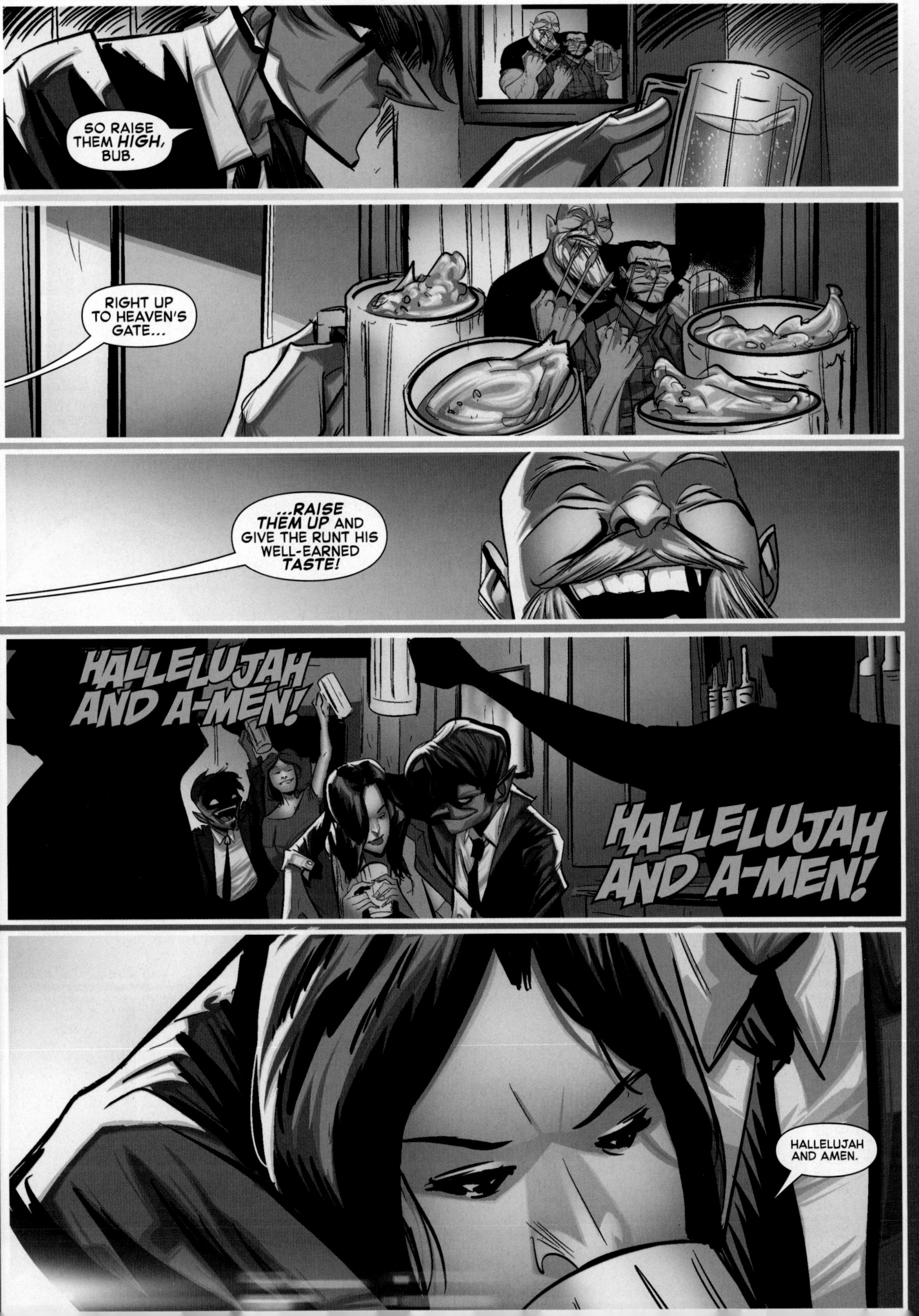
SO RAISE THEM HIGH, BUB.
RIGHT UP TO HEAVEN'S GATE...
...RAISE THEM UP AND GIVE THE RUNT HIS WELL-EARNED TASTE!
HALLELUJAH AND A-MEN!
HALLELUJAH AND A-MEN!
HALLELUJAH AND AMEN.

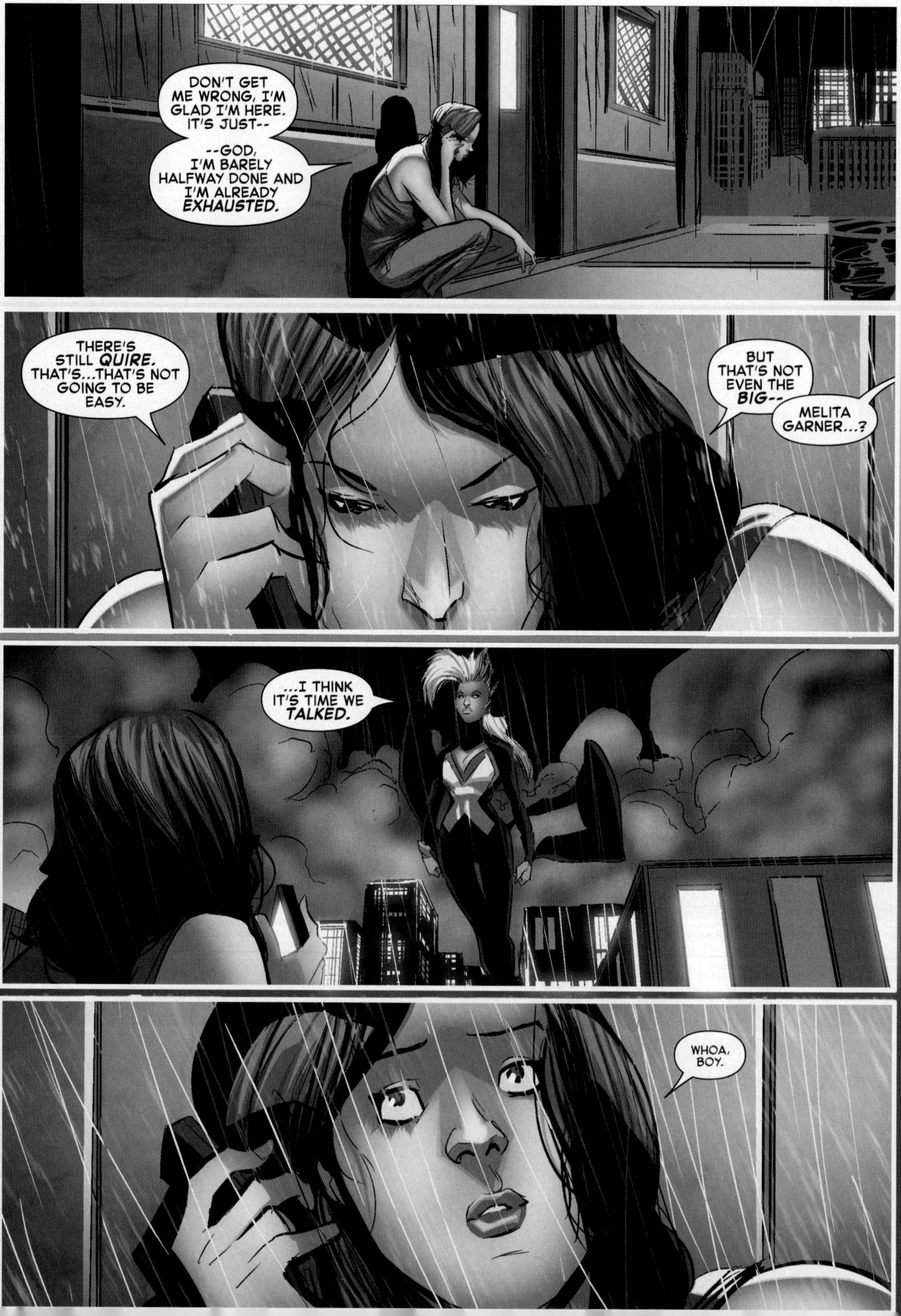
DON'T GET ME WRONG, I'M GLAD I'M HERE. IT'S JUST--
--GOD, I'M BARELY HALFWAY DONE AND I'M ALREADY EXHAUSTED.
THERE'S STILL QUIRE. THAT'S...THAT'S NOT GOING TO BE EASY.
BUT THAT'S NOT EVEN THE BIG--
MELITA GARNER...?
...I THINK IT'S TIME WE TALKED.
WHOA, BOY.

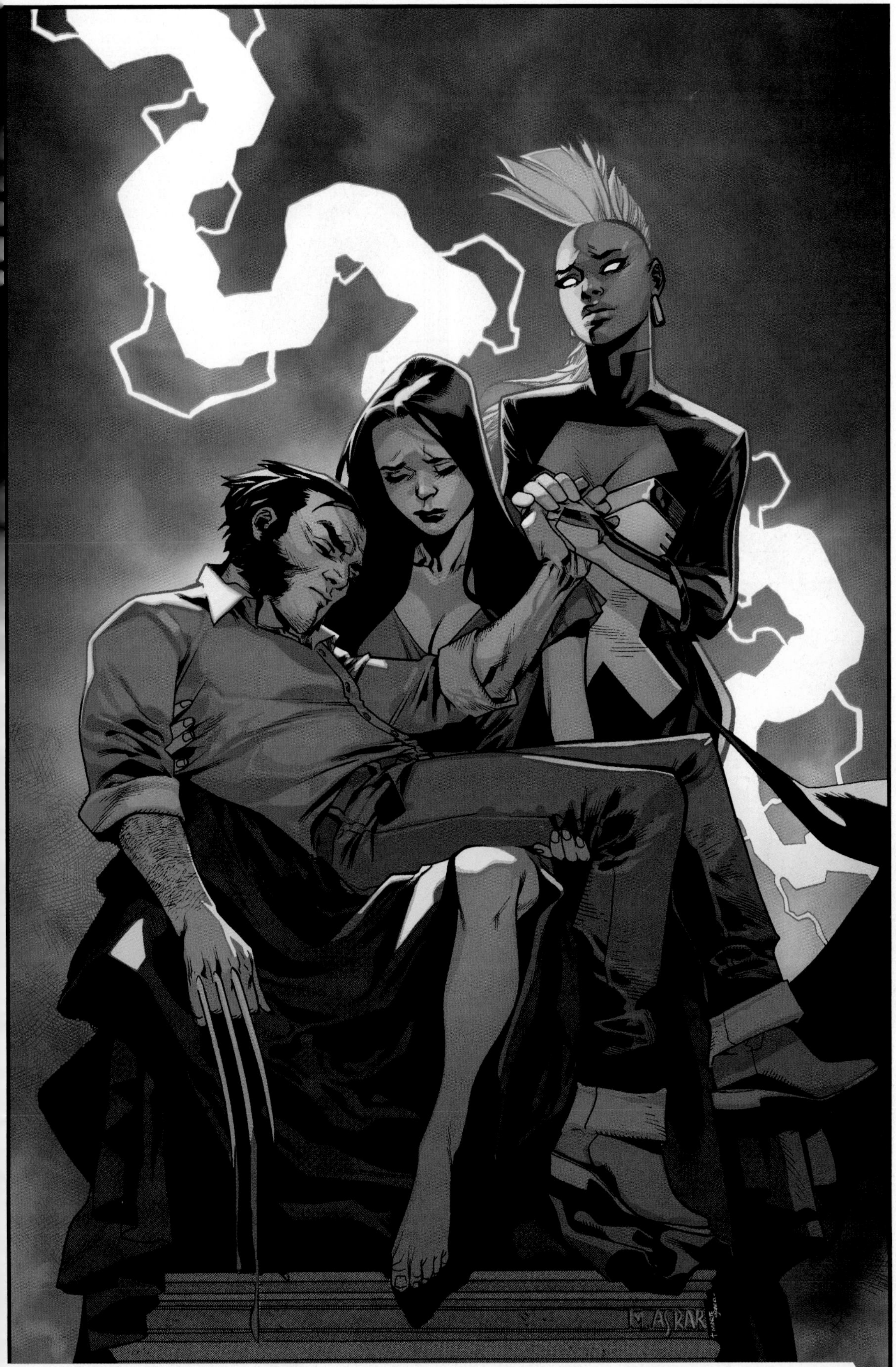
M. ASRAR

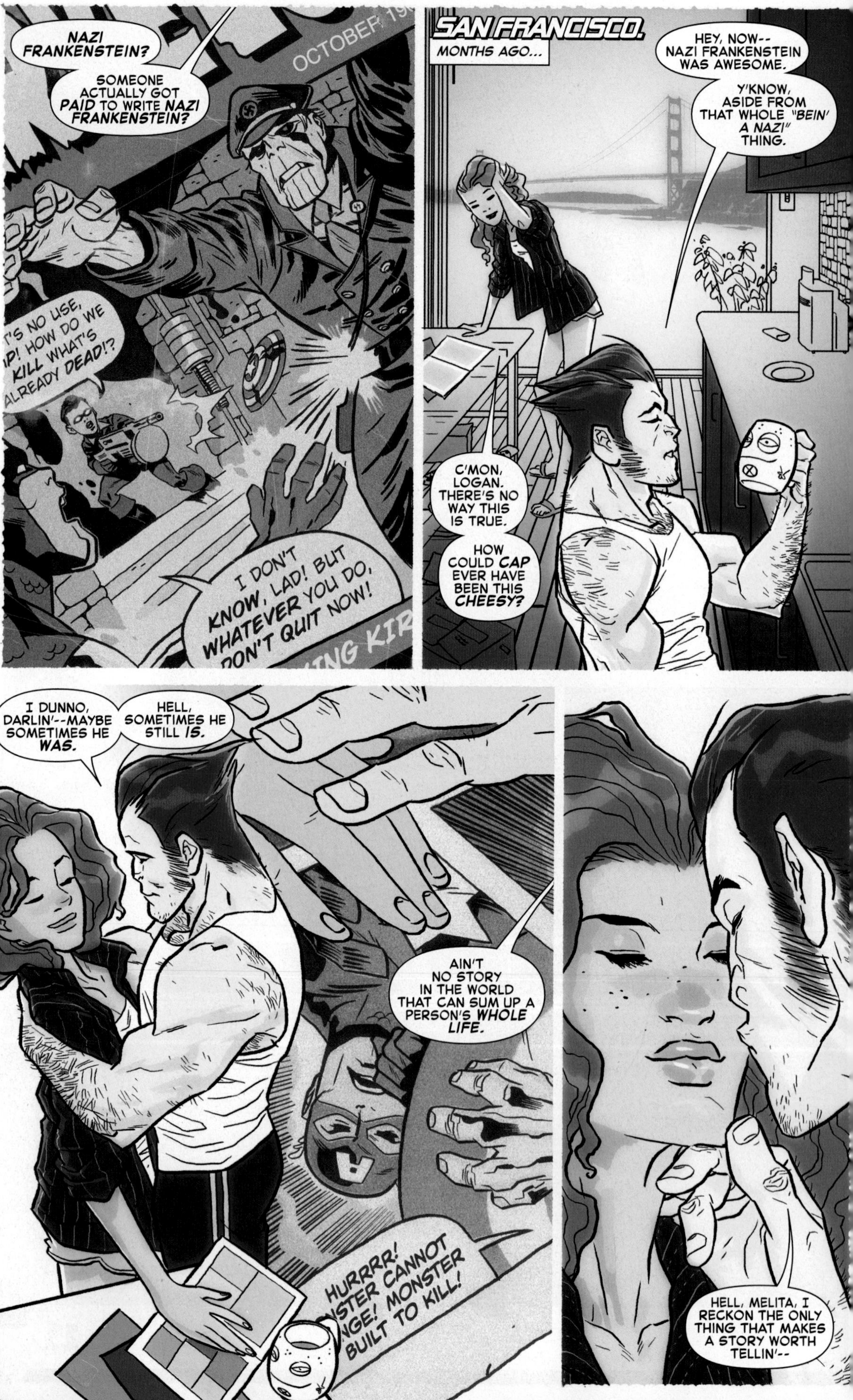
NAZI FRANKENSTEIN?
SOMEONE ACTUALLY GOT PAID TO WRITE NAZI FRANKENSTEIN?
OCTOBER
'S NO USE, P! HOW DO WE KILL WHAT'S ALREADY DEAD!?
I DON'T KNOW, LAD! BUT WHATEVER YOU DO, DON'T QUIT NOW!
SAN FRANCISCO.
MONTHS AGO...
HEY, NOW-- NAZI FRANKENSTEIN WAS AWESOME.
Y'KNOW, ASIDE FROM THAT WHOLE "BEIN' A NAZI" THING.
C'MON, LOGAN. THERE'S NO WAY THIS IS TRUE.
HOW COULD CAP EVER HAVE BEEN THIS CHEESY?
I DUNNO, DARLIN'--MAYBE SOMETIMES HE WAS.
HELL, SOMETIMES HE STILL IS.
AIN'T NO STORY IN THE WORLD THAT CAN SUM UP A PERSON'S WHOLE LIFE.
HURRRR! NSTER CANNOT NGE! MONSTER BUILT TO KILL!
HELL, MELITA, I RECKON THE ONLY THING THAT MAKES A STORY WORTH TELLIN'--

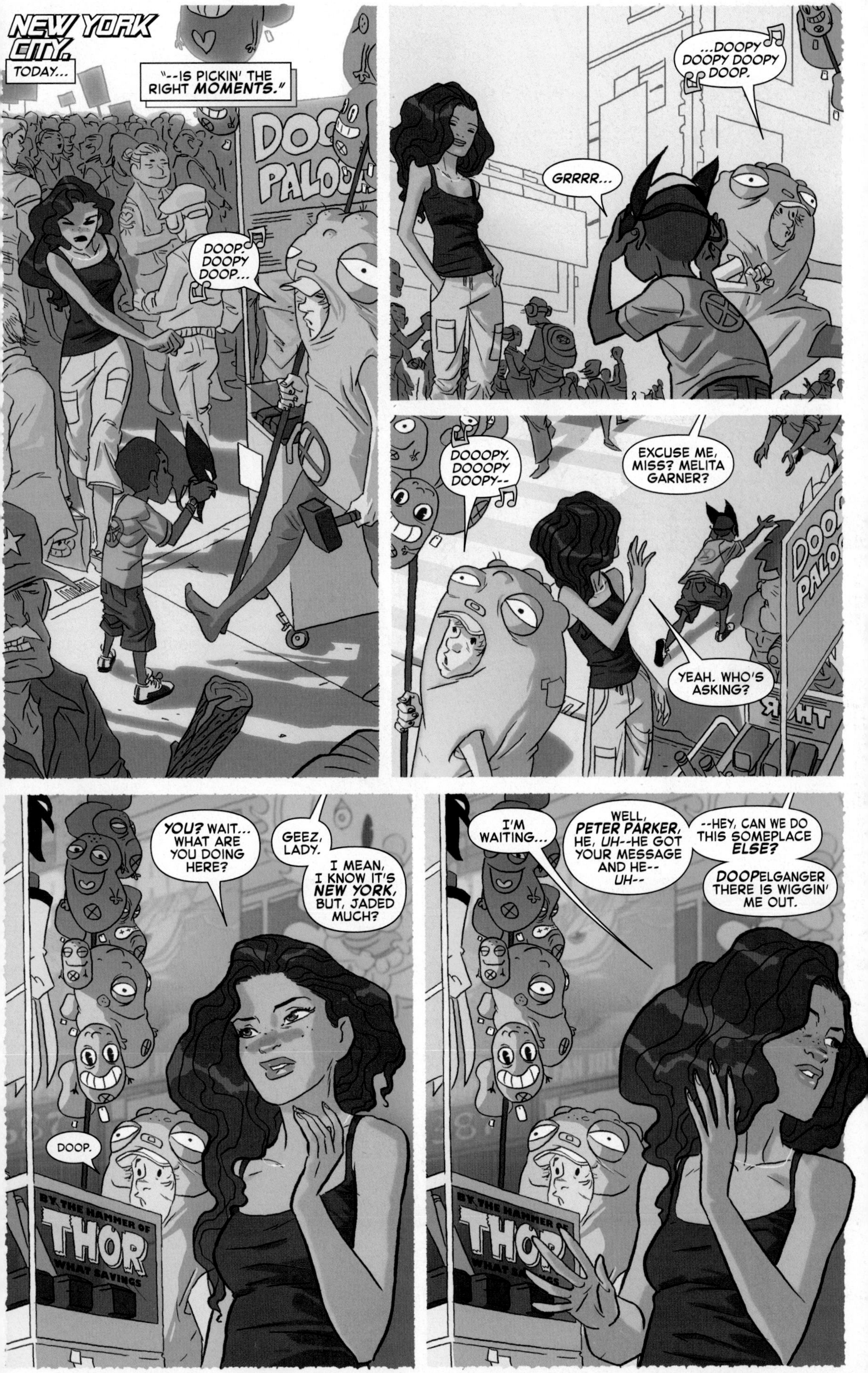
NEW YORK CITY.
TODAY...
"--IS PICKIN' THE RIGHT MOMENTS."
DOO PALOO
DOOP. DOOPY DOOP...
...DOOPY DOOPY DOOPY DOOP.
GRRRR...
DOOOPY. DOOOPY DOOPY--
EXCUSE ME, MISS? MELITA GARNER?
YEAH. WHO'S ASKING?
YOU? WAIT... WHAT ARE YOU DOING HERE?
GEEZ, LADY.
I MEAN, I KNOW IT'S NEW YORK, BUT, JADED MUCH?
DOOP.
BY THE HAMMER OF THOR WHAT SAVINGS
I'M WAITING...
WELL, PETER PARKER, HE, UH--HE GOT YOUR MESSAGE AND HE-- UH--
--HEY, CAN WE DO THIS SOMEPLACE ELSE?
DOOPELGANGER THERE IS WIGGIN' ME OUT.

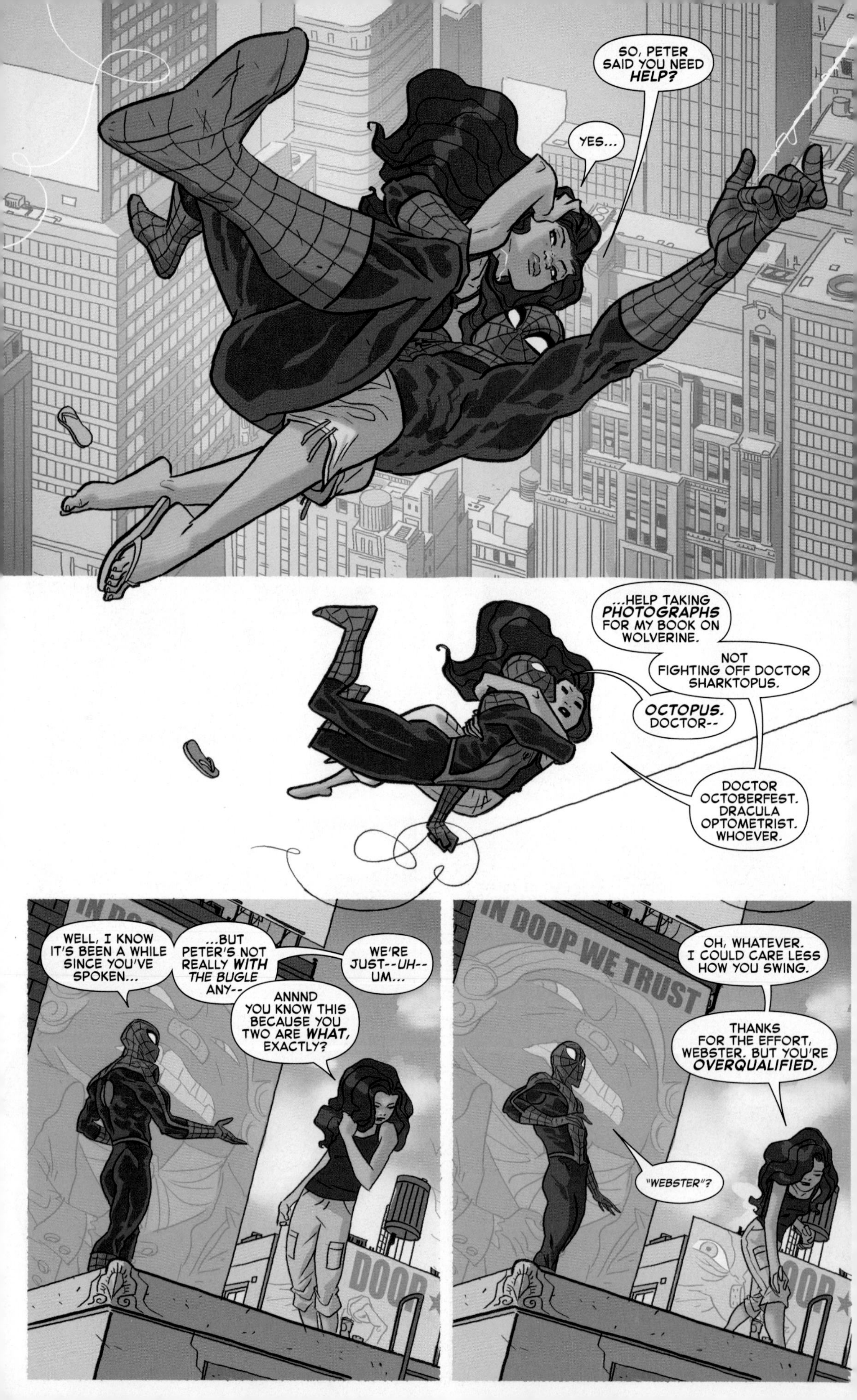
SO, PETER SAID YOU NEED HELP?
YES...
...HELP TAKING PHOTOGRAPHS FOR MY BOOK ON WOLVERINE.
NOT FIGHTING OFF DOCTOR SHARKTOPUS.
OCTOPUS. DOCTOR--
DOCTOR OCTOBERFEST. DRACULA OPTOMETRIST. WHOEVER.
WELL, I KNOW IT'S BEEN A WHILE SINCE YOU'VE SPOKEN...
...BUT PETER'S NOT REALLY WITH THE BUGLE ANY--
WE'RE JUST--UH-- UM...
ANNND YOU KNOW THIS BECAUSE YOU TWO ARE WHAT, EXACTLY?
IN DOOP WE TRUST
DOOP
OH, WHATEVER. I COULD CARE LESS HOW YOU SWING.
THANKS FOR THE EFFORT, WEBSTER. BUT YOU'RE OVERQUALIFIED.
"WEBSTER"?

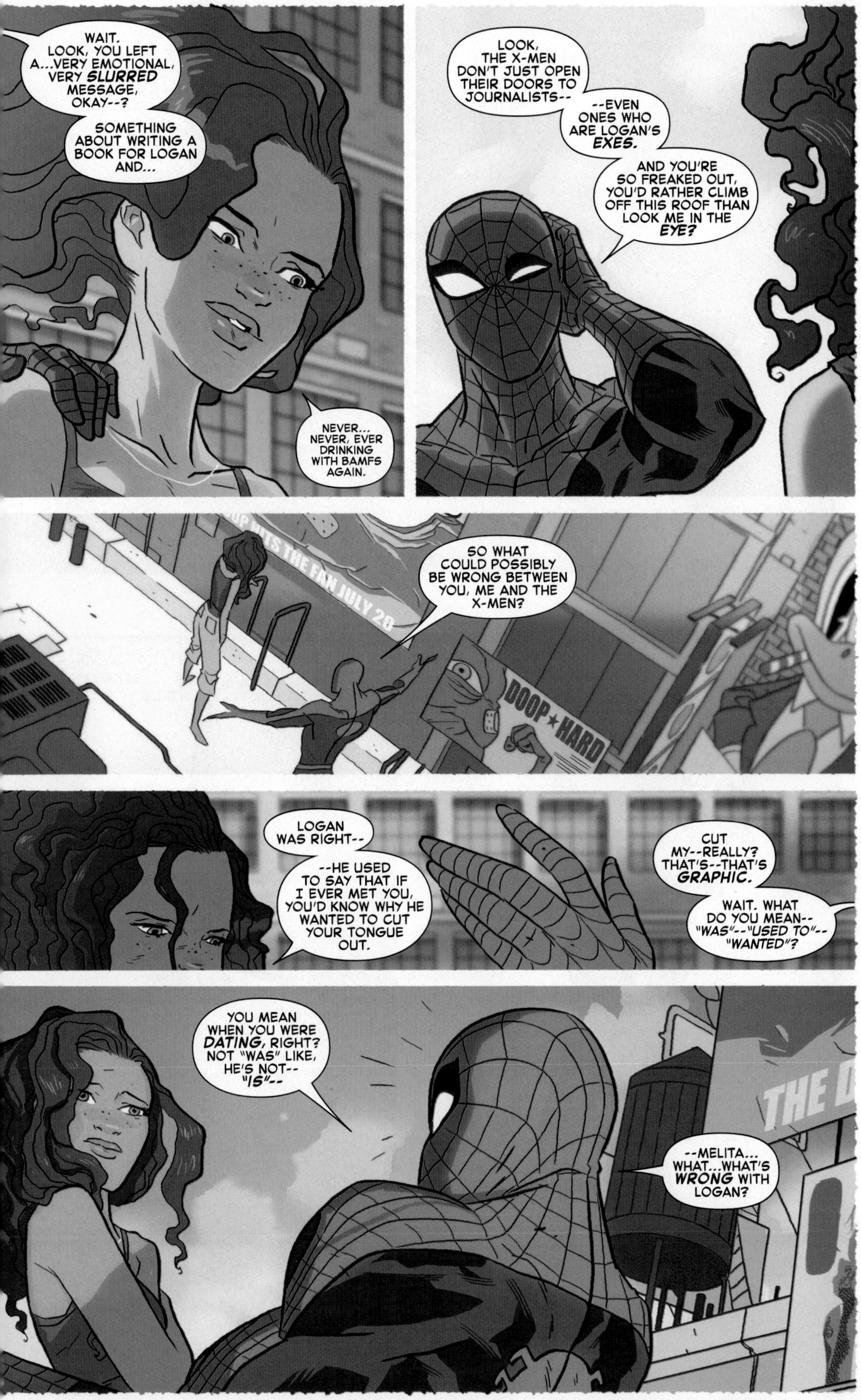
WAIT. LOOK, YOU LEFT A...VERY EMOTIONAL, VERY SLURRED MESSAGE, OKAY--?
SOMETHING ABOUT WRITING A BOOK FOR LOGAN AND...
NEVER... NEVER, EVER DRINKING WITH BAMFS AGAIN.
LOOK, THE X-MEN DON'T JUST OPEN THEIR DOORS TO JOURNALISTS--
--EVEN ONES WHO ARE LOGAN'S EXES.
AND YOU'RE SO FREAKED OUT, YOU'D RATHER CLIMB OFF THIS ROOF THAN LOOK ME IN THE EYE?
HITS THE FAN JULY 20
SO WHAT COULD POSSIBLY BE WRONG BETWEEN YOU, ME AND THE X-MEN?
DOOP ★ HARD
LOGAN WAS RIGHT--
--HE USED TO SAY THAT IF I EVER MET YOU, YOU'D KNOW WHY HE WANTED TO CUT YOUR TONGUE OUT.
CUT MY--REALLY? THAT'S--THAT'S GRAPHIC.
WAIT. WHAT DO YOU MEAN-- "WAS"--"USED TO"-- "WANTED"?
YOU MEAN WHEN YOU WERE DATING, RIGHT? NOT "WAS" LIKE, HE'S NOT-- "IS"--
--MELITA... WHAT...WHAT'S WRONG WITH LOGAN?

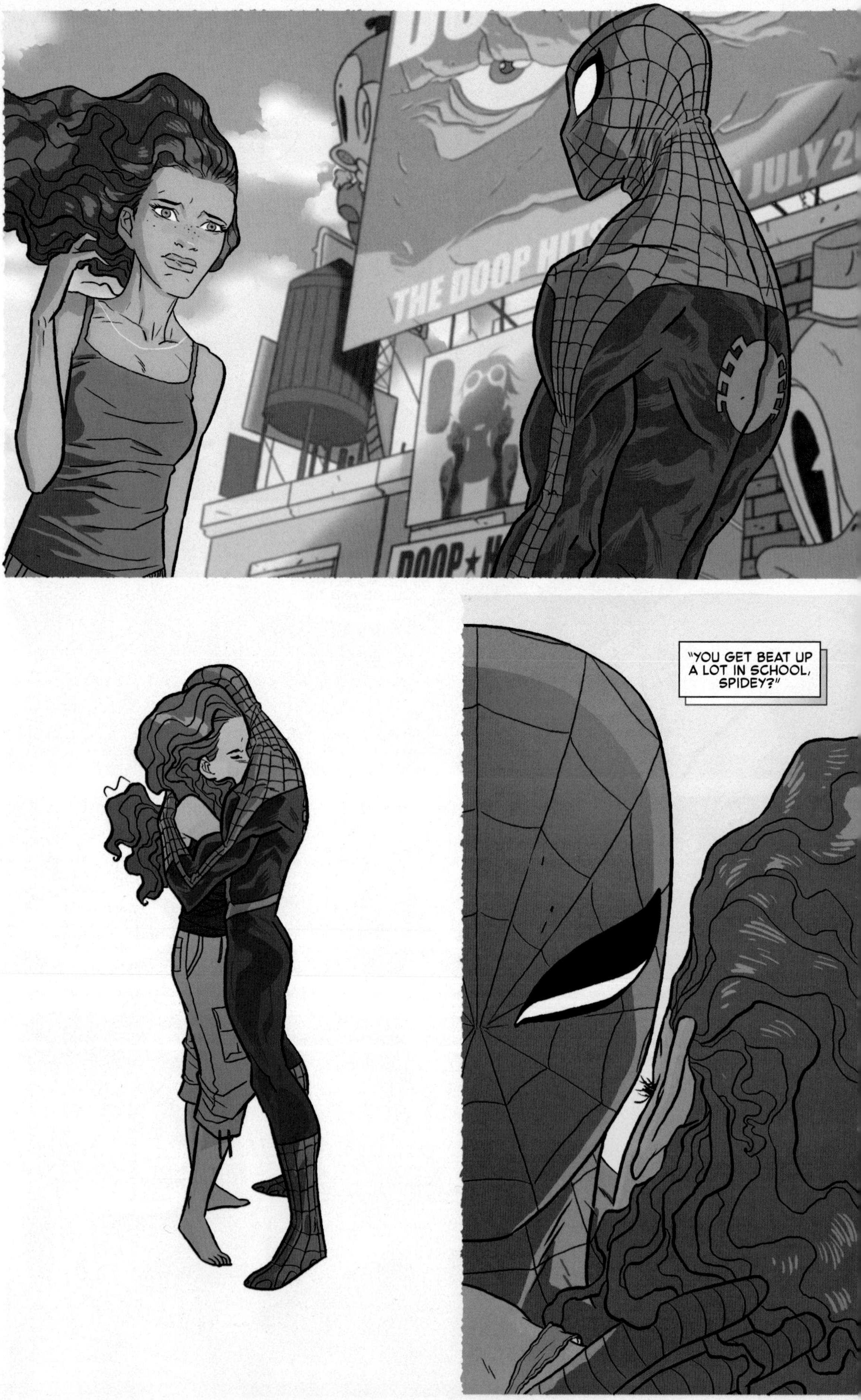
"YOU GET BEAT UP A LOT IN SCHOOL, SPIDEY?"

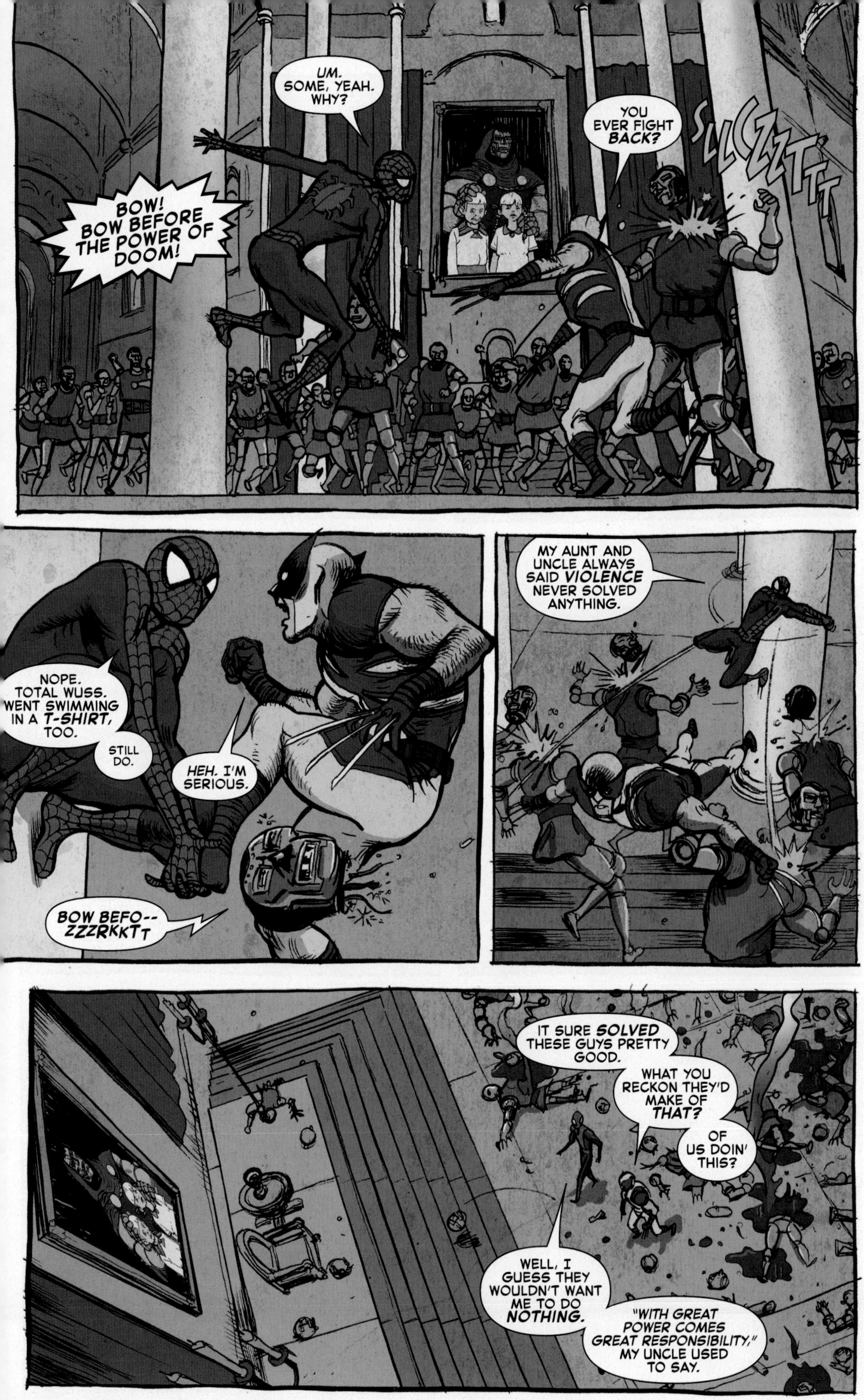
BOW! BOW BEFORE THE POWER OF DOOM!
UM. SOME, YEAH. WHY?
YOU EVER FIGHT BACK?
SLLCZZZTTT
NOPE. TOTAL WUSS. WENT SWIMMING IN A T-SHIRT, TOO.
STILL DO.
HEH. I'M SERIOUS.
BOW BEFO-- ZZZRKKTT
MY AUNT AND UNCLE ALWAYS SAID VIOLENCE NEVER SOLVED ANYTHING.
IT SURE SOLVED THESE GUYS PRETTY GOOD.
WHAT YOU RECKON THEY'D MAKE OF THAT?
OF US DOIN' THIS?
WELL, I GUESS THEY WOULDN'T WANT ME TO DO NOTHING.
"WITH GREAT POWER COMES GREAT RESPONSIBILITY," MY UNCLE USED TO SAY.

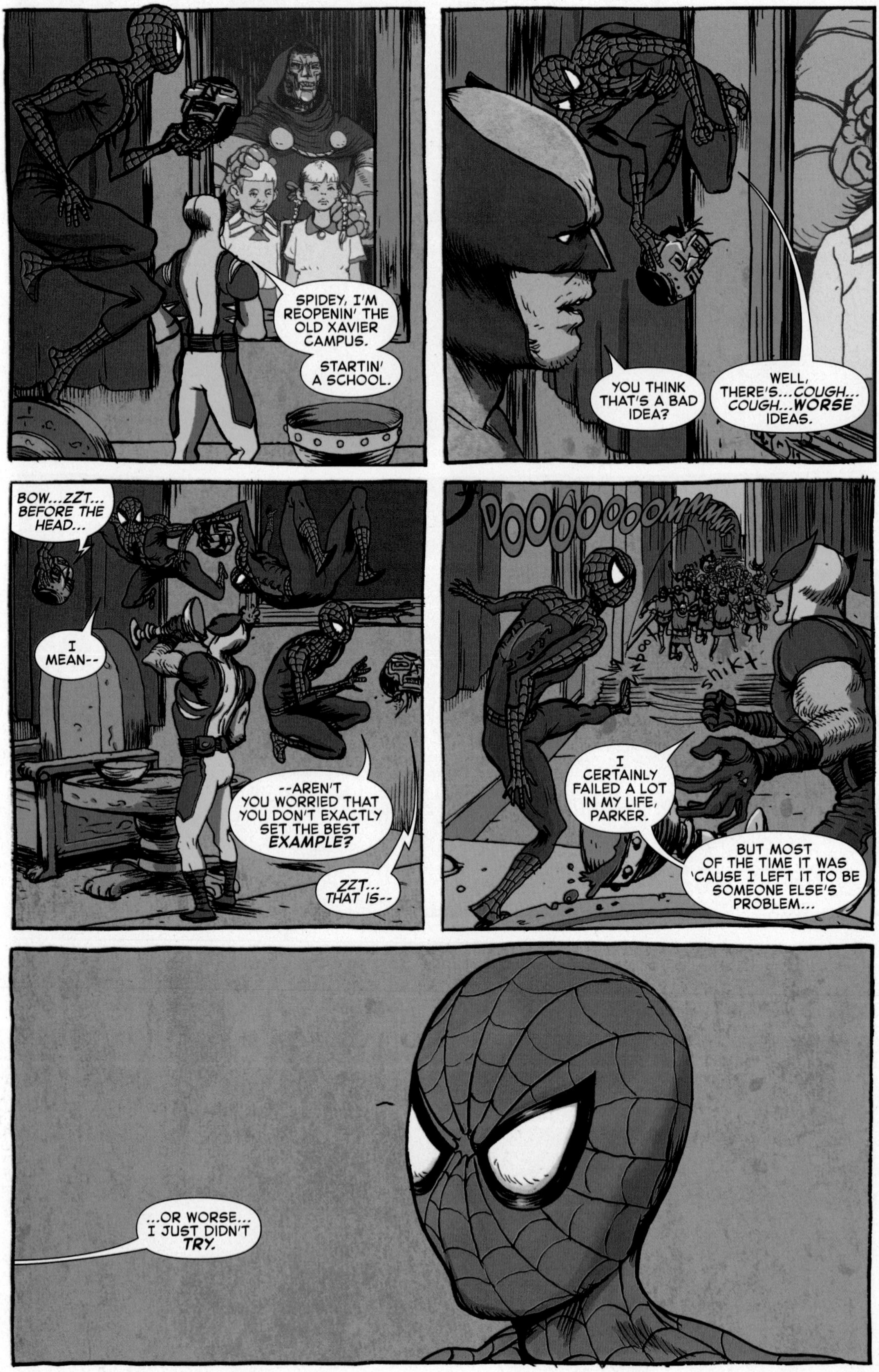
SPIDEY, I'M REOPENIN' THE OLD XAVIER CAMPUS.
STARTIN' A SCHOOL.
YOU THINK THAT'S A BAD IDEA?
WELL, THERE'S...COUGH... COUGH...WORSE IDEAS.
BOW...ZZT... BEFORE THE HEAD...
I MEAN--
--AREN'T YOU WORRIED THAT YOU DON'T EXACTLY SET THE BEST EXAMPLE?
ZZT... THAT IS--
DOOOOOOOOMMMM!
shikt
I CERTAINLY FAILED A LOT IN MY LIFE, PARKER.
BUT MOST OF THE TIME IT WAS 'CAUSE I LEFT IT TO BE SOMEONE ELSE'S PROBLEM...
...OR WORSE... I JUST DIDN'T TRY.

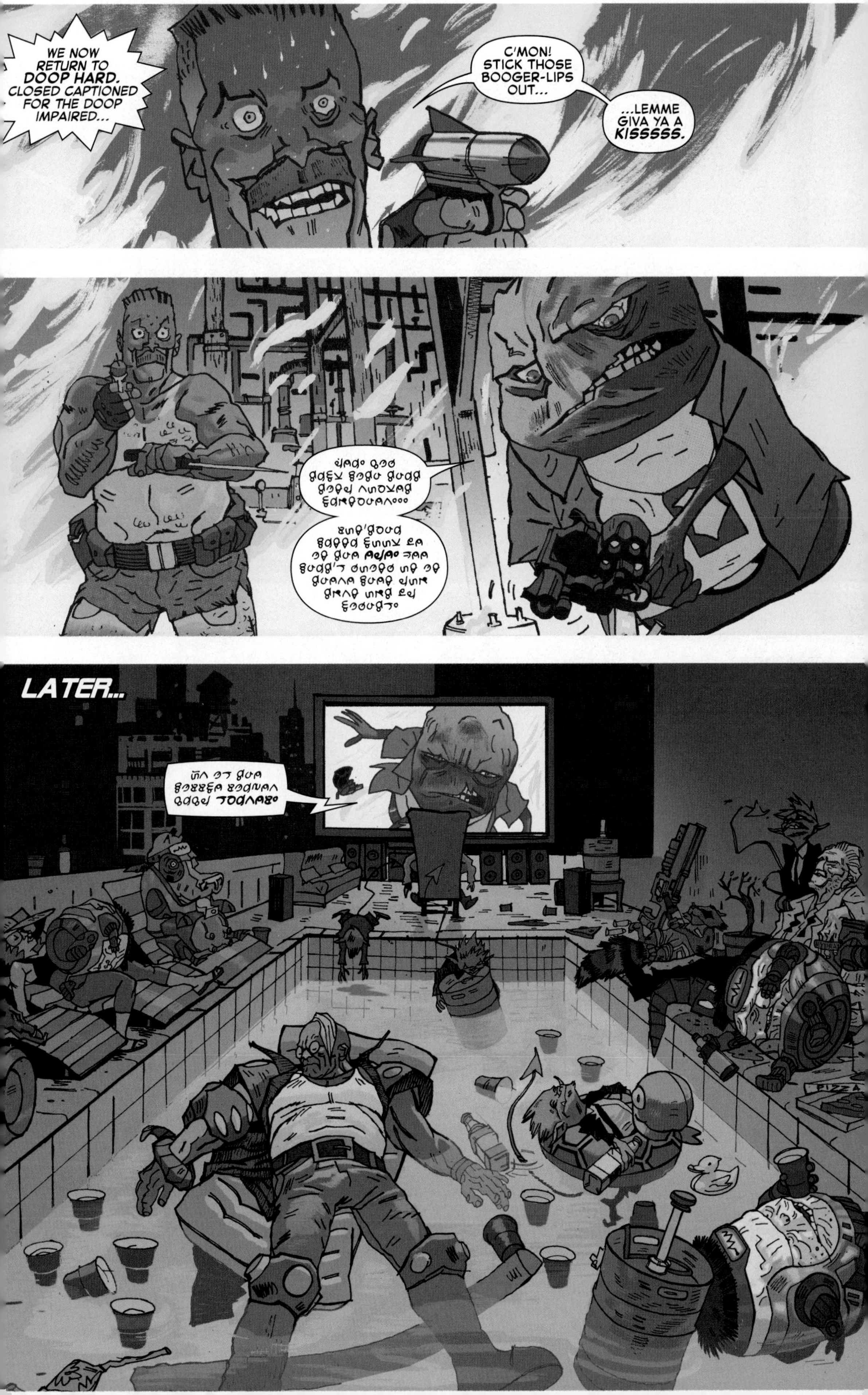
WE NOW RETURN TO DOOP HARD. CLOSED CAPTIONED FOR THE DOOP IMPAIRED...
C'MON! STICK THOSE BOOGER-LIPS OUT...
...LEMME GIVA YA A KISSSSS.
LATER...
PIZZA

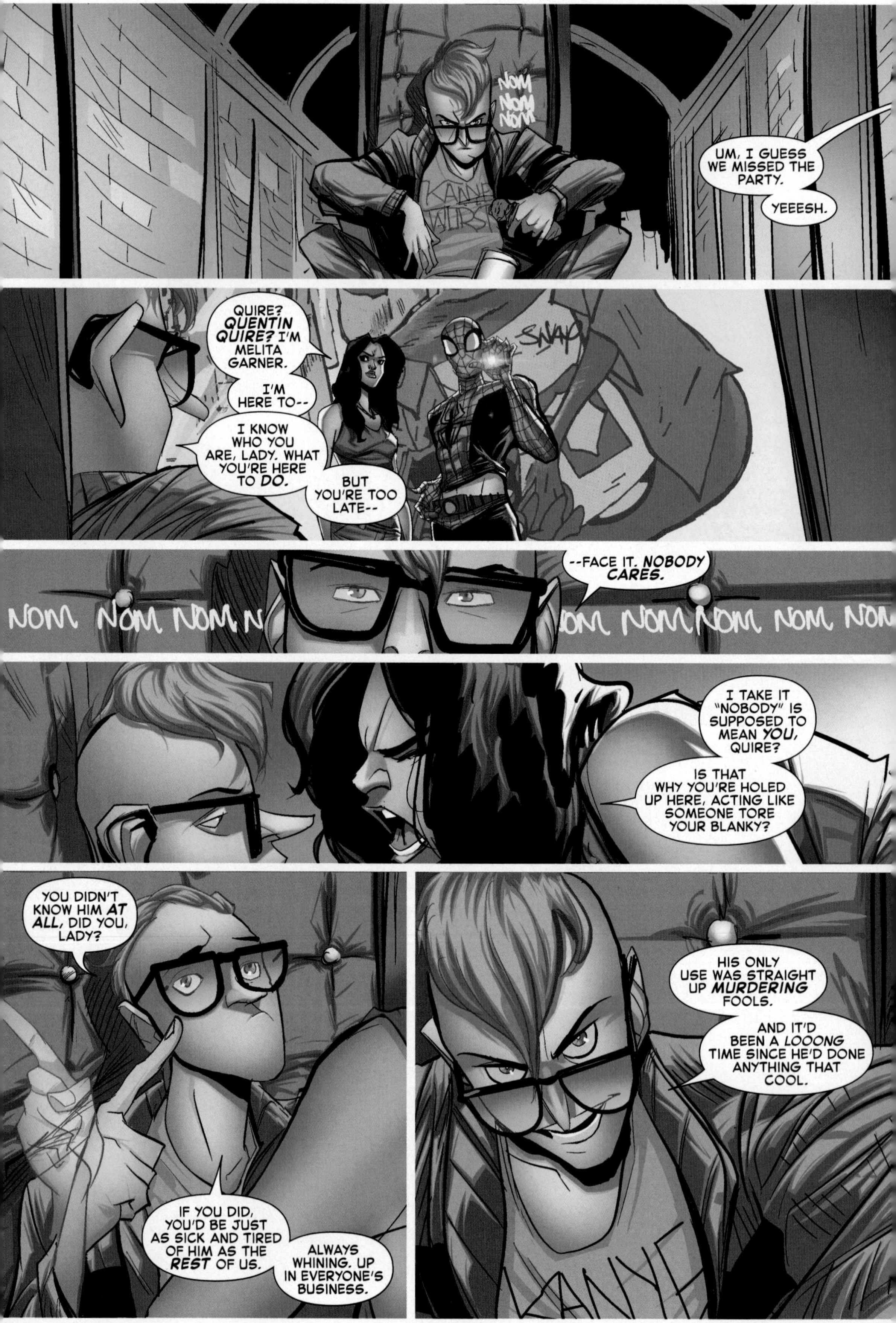
NOM NOM NOM
UM, I GUESS WE MISSED THE PARTY.
YEEESH.
QUIRE? QUENTIN QUIRE? I'M MELITA GARNER.
I'M HERE TO--
I KNOW WHO YOU ARE, LADY. WHAT YOU'RE HERE TO DO.
BUT YOU'RE TOO LATE--
--FACE IT. NOBODY CARES.
NOM NOM NOM N
NOM NOM NOM NOM NON
I TAKE IT "NOBODY" IS SUPPOSED TO MEAN YOU, QUIRE?
IS THAT WHY YOU'RE HOLED UP HERE, ACTING LIKE SOMEONE TORE YOUR BLANKY?
YOU DIDN'T KNOW HIM AT ALL, DID YOU, LADY?
IF YOU DID, YOU'D BE JUST AS SICK AND TIRED OF HIM AS THE REST OF US.
ALWAYS WHINING. UP IN EVERYONE'S BUSINESS.
HIS ONLY USE WAS STRAIGHT UP MURDERING FOOLS.
AND IT'D BEEN A LOOONG TIME SINCE HE'D DONE ANYTHING THAT COOL.

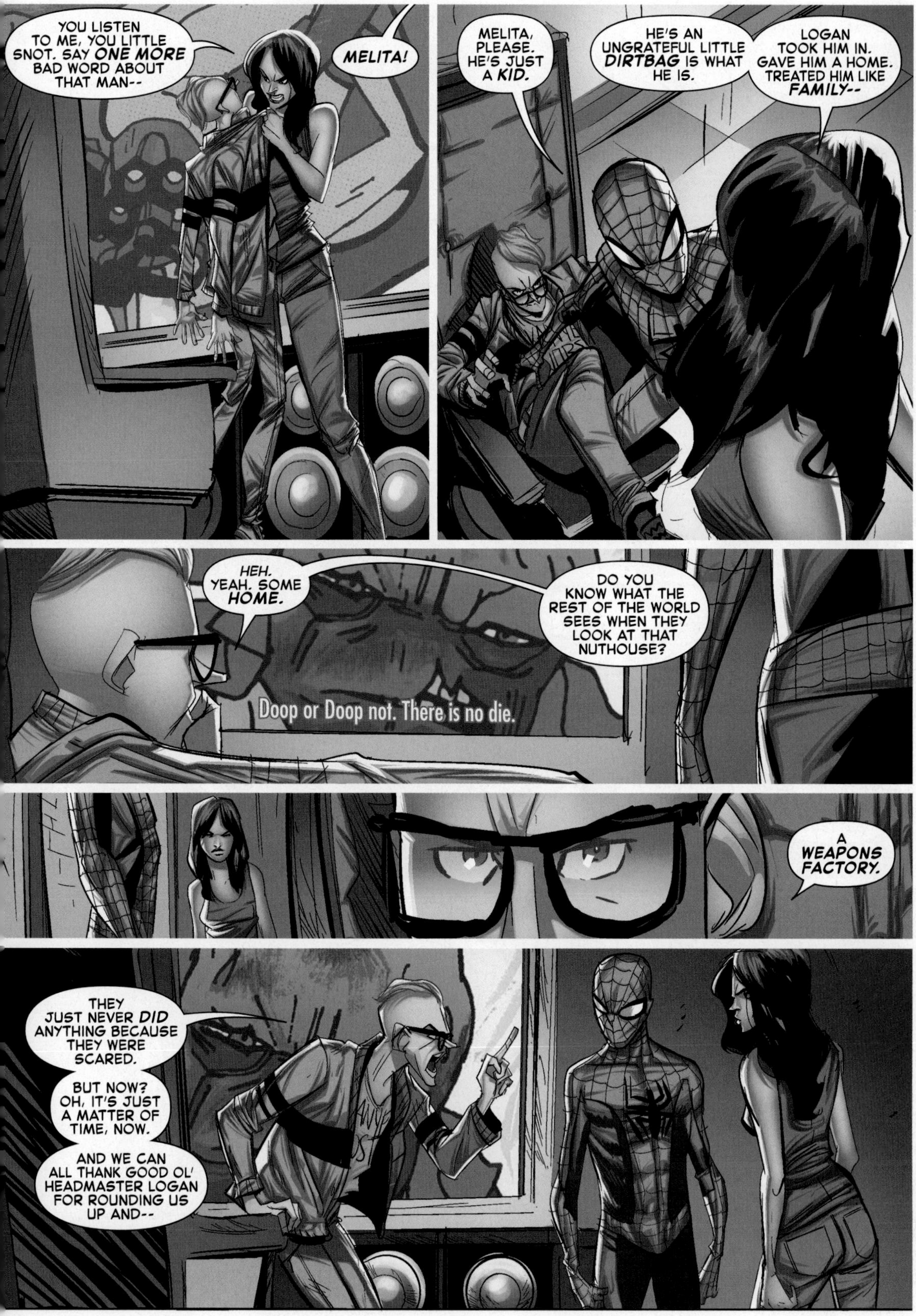

YOU LISTEN TO ME, YOU LITTLE SNOT. SAY ONE MORE BAD WORD ABOUT THAT MAN--
MELITA!
MELITA, PLEASE. HE'S JUST A KID.
HE'S AN UNGRATEFUL LITTLE DIRTBAG IS WHAT HE IS.
LOGAN TOOK HIM IN. GAVE HIM A HOME. TREATED HIM LIKE FAMILY--
HEH. YEAH. SOME HOME.
DO YOU KNOW WHAT THE REST OF THE WORLD SEES WHEN THEY LOOK AT THAT NUTHOUSE?
Doop or Doop not. There is no die.
A WEAPONS FACTORY.
THEY JUST NEVER DID ANYTHING BECAUSE THEY WERE SCARED.
BUT NOW? OH, IT'S JUST A MATTER OF TIME, NOW.
AND WE CAN ALL THANK GOOD OL' HEADMASTER LOGAN FOR ROUNDING US UP AND--

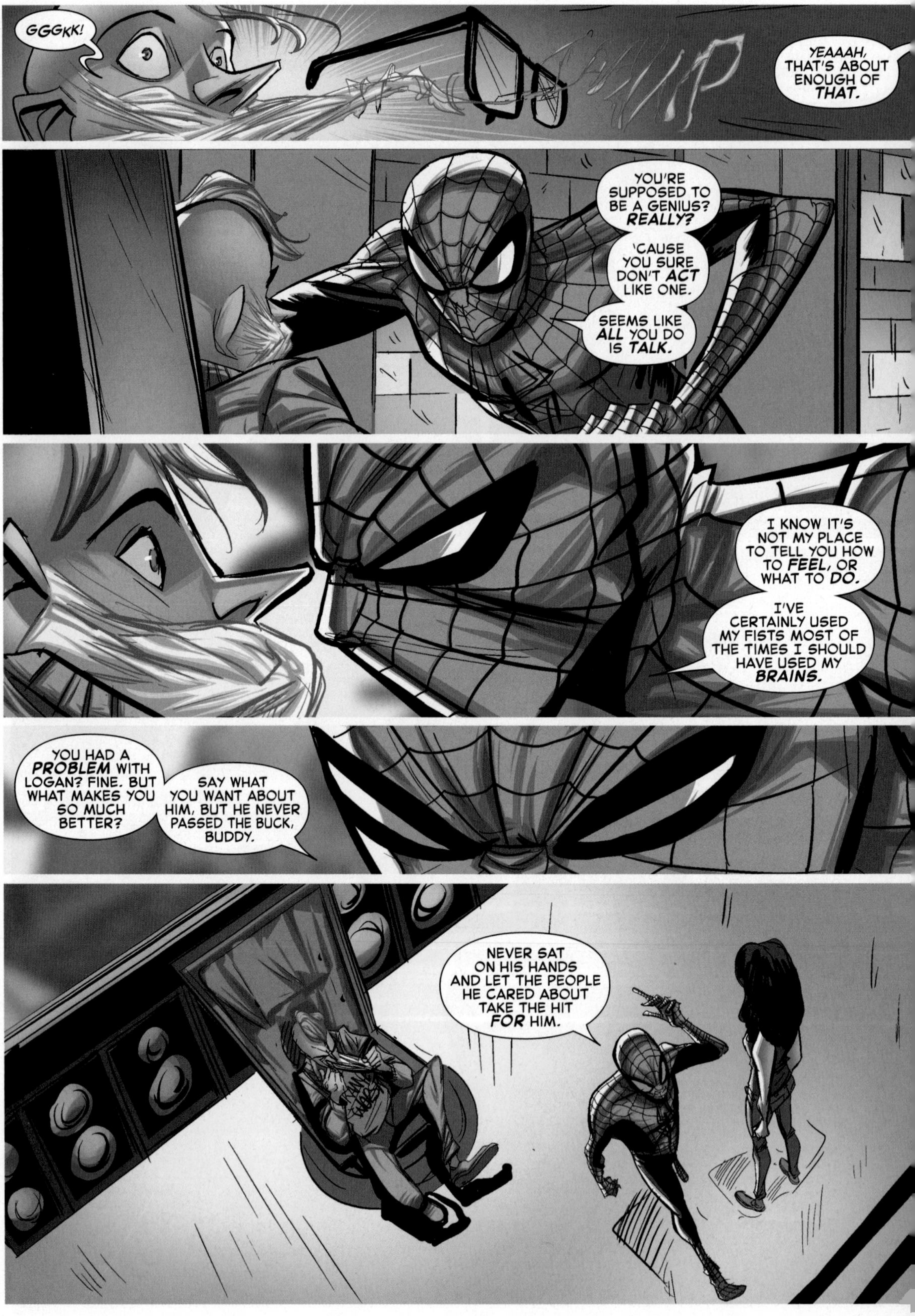

GGGKK!
THWIP
YEAAAH, THAT'S ABOUT ENOUGH OF THAT.
YOU'RE SUPPOSED TO BE A GENIUS? REALLY?
'CAUSE YOU SURE DON'T ACT LIKE ONE.
SEEMS LIKE ALL YOU DO IS TALK.
I KNOW IT'S NOT MY PLACE TO TELL YOU HOW TO FEEL, OR WHAT TO DO.
I'VE CERTAINLY USED MY FISTS MOST OF THE TIMES I SHOULD HAVE USED MY BRAINS.
YOU HAD A PROBLEM WITH LOGAN? FINE. BUT WHAT MAKES YOU SO MUCH BETTER?
SAY WHAT YOU WANT ABOUT HIM, BUT HE NEVER PASSED THE BUCK, BUDDY.
NEVER SAT ON HIS HANDS AND LET THE PEOPLE HE CARED ABOUT TAKE THE HIT FOR HIM.

HEH. HILARIOUS.

YOU STRUT IN HERE LIKE A COWBOY--WITH NO CONCERN FOR WHAT I COULD DO, OR SEE, OR SAY?

ALL THAT TRUST JUST 'CAUSE LOGAN TOLD YOU I'M A GOOD KID DEEP DOWN?

YEAH, MAYBE THAT'S IT.

OR MAYBE YOU JUST KNOW HOW BORING YOU REALLY ARE.

WELL, LIE TO YOURSELF ALL YOU WANT.

I KNOW WHAT SHE SAW.

WHAT YOU REALLY THINK.

WHAT I THINK IS YOU NEED TO SPEND SOME OF THAT MONEY OF YOURS AT THE BARBERSHOP, PLAYBOY.

ANNND WE'RE DONE HERE. SEE YA AROUND, QUIRE.

𝔊𝔲𝔡𝔤𝔢𝔯 𝔢𝔤𝔢 𝔰𝔬𝔢 𝔯𝔞𝔤𝔬𝔞𝔳𝔰𝔬 𝔒𝔲𝔰𝔲𝔫𝔢𝔳𝔞𝔢 𝔰𝔞𝔤𝔰𝔰𝔢𝔳𝔬

YOU SAY THAT EVERY TIME, SON.

YOU SAY THAT EVERY TIME.

NOT IF I SEE YOU FIRST, SPIDER-MAN.

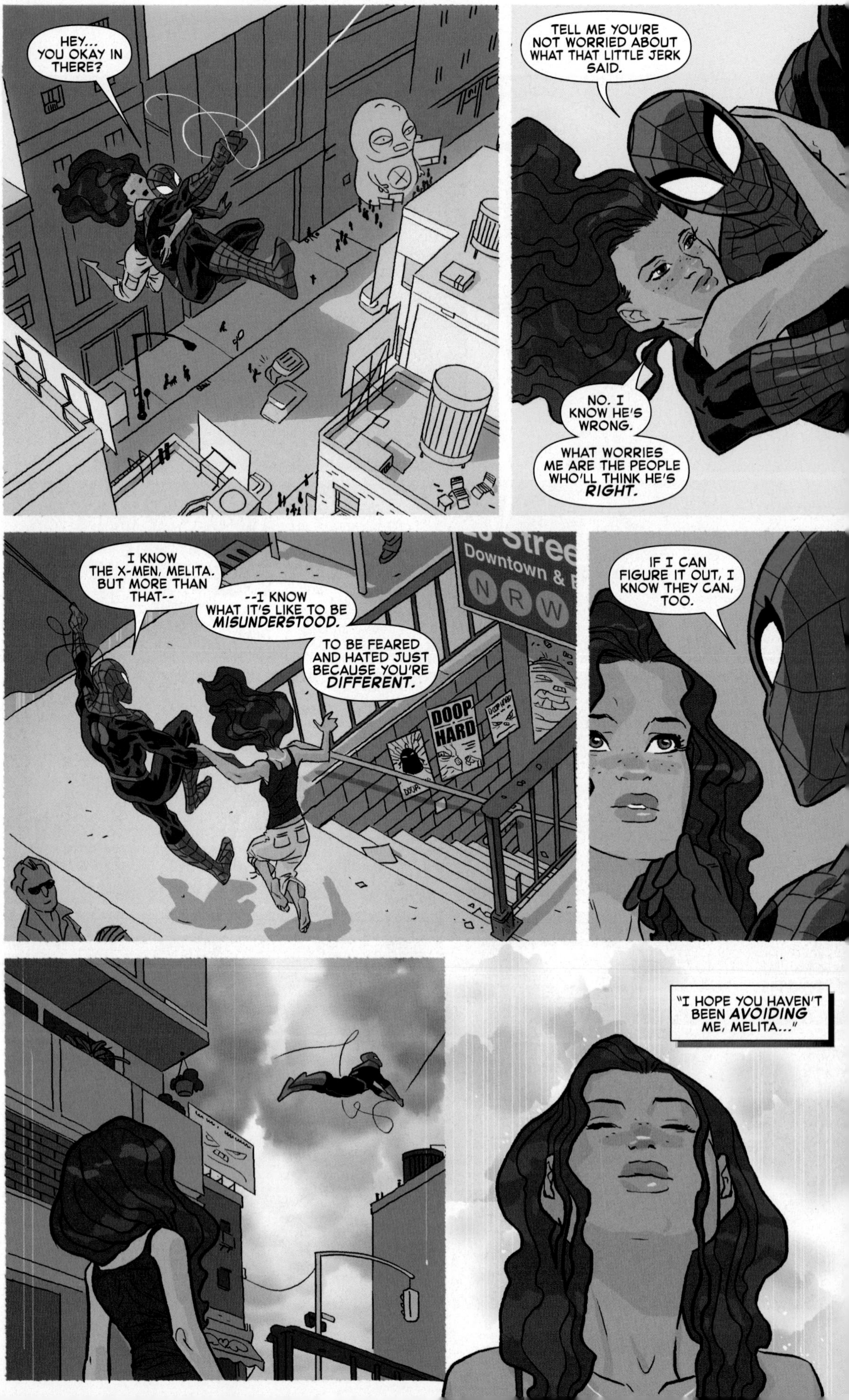
HEY... YOU OKAY IN THERE?
TELL ME YOU'RE NOT WORRIED ABOUT WHAT THAT LITTLE JERK SAID.
NO. I KNOW HE'S WRONG.
WHAT WORRIES ME ARE THE PEOPLE WHO'LL THINK HE'S RIGHT.
I KNOW THE X-MEN, MELITA. BUT MORE THAN THAT--
--I KNOW WHAT IT'S LIKE TO BE MISUNDERSTOOD.
TO BE FEARED AND HATED JUST BECAUSE YOU'RE DIFFERENT.
Downtown &
N R W
DOOP HARD
IF I CAN FIGURE IT OUT, I KNOW THEY CAN, TOO.
"I HOPE YOU HAVEN'T BEEN AVOIDING ME, MELITA..."

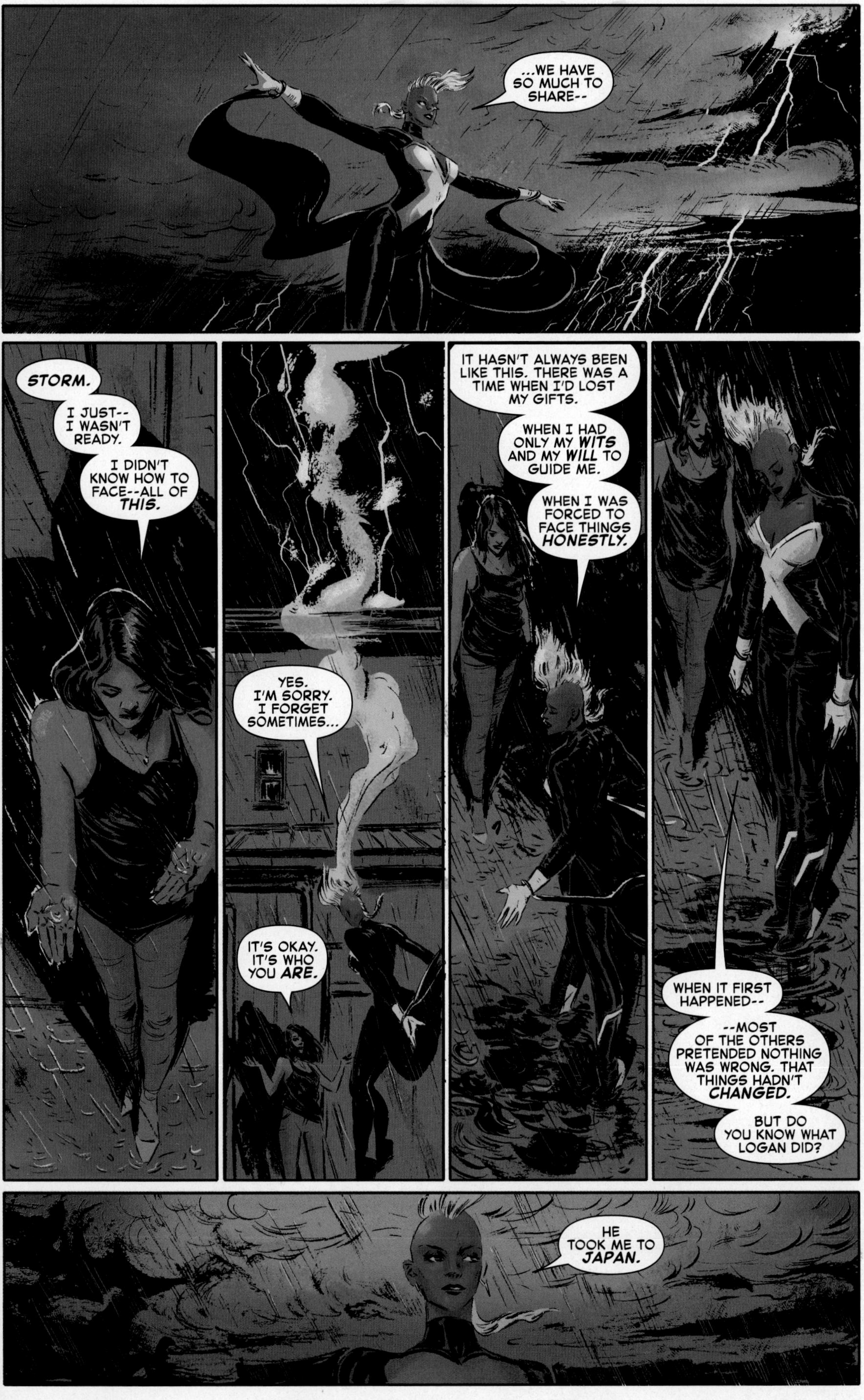
...WE HAVE SO MUCH TO SHARE--
STORM.
I JUST-- I WASN'T READY.
I DIDN'T KNOW HOW TO FACE--ALL OF THIS.
YES. I'M SORRY. I FORGET SOMETIMES...
IT'S OKAY. IT'S WHO YOU ARE.
IT HASN'T ALWAYS BEEN LIKE THIS. THERE WAS A TIME WHEN I'D LOST MY GIFTS.
WHEN I HAD ONLY MY WITS AND MY WILL TO GUIDE ME.
WHEN I WAS FORCED TO FACE THINGS HONESTLY.
WHEN IT FIRST HAPPENED--
--MOST OF THE OTHERS PRETENDED NOTHING WAS WRONG. THAT THINGS HADN'T CHANGED.
BUT DO YOU KNOW WHAT LOGAN DID?
HE TOOK ME TO JAPAN.

各停 LOCAL 新宿 SHINJUKU

OF COURSE....

WHEREVER WOLVERINE WENT IN JAPAN....

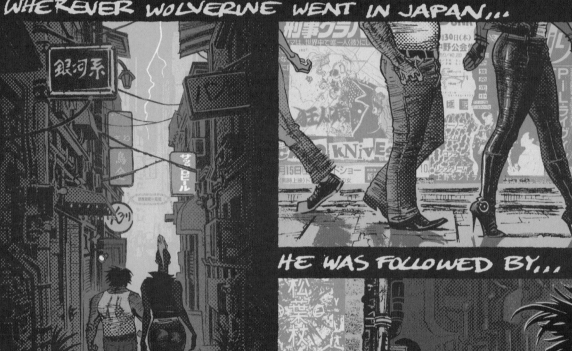

HE WAS FOLLOWED BY....

..THE HAND....

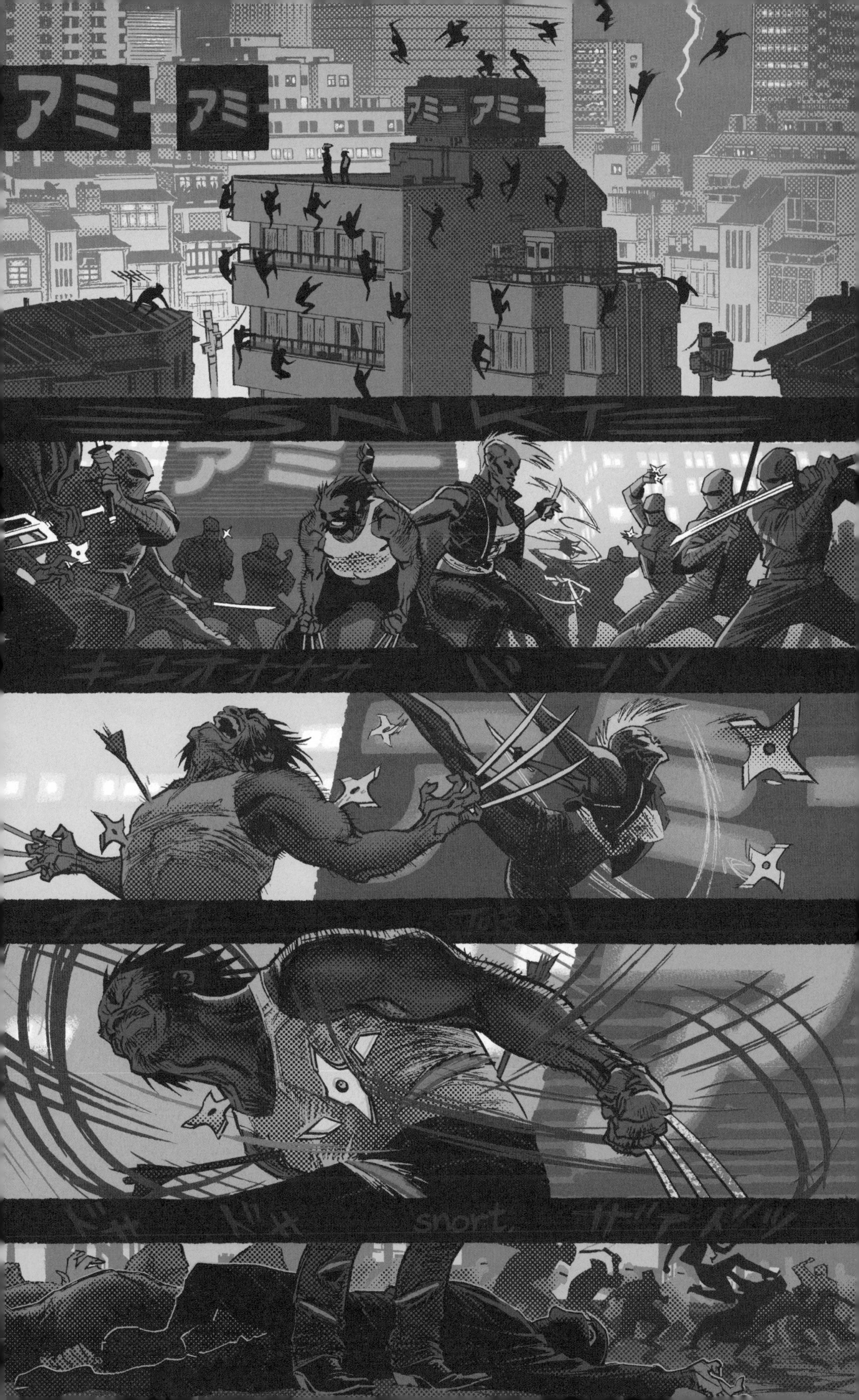
アミー
アミー
アミー
アミー
SNIKT
snort

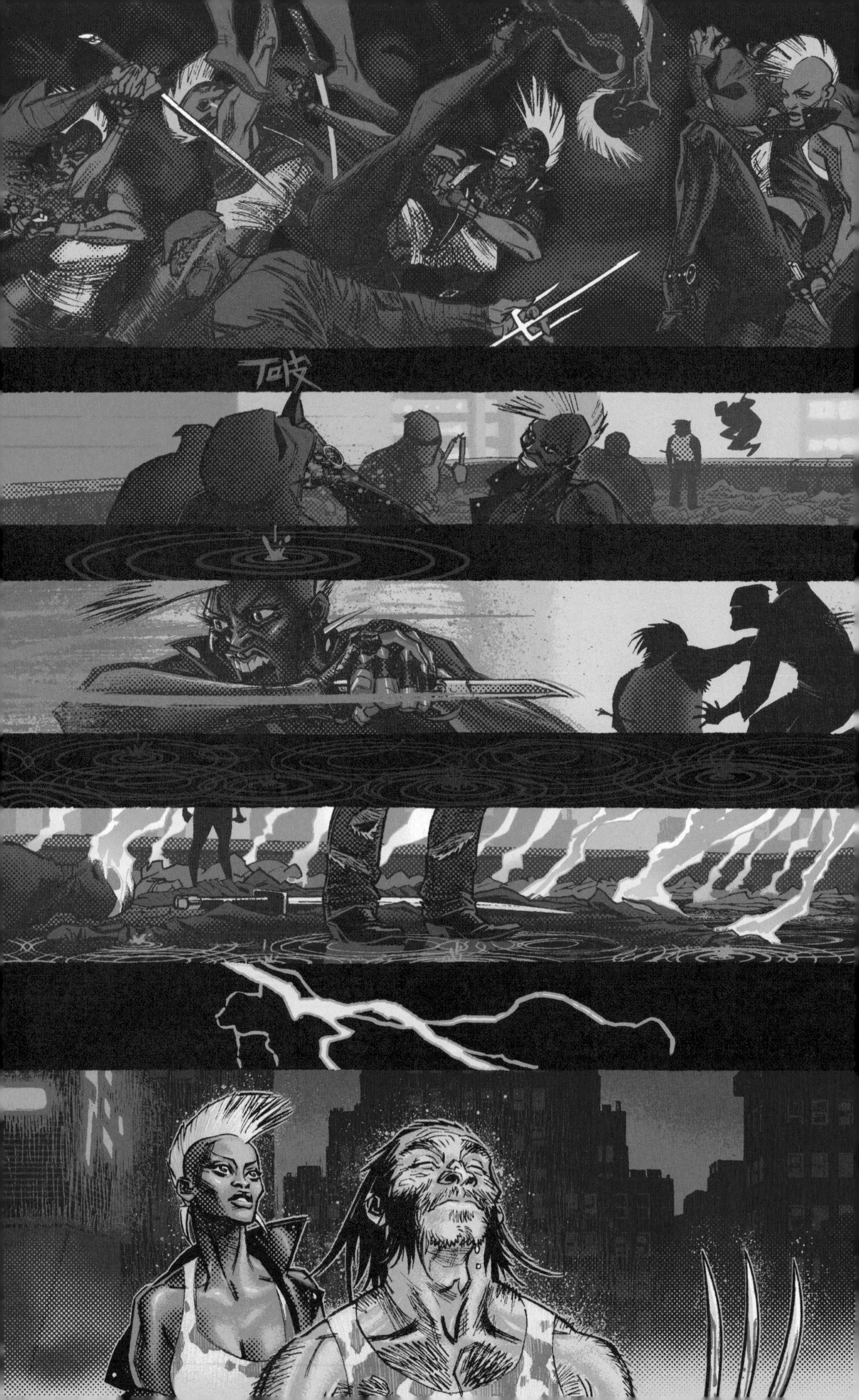
TOK

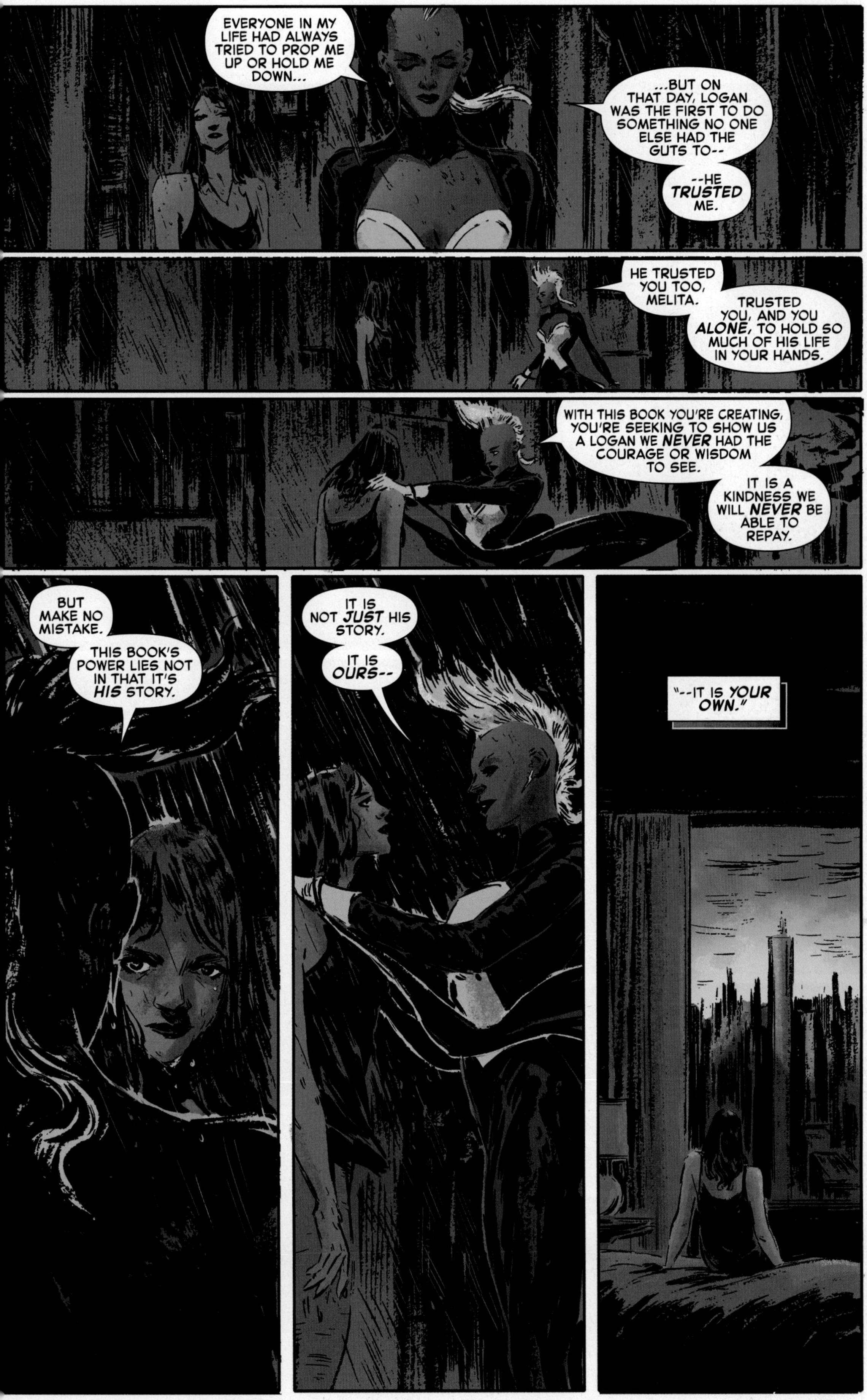
EVERYONE IN MY LIFE HAD ALWAYS TRIED TO PROP ME UP OR HOLD ME DOWN...
...BUT ON THAT DAY, LOGAN WAS THE FIRST TO DO SOMETHING NO ONE ELSE HAD THE GUTS TO--
--HE TRUSTED ME.
HE TRUSTED YOU TOO, MELITA.
TRUSTED YOU, AND YOU ALONE, TO HOLD SO MUCH OF HIS LIFE IN YOUR HANDS.
WITH THIS BOOK YOU'RE CREATING, YOU'RE SEEKING TO SHOW US A LOGAN WE NEVER HAD THE COURAGE OR WISDOM TO SEE.
IT IS A KINDNESS WE WILL NEVER BE ABLE TO REPAY.
BUT MAKE NO MISTAKE.
THIS BOOK'S POWER LIES NOT IN THAT IT'S HIS STORY.
IT IS NOT JUST HIS STORY.
IT IS OURS--
"--IT IS YOUR OWN."

EPILOGUE.

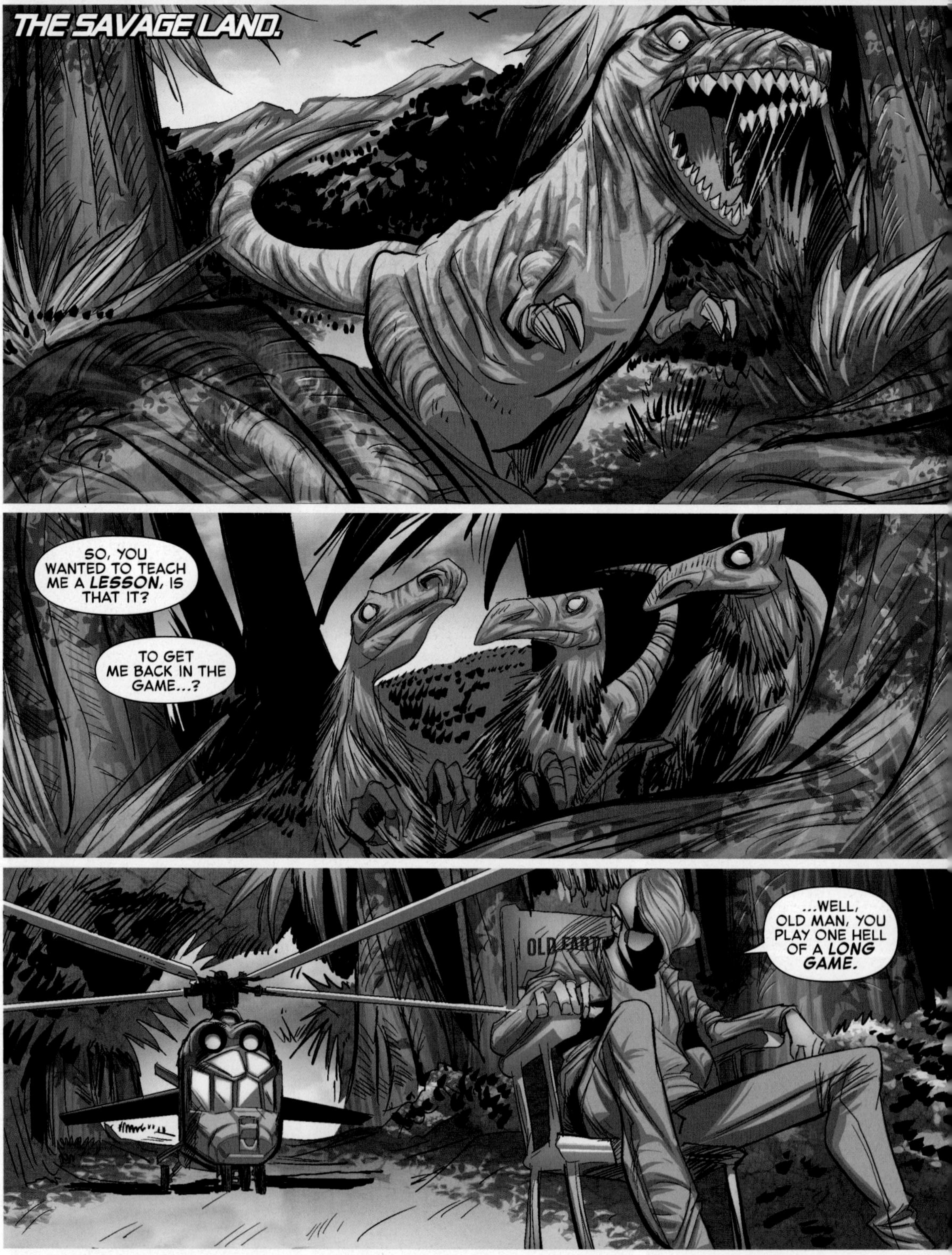
THE SAVAGE LAND.
SO, YOU WANTED TO TEACH ME A *LESSON*, IS THAT IT?
TO GET ME BACK IN THE GAME...?
...WELL, OLD MAN, YOU PLAY ONE HELL OF A *LONG GAME.*

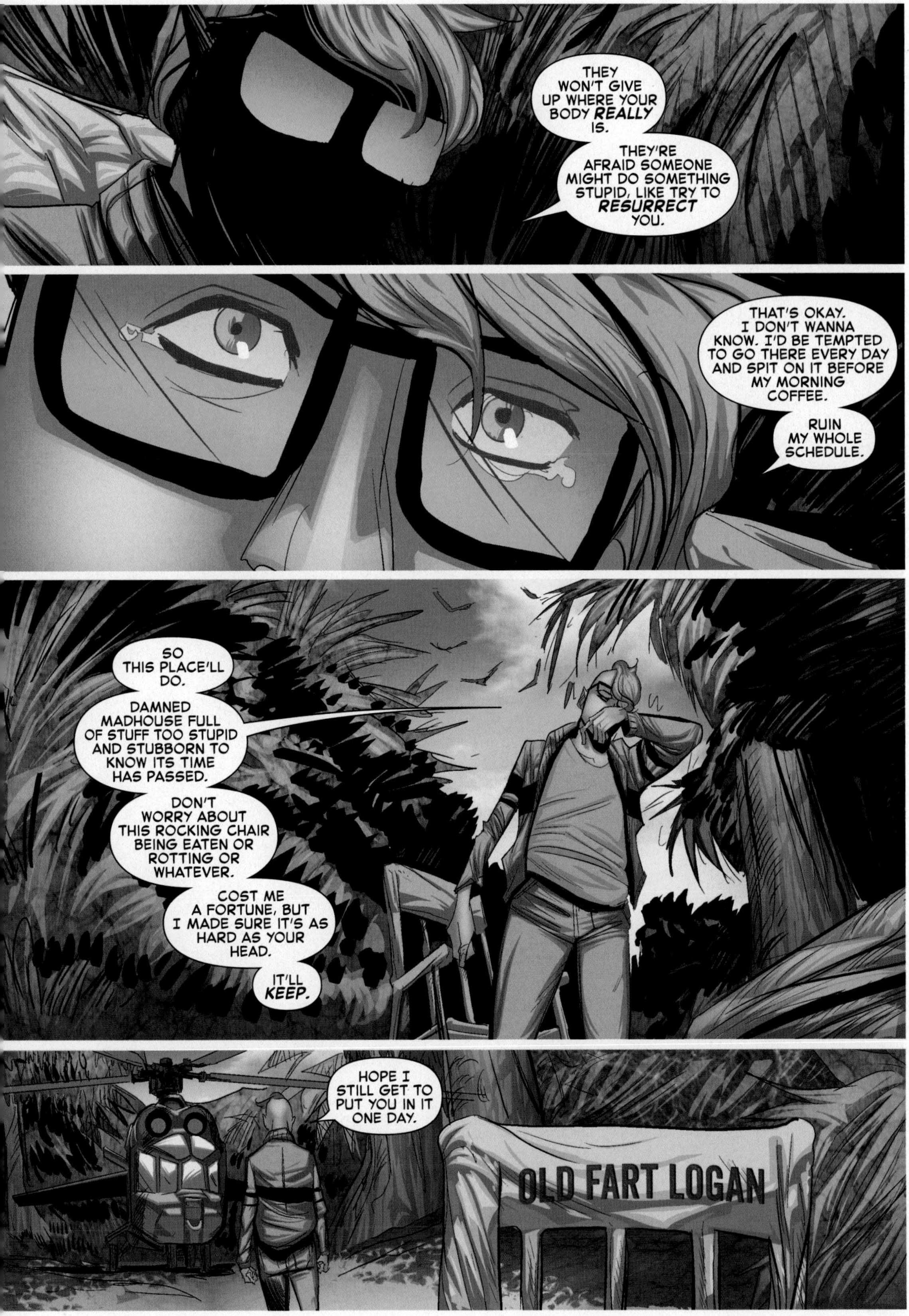

THEY WON'T GIVE UP WHERE YOUR BODY *REALLY* IS.
THEY'RE AFRAID SOMEONE MIGHT DO SOMETHING STUPID, LIKE TRY TO *RESURRECT* YOU.
THAT'S OKAY. I DON'T WANNA KNOW. I'D BE TEMPTED TO GO THERE EVERY DAY AND SPIT ON IT BEFORE MY MORNING COFFEE.
RUIN MY WHOLE SCHEDULE.
SO THIS PLACE'LL DO.
DAMNED MADHOUSE FULL OF STUFF TOO STUPID AND STUBBORN TO KNOW ITS TIME HAS PASSED.
DON'T WORRY ABOUT THIS ROCKING CHAIR BEING EATEN OR ROTTING OR WHATEVER.
COST ME A FORTUNE, BUT I MADE SURE IT'S AS HARD AS YOUR HEAD.
IT'LL *KEEP.*
HOPE I STILL GET TO PUT YOU IN IT ONE DAY.
OLD FART LOGAN

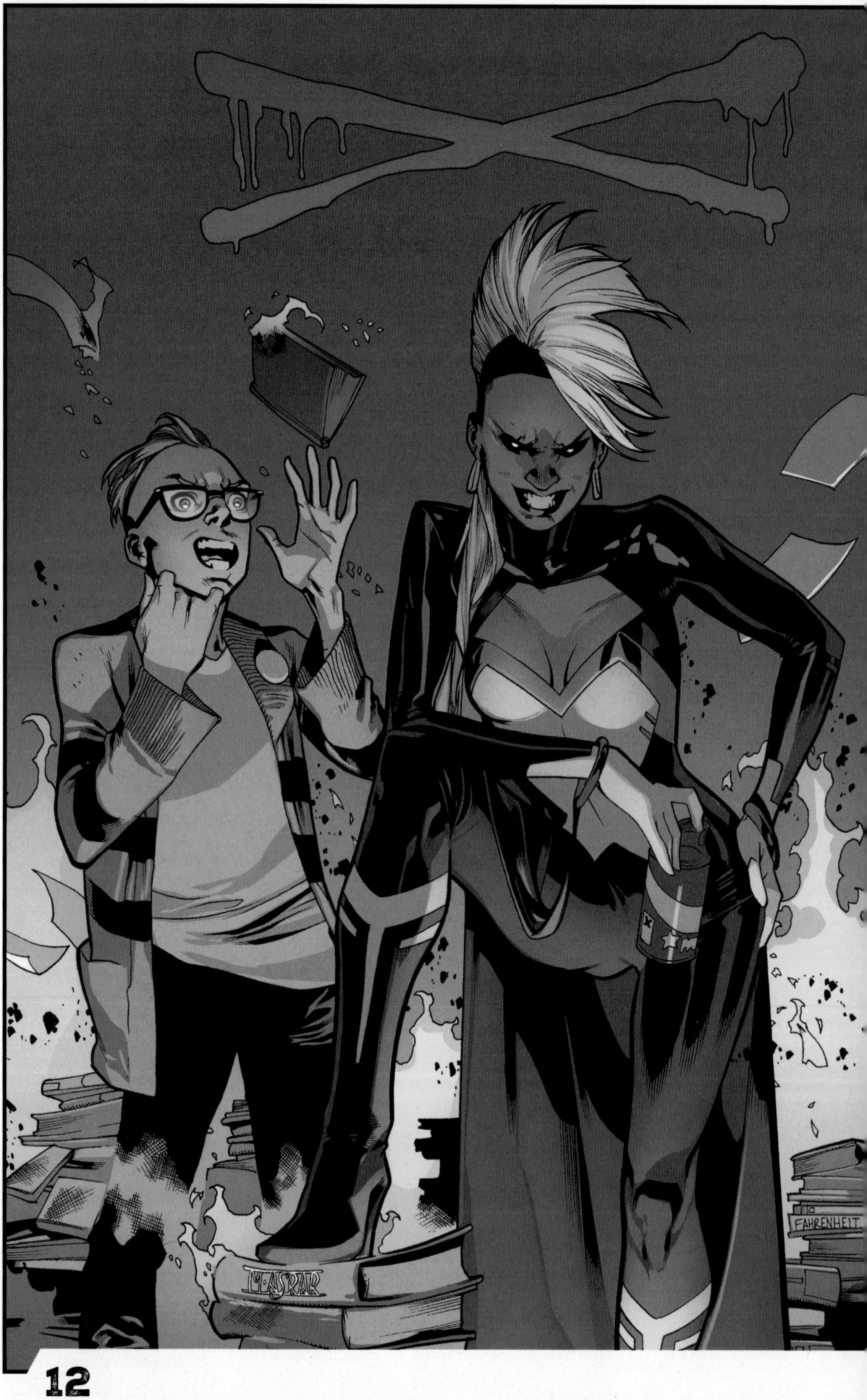
FAHRENHEIT

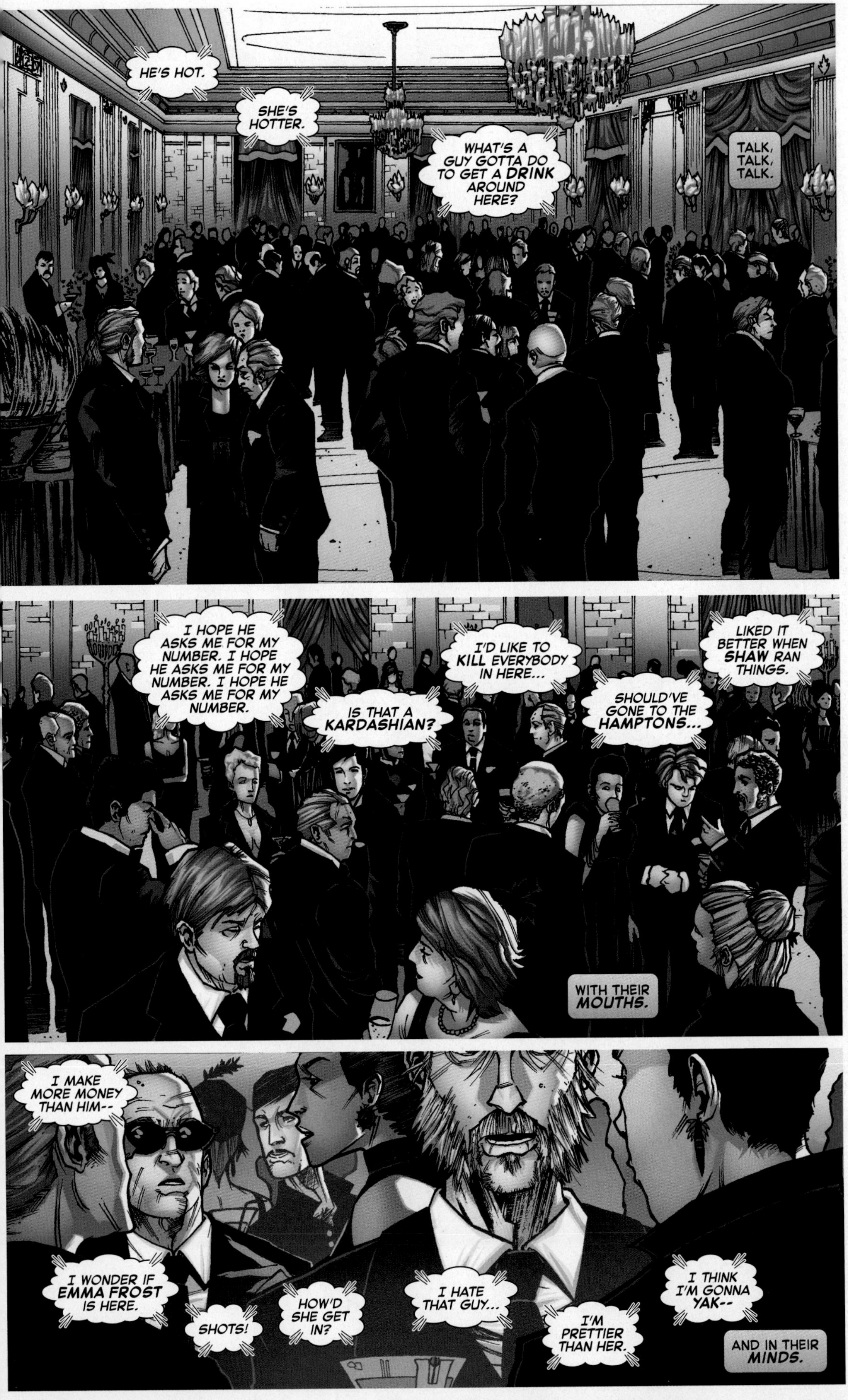
HE'S HOT.
SHE'S HOTTER.
WHAT'S A GUY GOTTA DO TO GET A DRINK AROUND HERE?
TALK, TALK, TALK.
I HOPE HE ASKS ME FOR MY NUMBER. I HOPE HE ASKS ME FOR MY NUMBER. I HOPE HE ASKS ME FOR MY NUMBER.
IS THAT A KARDASHIAN?
I'D LIKE TO KILL EVERYBODY IN HERE...
SHOULD'VE GONE TO THE HAMPTONS...
LIKED IT BETTER WHEN SHAW RAN THINGS.
WITH THEIR MOUTHS.
I MAKE MORE MONEY THAN HIM--
I WONDER IF EMMA FROST IS HERE.
SHOTS!
HOW'D SHE GET IN?
I HATE THAT GUY...
I'M PRETTIER THAN HER.
I THINK I'M GONNA YAK--
AND IN THEIR MINDS.

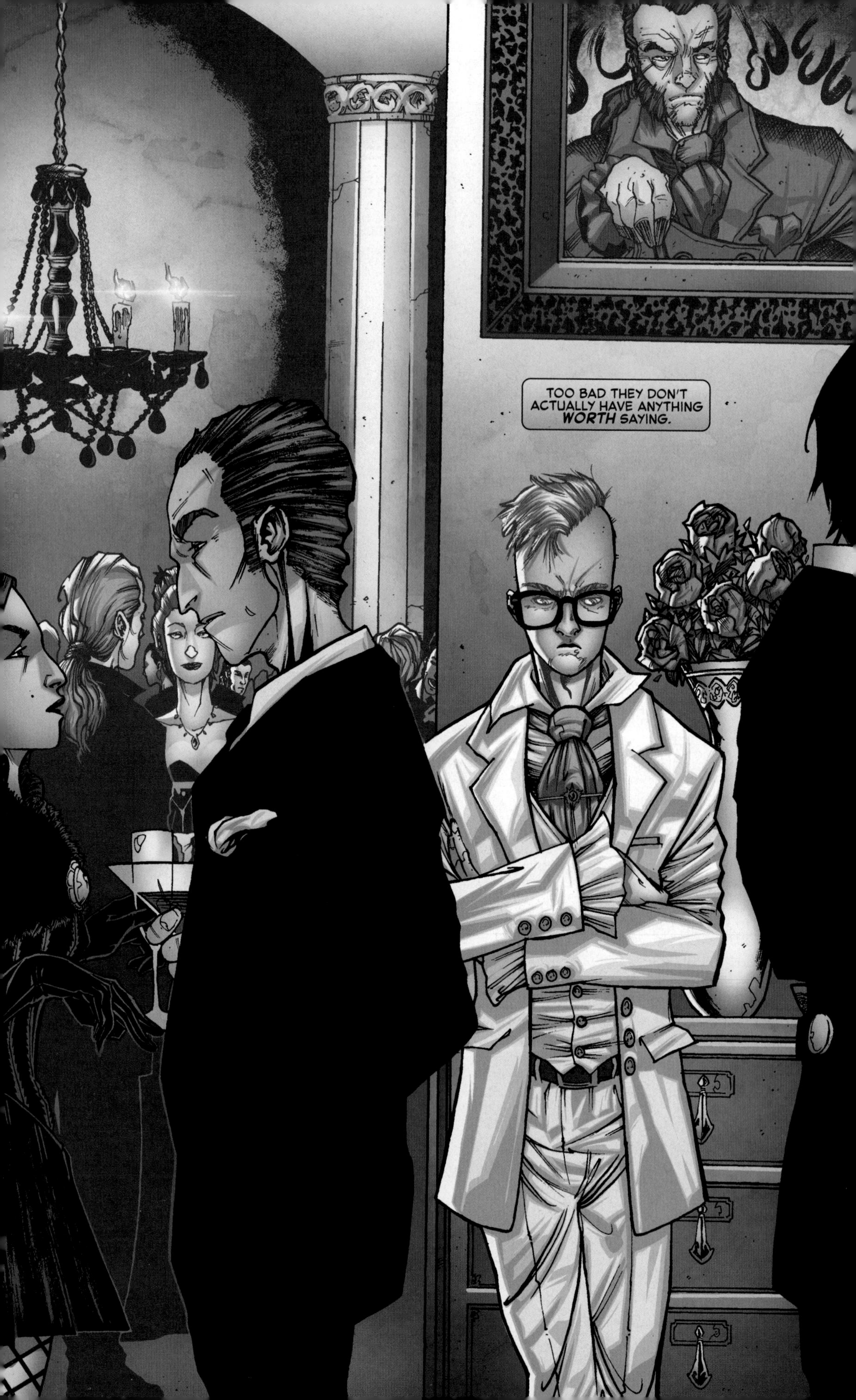
TOO BAD THEY DON'T ACTUALLY HAVE ANYTHING WORTH SAYING.

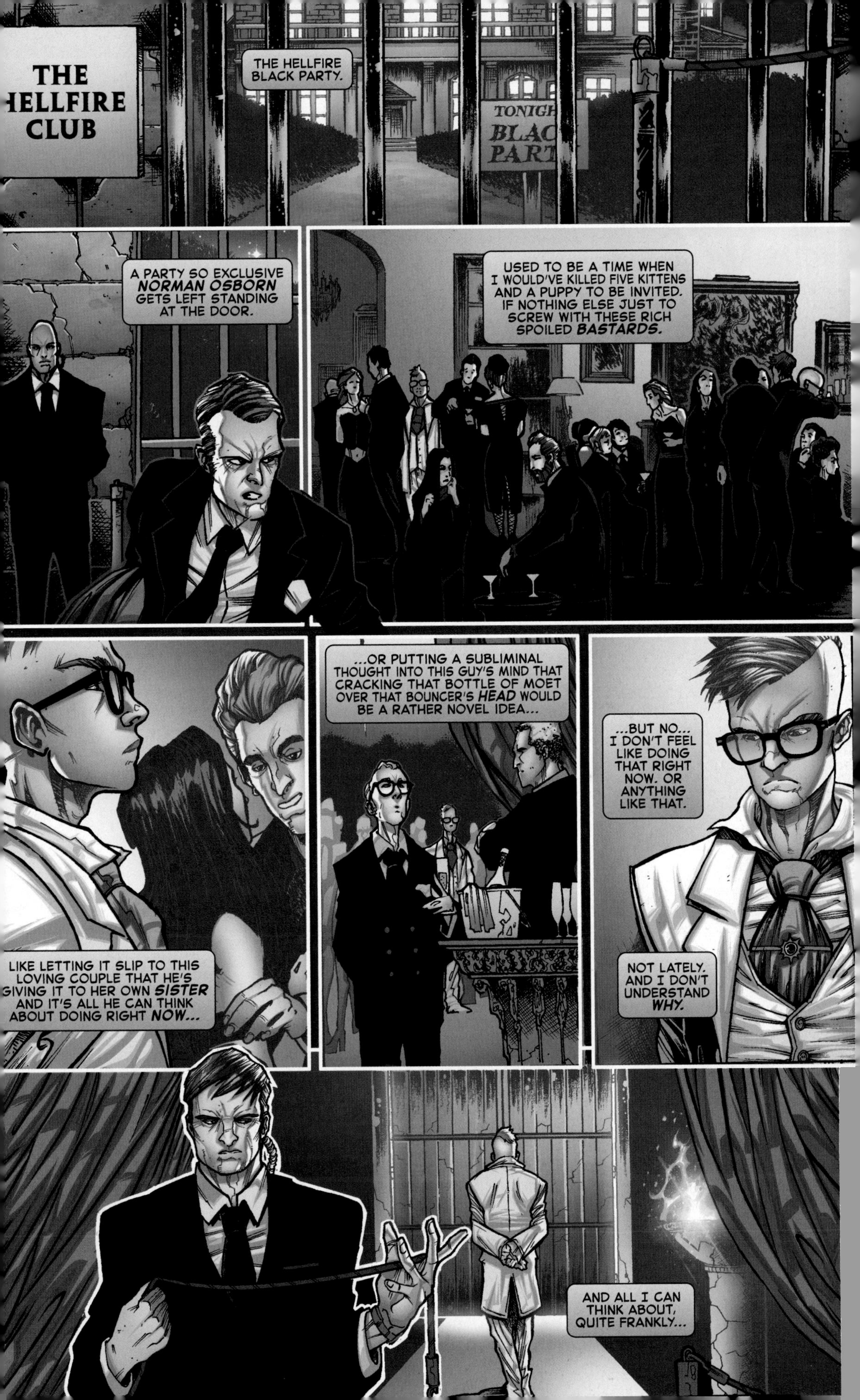
THE HELLFIRE CLUB
THE HELLFIRE BLACK PARTY.
TONIGH BLAC PART
A PARTY SO EXCLUSIVE NORMAN OSBORN GETS LEFT STANDING AT THE DOOR.
USED TO BE A TIME WHEN I WOULD'VE KILLED FIVE KITTENS AND A PUPPY TO BE INVITED. IF NOTHING ELSE JUST TO SCREW WITH THESE RICH SPOILED BASTARDS.
LIKE LETTING IT SLIP TO THIS LOVING COUPLE THAT HE'S GIVING IT TO HER OWN SISTER AND IT'S ALL HE CAN THINK ABOUT DOING RIGHT NOW...
...OR PUTTING A SUBLIMINAL THOUGHT INTO THIS GUY'S MIND THAT CRACKING THAT BOTTLE OF MOET OVER THAT BOUNCER'S HEAD WOULD BE A RATHER NOVEL IDEA...
...BUT NO... I DON'T FEEL LIKE DOING THAT RIGHT NOW. OR ANYTHING LIKE THAT.
NOT LATELY. AND I DON'T UNDERSTAND WHY.
AND ALL I CAN THINK ABOUT, QUITE FRANKLY...

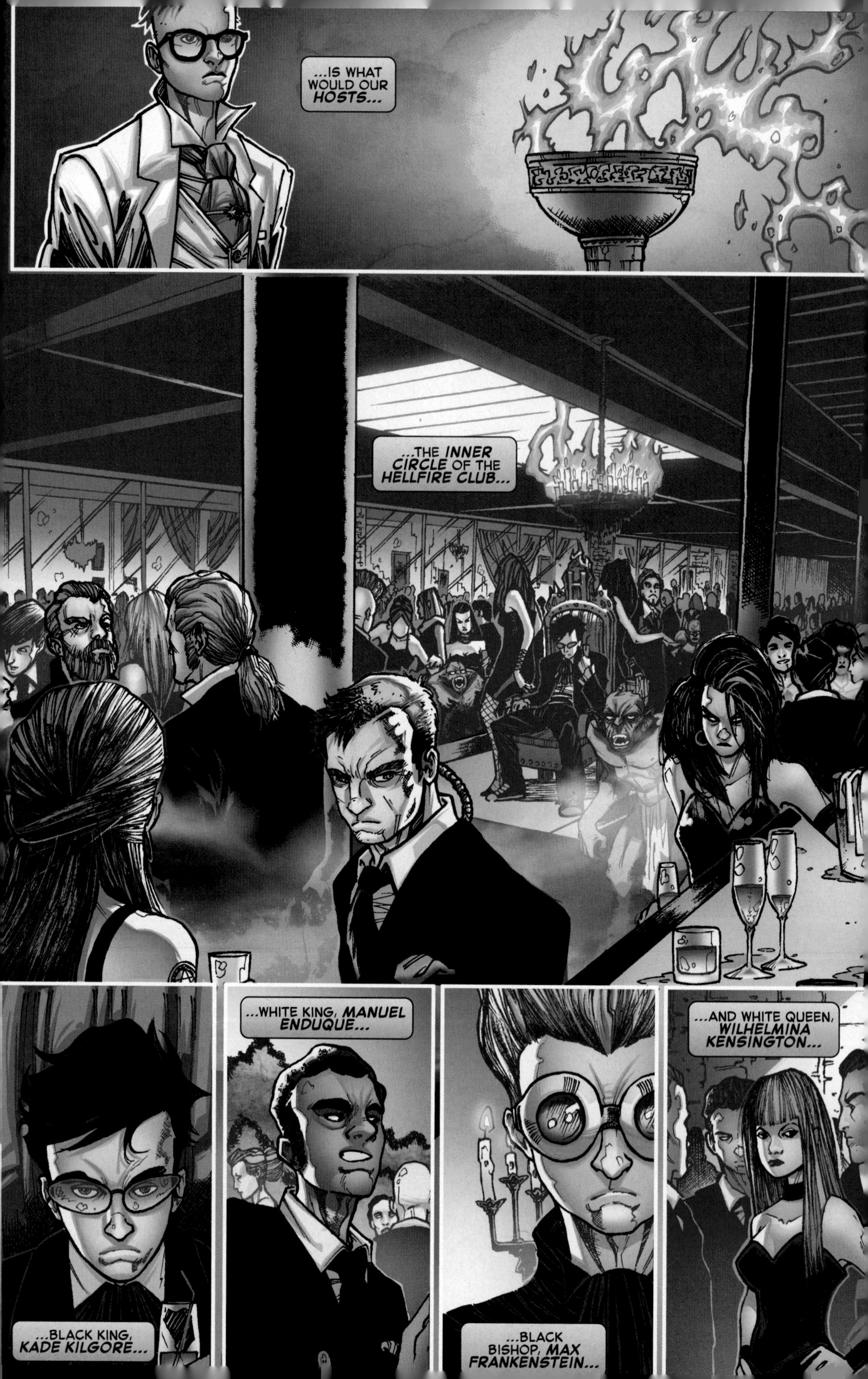
...IS WHAT WOULD OUR HOSTS...
...THE INNER CIRCLE OF THE HELLFIRE CLUB...
...BLACK KING, KADE KILGORE...
...WHITE KING, MANUEL ENDUQUE...
...BLACK BISHOP, MAX FRANKENSTEIN...
...AND WHITE QUEEN, WILHELMINA KENSINGTON...

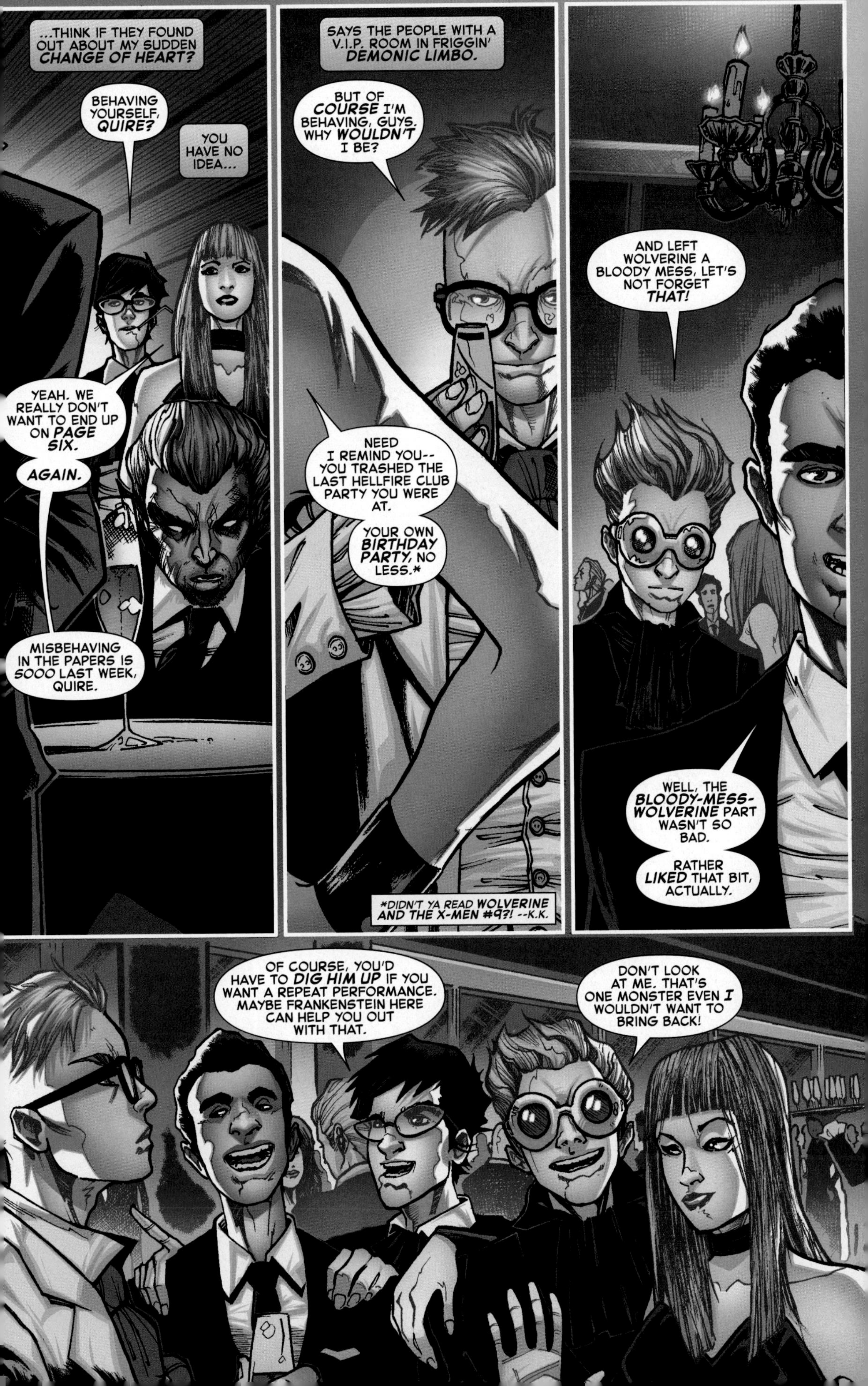
...THINK IF THEY FOUND OUT ABOUT MY SUDDEN CHANGE OF HEART?
BEHAVING YOURSELF, QUIRE?
YOU HAVE NO IDEA...
YEAH. WE REALLY DON'T WANT TO END UP ON PAGE SIX.
AGAIN.
MISBEHAVING IN THE PAPERS IS SOOO LAST WEEK, QUIRE.
SAYS THE PEOPLE WITH A V.I.P. ROOM IN FRIGGIN' DEMONIC LIMBO.
BUT OF COURSE I'M BEHAVING, GUYS. WHY WOULDN'T I BE?
NEED I REMIND YOU-- YOU TRASHED THE LAST HELLFIRE CLUB PARTY YOU WERE AT.
YOUR OWN BIRTHDAY PARTY, NO LESS.*
*DIDN'T YA READ WOLVERINE AND THE X-MEN #9?! --K.K.
AND LEFT WOLVERINE A BLOODY MESS, LET'S NOT FORGET THAT!
WELL, THE BLOODY-MESS-WOLVERINE PART WASN'T SO BAD.
RATHER LIKED THAT BIT, ACTUALLY.
OF COURSE, YOU'D HAVE TO DIG HIM UP IF YOU WANT A REPEAT PERFORMANCE. MAYBE FRANKENSTEIN HERE CAN HELP YOU OUT WITH THAT.
DON'T LOOK AT ME. THAT'S ONE MONSTER EVEN I WOULDN'T WANT TO BRING BACK!

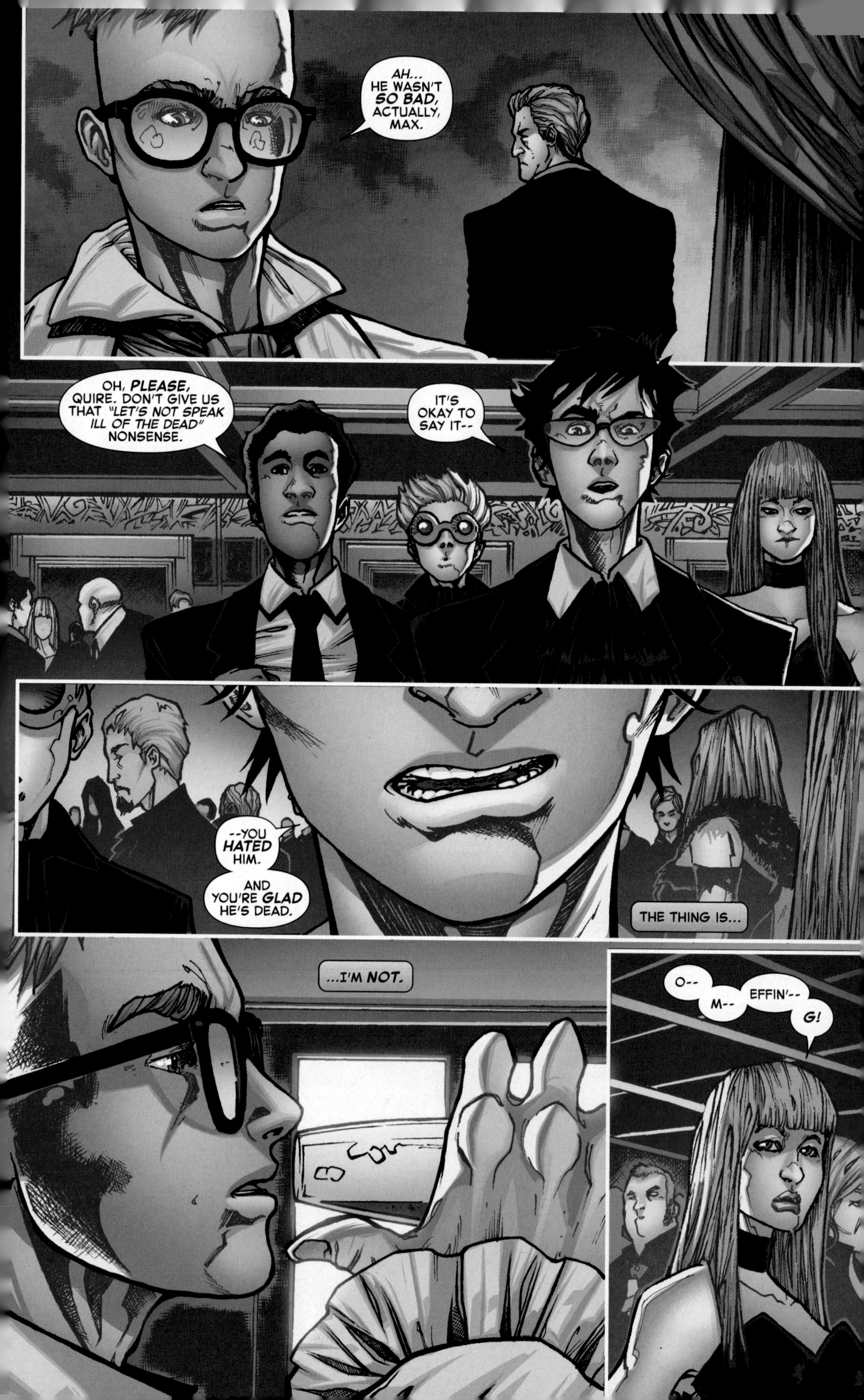
AH... HE WASN'T SO BAD, ACTUALLY, MAX.
OH, PLEASE, QUIRE. DON'T GIVE US THAT "LET'S NOT SPEAK ILL OF THE DEAD" NONSENSE.
IT'S OKAY TO SAY IT--
--YOU HATED HIM.
AND YOU'RE GLAD HE'S DEAD.
THE THING IS...
...I'M NOT.
O--
M--
EFFIN'--
G!

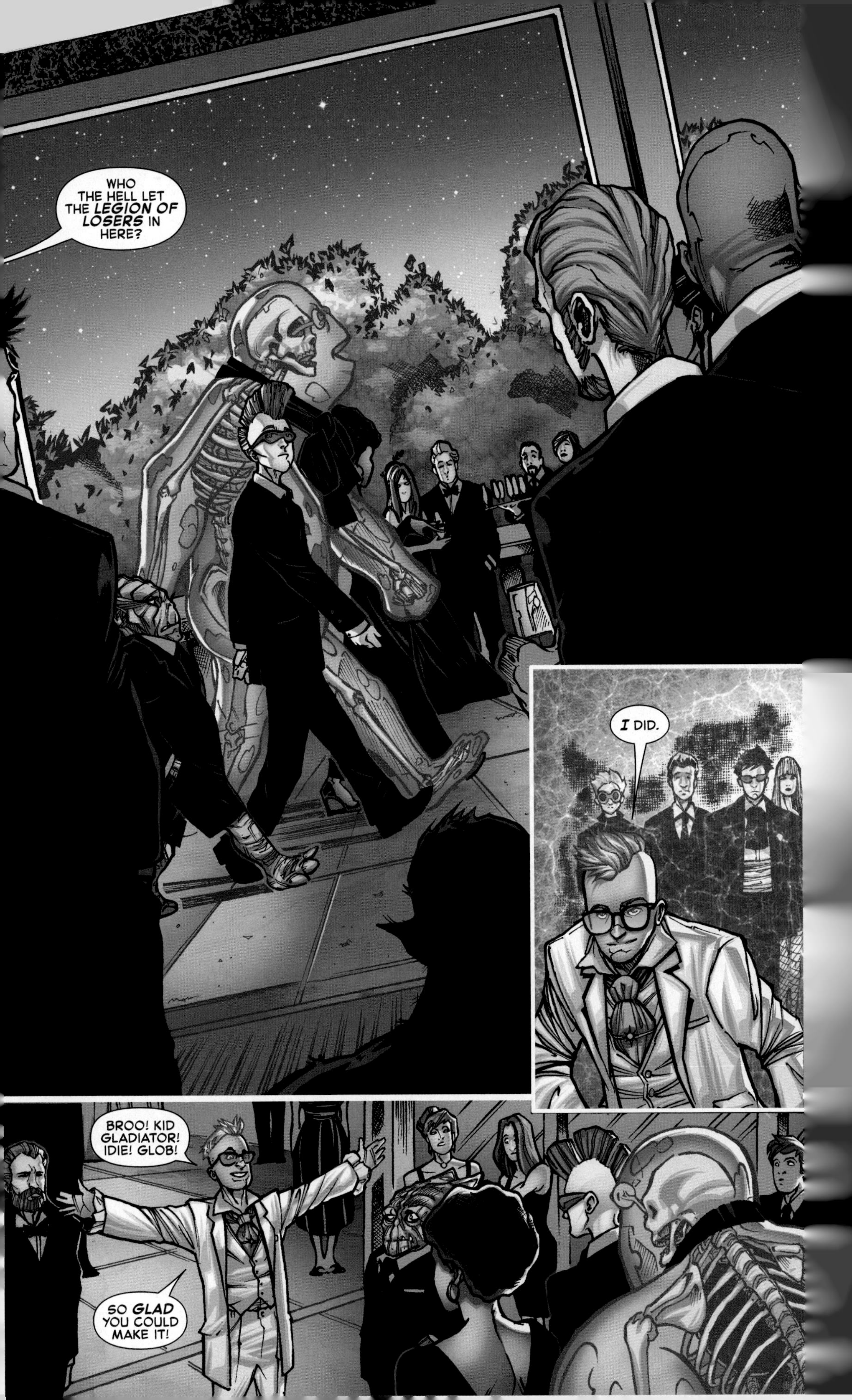
WHO THE HELL LET THE *LEGION OF LOSERS* IN HERE?
I DID.
BROO! KID GLADIATOR! IDIE! GLOB!
SO *GLAD* YOU COULD MAKE IT!

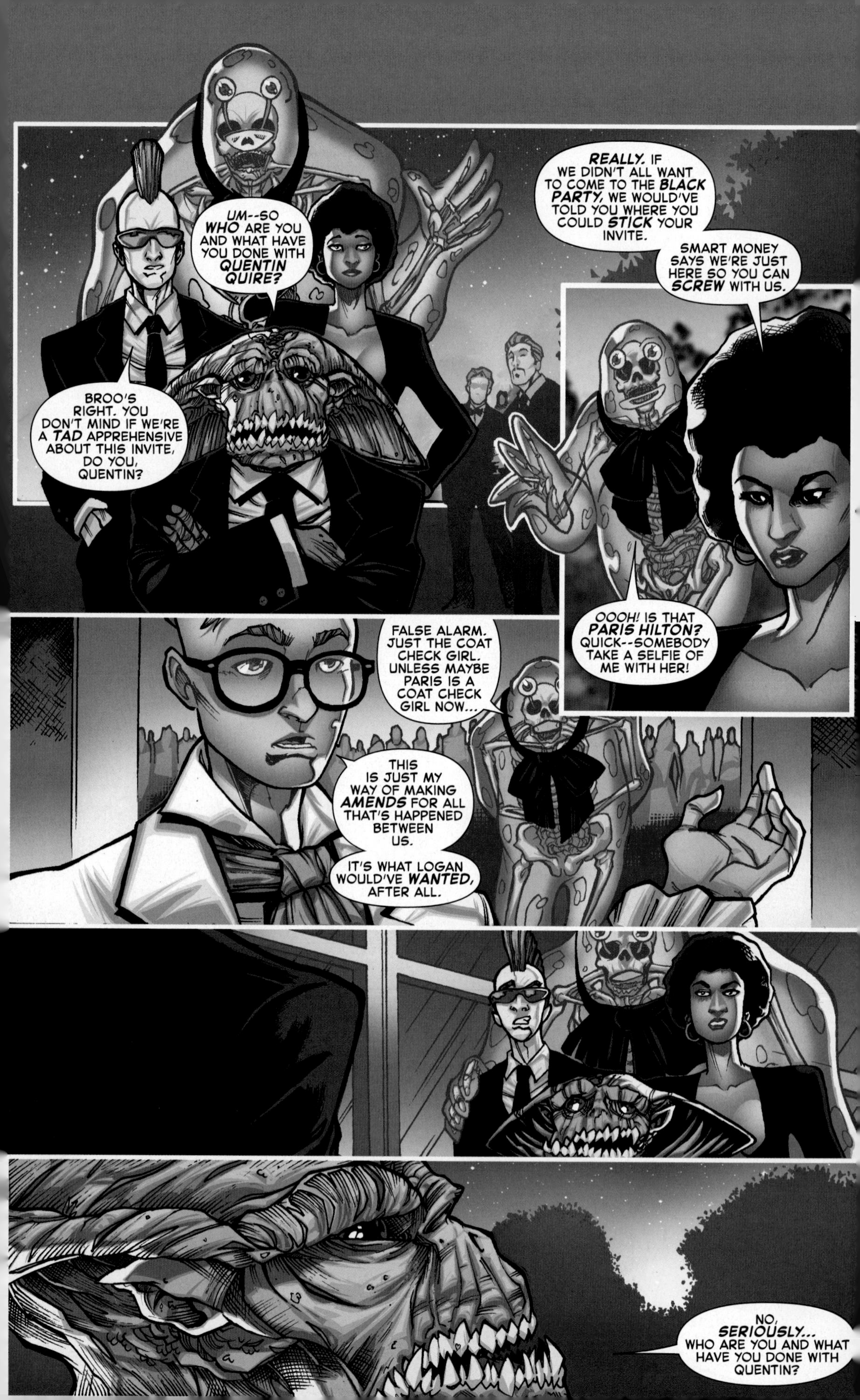
UM--SO WHO ARE YOU AND WHAT HAVE YOU DONE WITH QUENTIN QUIRE?
BROO'S RIGHT. YOU DON'T MIND IF WE'RE A TAD APPREHENSIVE ABOUT THIS INVITE, DO YOU, QUENTIN?
REALLY. IF WE DIDN'T ALL WANT TO COME TO THE BLACK PARTY, WE WOULD'VE TOLD YOU WHERE YOU COULD STICK YOUR INVITE.
SMART MONEY SAYS WE'RE JUST HERE SO YOU CAN SCREW WITH US.
OOOH! IS THAT PARIS HILTON? QUICK--SOMEBODY TAKE A SELFIE OF ME WITH HER!
FALSE ALARM. JUST THE COAT CHECK GIRL. UNLESS MAYBE PARIS IS A COAT CHECK GIRL NOW...
THIS IS JUST MY WAY OF MAKING AMENDS FOR ALL THAT'S HAPPENED BETWEEN US.
IT'S WHAT LOGAN WOULD'VE WANTED, AFTER ALL.
NO, SERIOUSLY... WHO ARE YOU AND WHAT HAVE YOU DONE WITH QUENTIN?

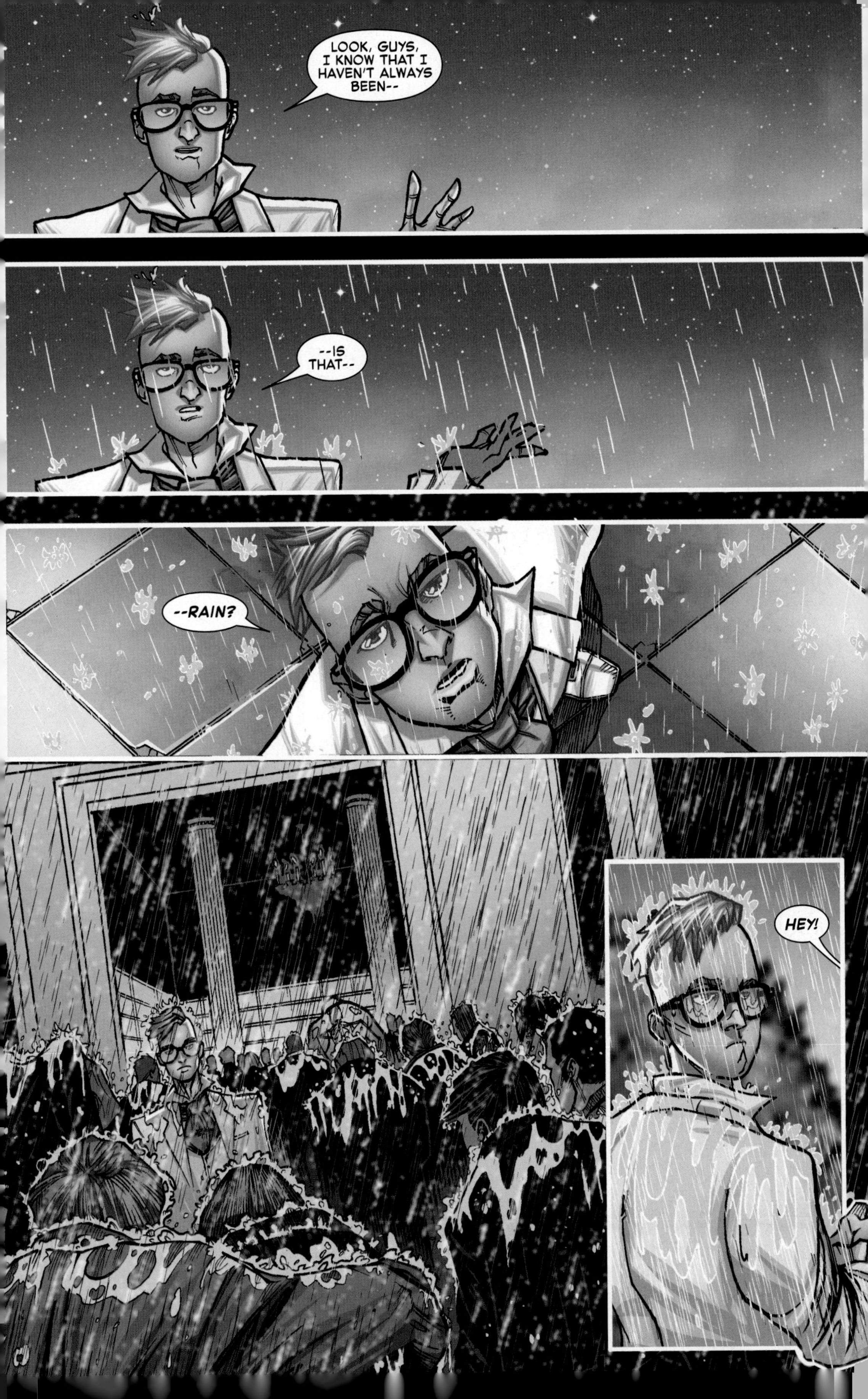
LOOK, GUYS, I KNOW THAT I HAVEN'T ALWAYS BEEN--
--IS THAT--
--RAIN?
HEY!

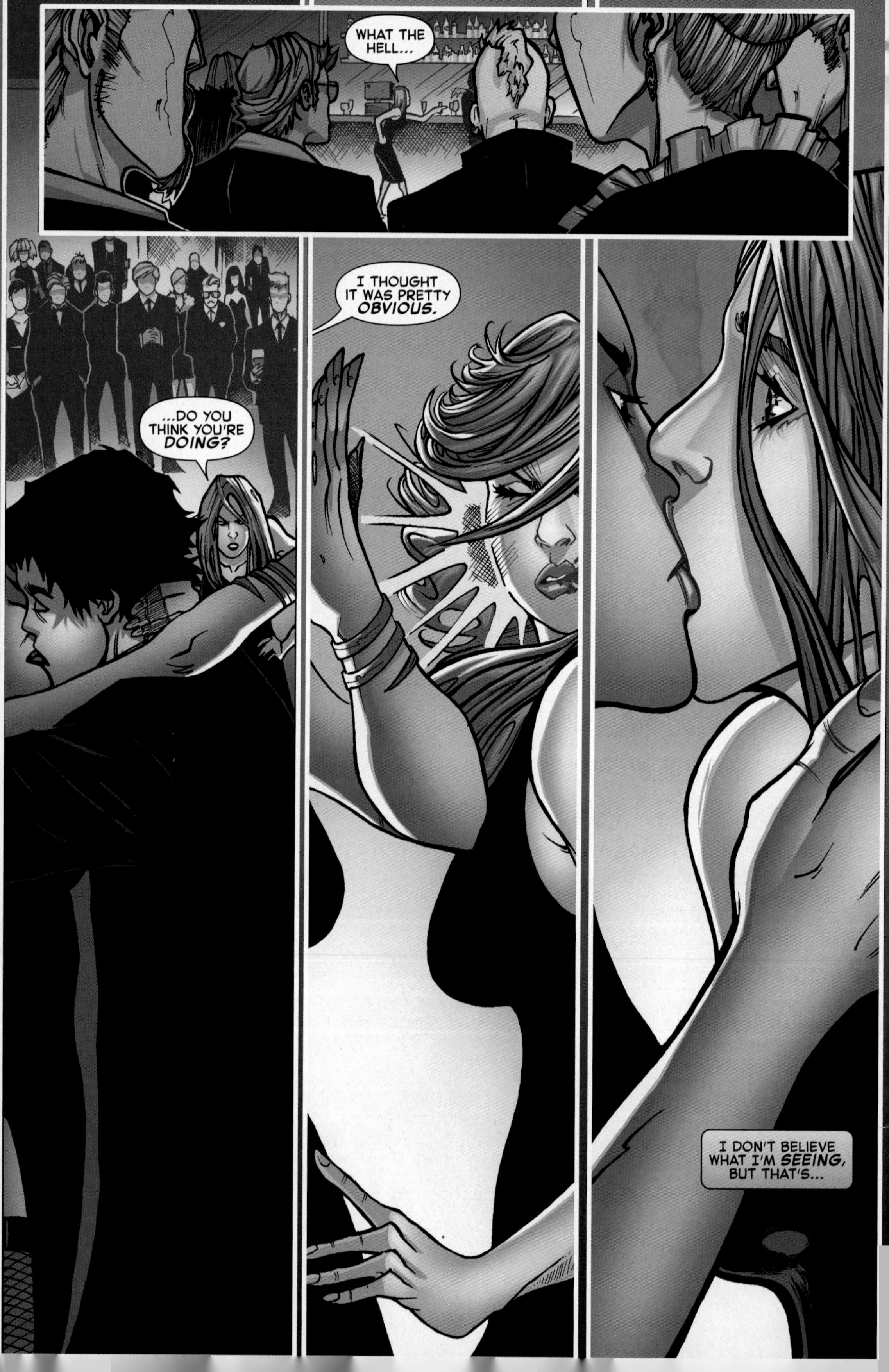
WHAT THE HELL...
...DO YOU THINK YOU'RE DOING?
I THOUGHT IT WAS PRETTY OBVIOUS.
I DON'T BELIEVE WHAT I'M SEEING, BUT THAT'S...

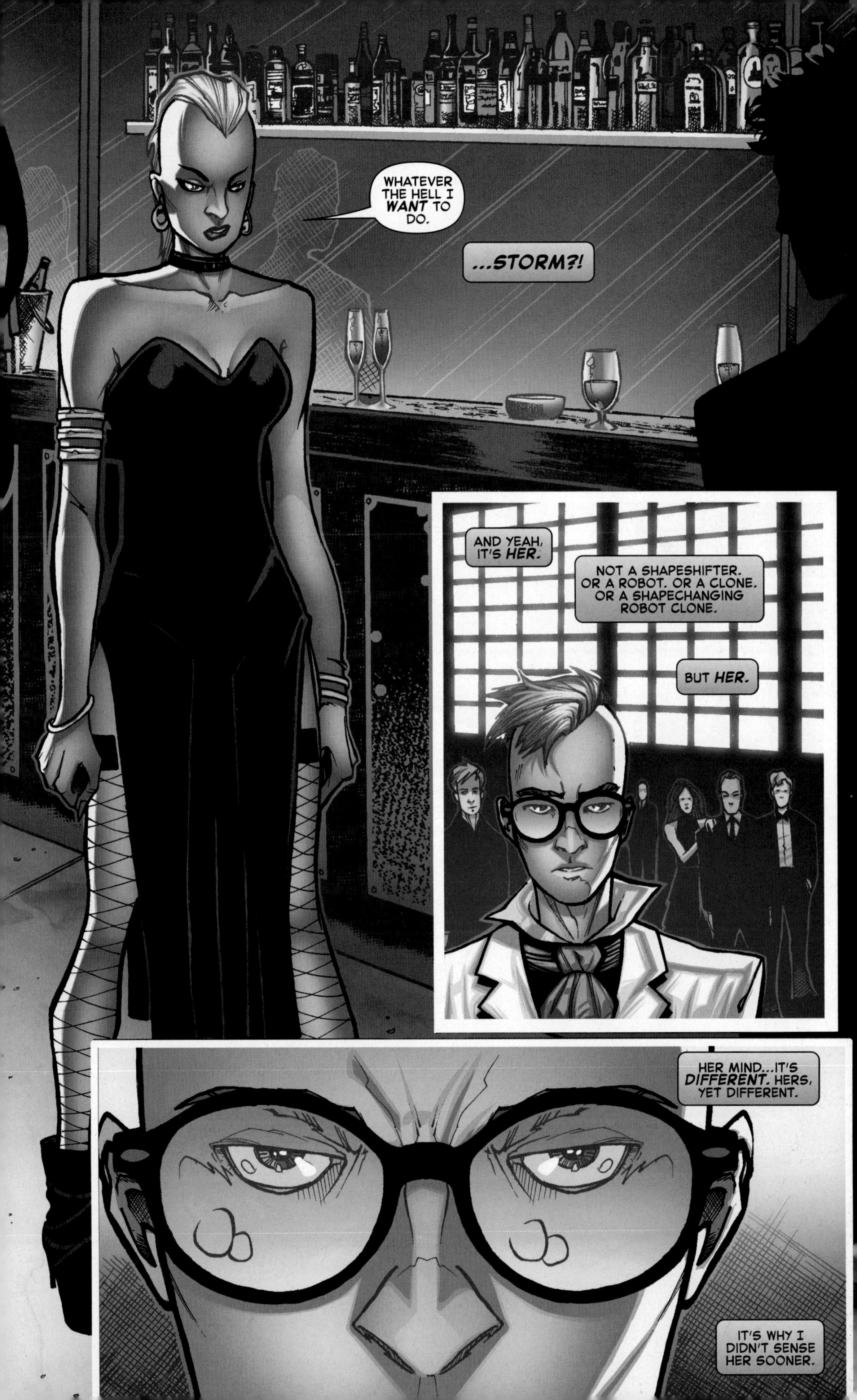
WHATEVER THE HELL I *WANT* TO DO.
...*STORM?!*
AND YEAH, IT'S *HER.*
NOT A SHAPESHIFTER. OR A ROBOT. OR A CLONE. OR A SHAPECHANGING ROBOT CLONE.
BUT *HER.*
HER MIND...IT'S *DIFFERENT.* HERS, YET DIFFERENT.
IT'S WHY I DIDN'T SENSE HER SOONER.

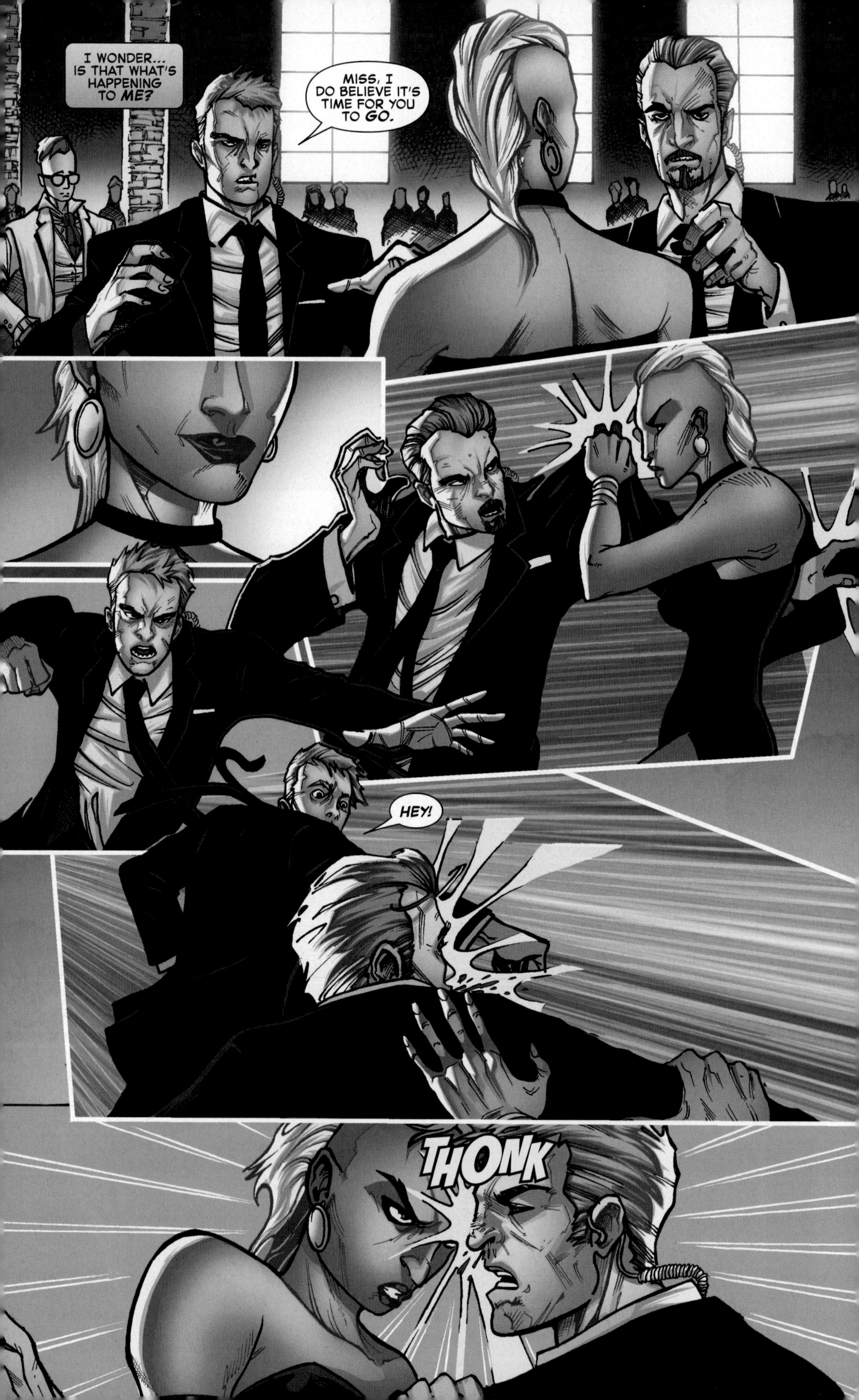
I WONDER... IS THAT WHAT'S HAPPENING TO ME?
MISS, I DO BELIEVE IT'S TIME FOR YOU TO GO.
HEY!
THONK

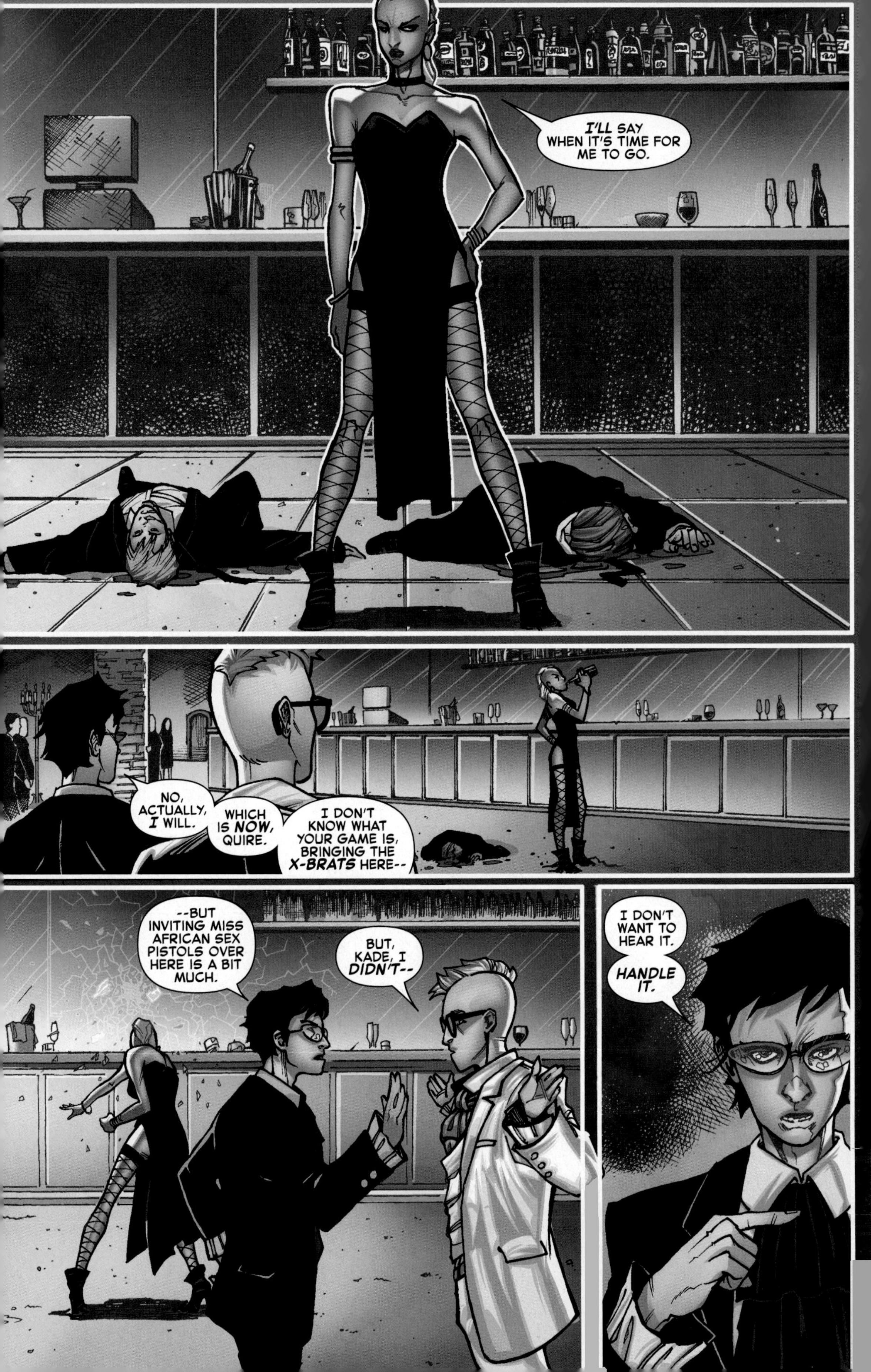
I'LL SAY WHEN IT'S TIME FOR ME TO GO.
NO, ACTUALLY, I WILL.
WHICH IS NOW, QUIRE.
I DON'T KNOW WHAT YOUR GAME IS, BRINGING THE X-BRATS HERE--
--BUT INVITING MISS AFRICAN SEX PISTOLS OVER HERE IS A BIT MUCH.
BUT, KADE, I DIDN'T--
I DON'T WANT TO HEAR IT.
HANDLE IT.

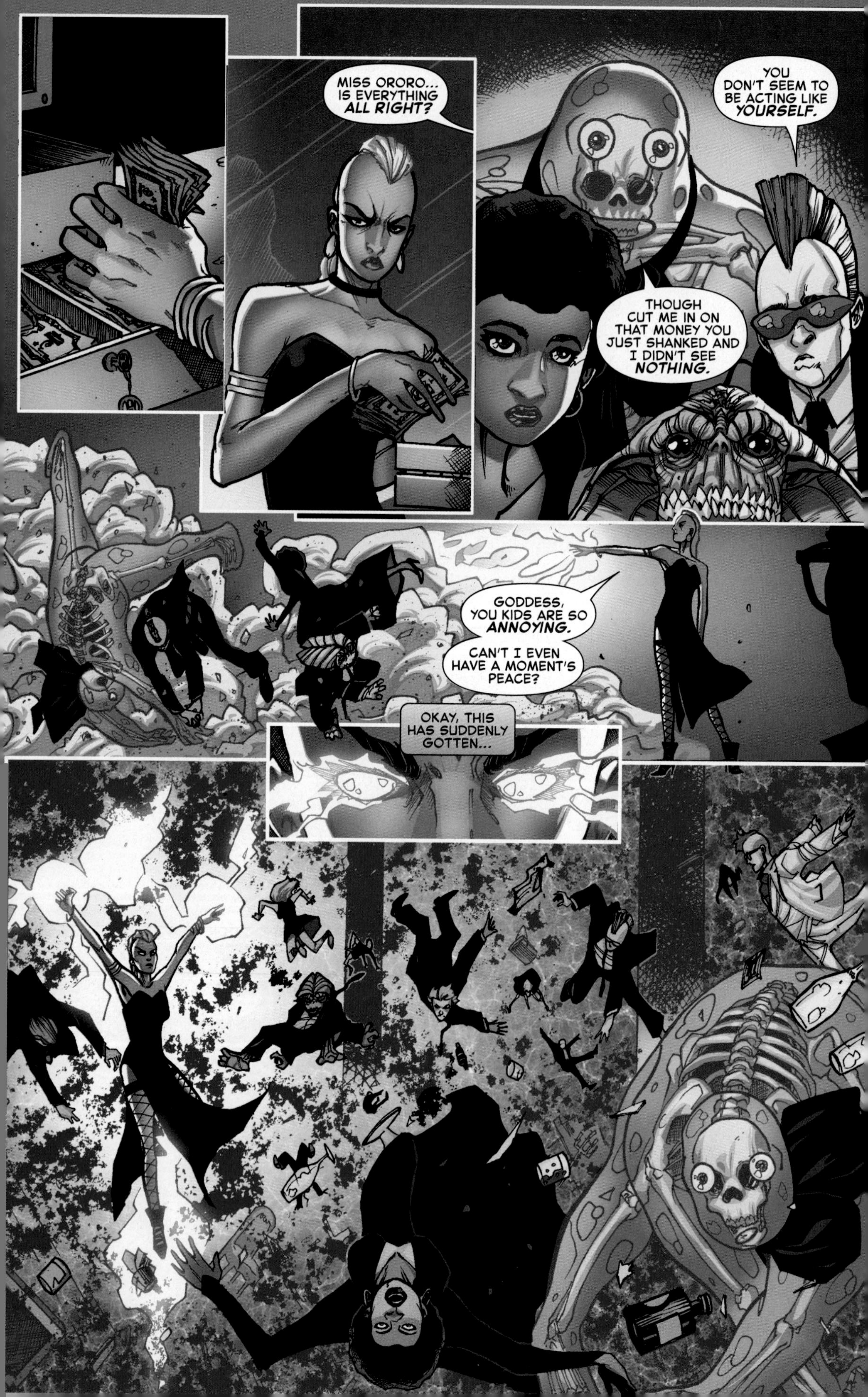
MISS ORORO... IS EVERYTHING ALL RIGHT?
YOU DON'T SEEM TO BE ACTING LIKE YOURSELF.
THOUGH CUT ME IN ON THAT MONEY YOU JUST SHANKED AND I DIDN'T SEE NOTHING.
GODDESS, YOU KIDS ARE SO ANNOYING.
CAN'T I EVEN HAVE A MOMENT'S PEACE?
OKAY, THIS HAS SUDDENLY GOTTEN...

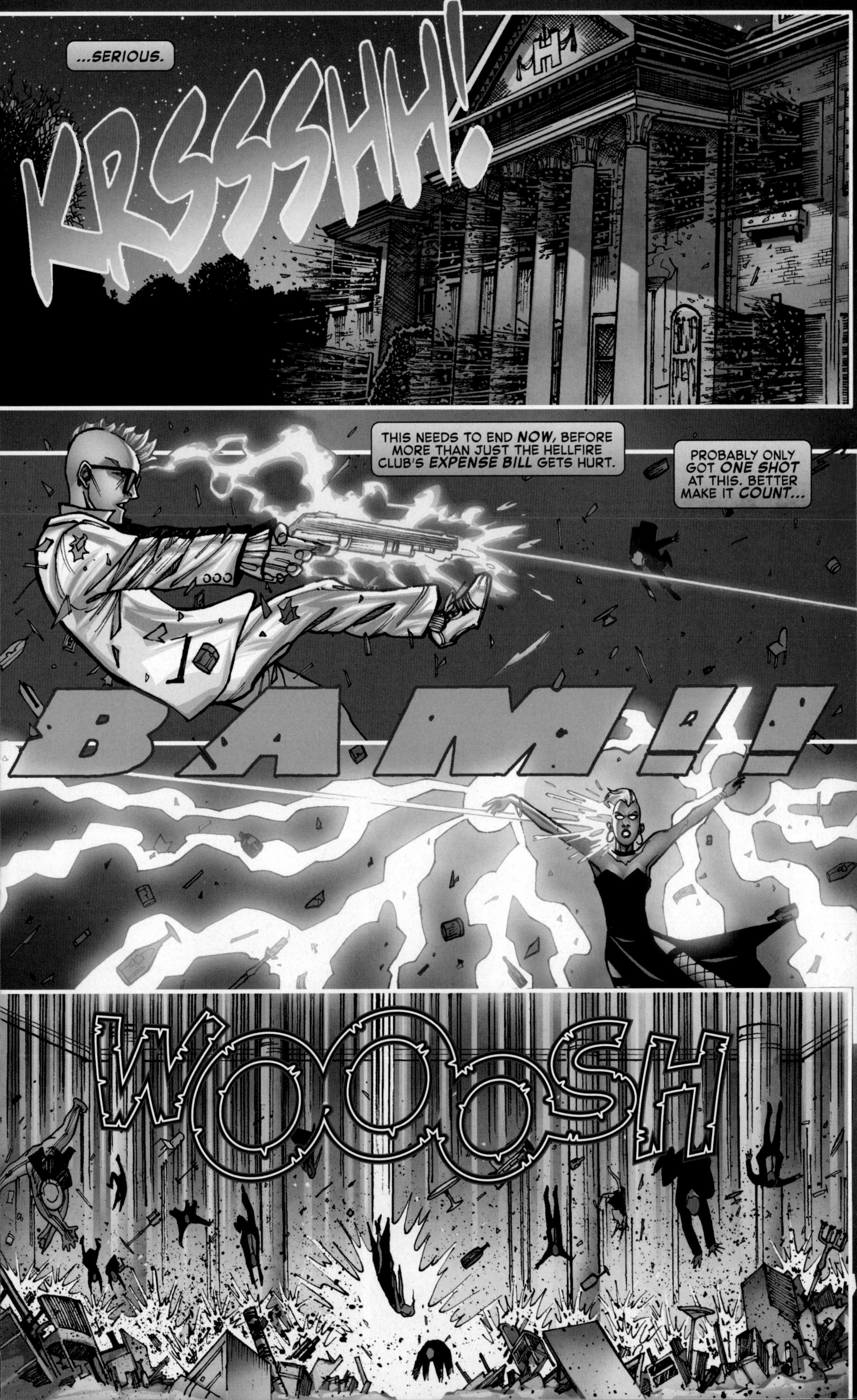
...SERIOUS.
KRSSSHH!
THIS NEEDS TO END NOW, BEFORE MORE THAN JUST THE HELLFIRE CLUB'S EXPENSE BILL GETS HURT.
PROBABLY ONLY GOT ONE SHOT AT THIS. BETTER MAKE IT COUNT...
BAM!!!
WOOOSH

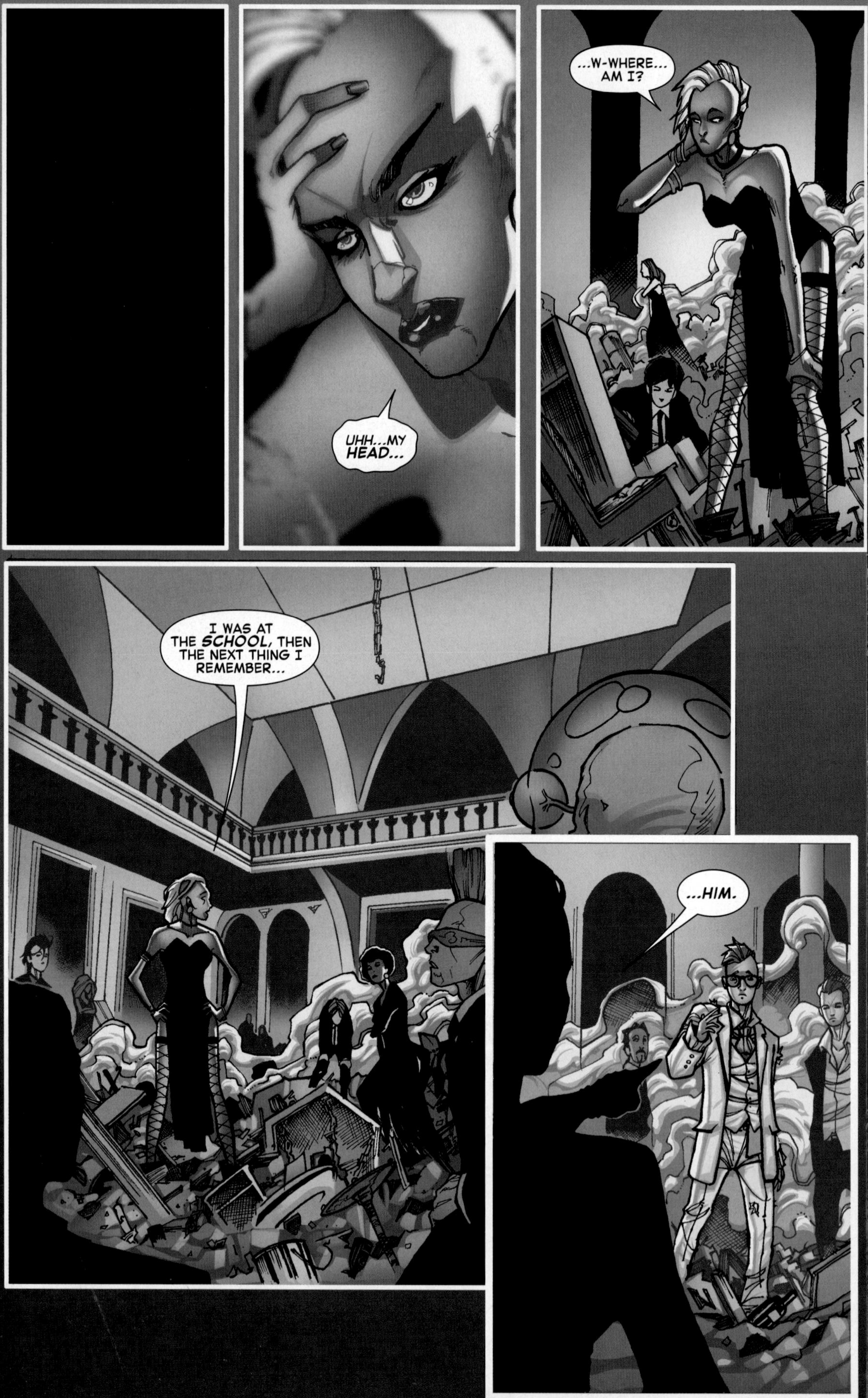
UHH...MY HEAD...
...W-WHERE... AM I?
I WAS AT THE SCHOOL, THEN THE NEXT THING I REMEMBER...
...HIM.

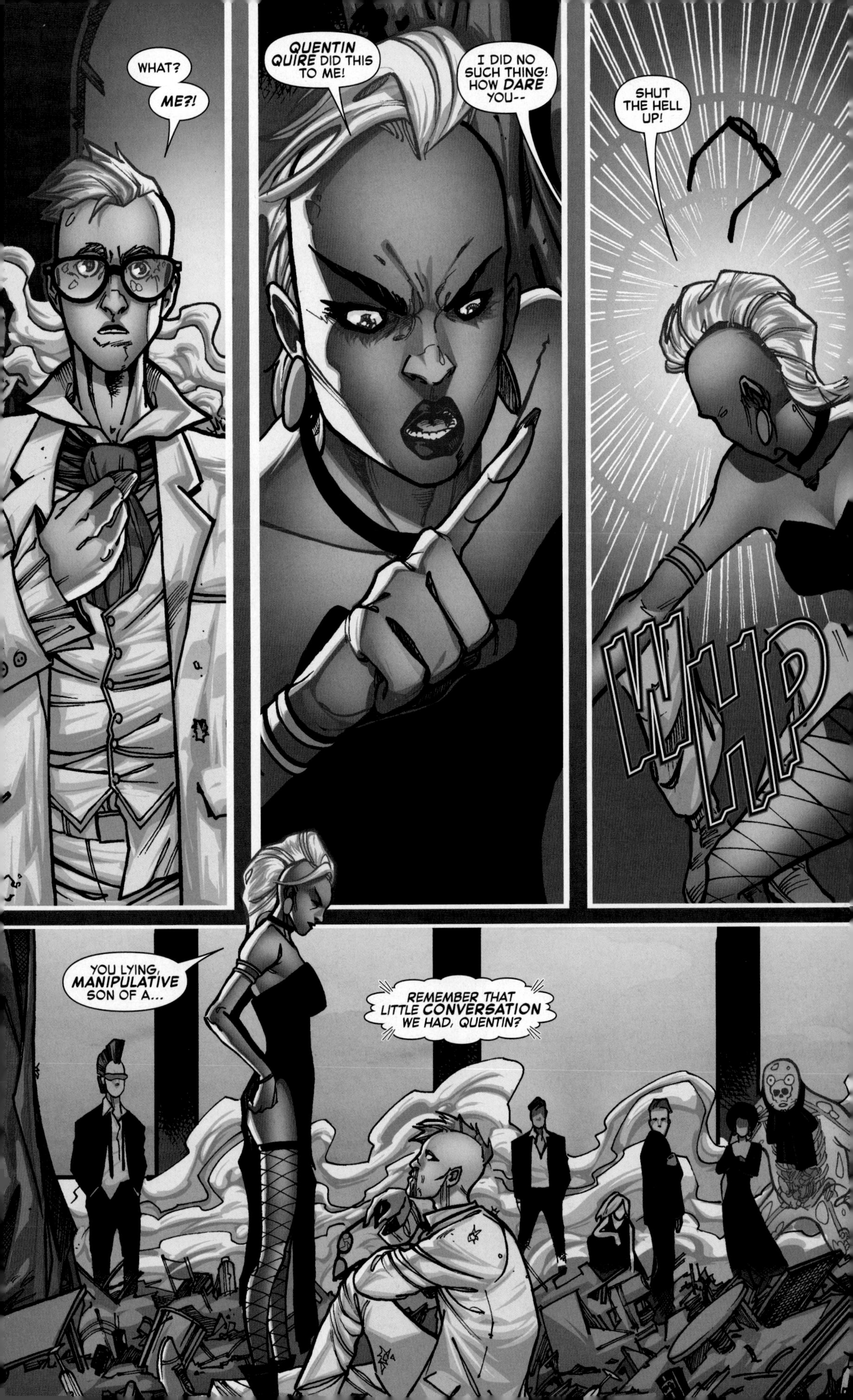
WHAT?
ME?!
QUENTIN QUIRE DID THIS TO ME!
I DID NO SUCH THING! HOW DARE YOU--
SHUT THE HELL UP!
WHP
YOU LYING, MANIPULATIVE SON OF A...
REMEMBER THAT LITTLE CONVERSATION WE HAD, QUENTIN?

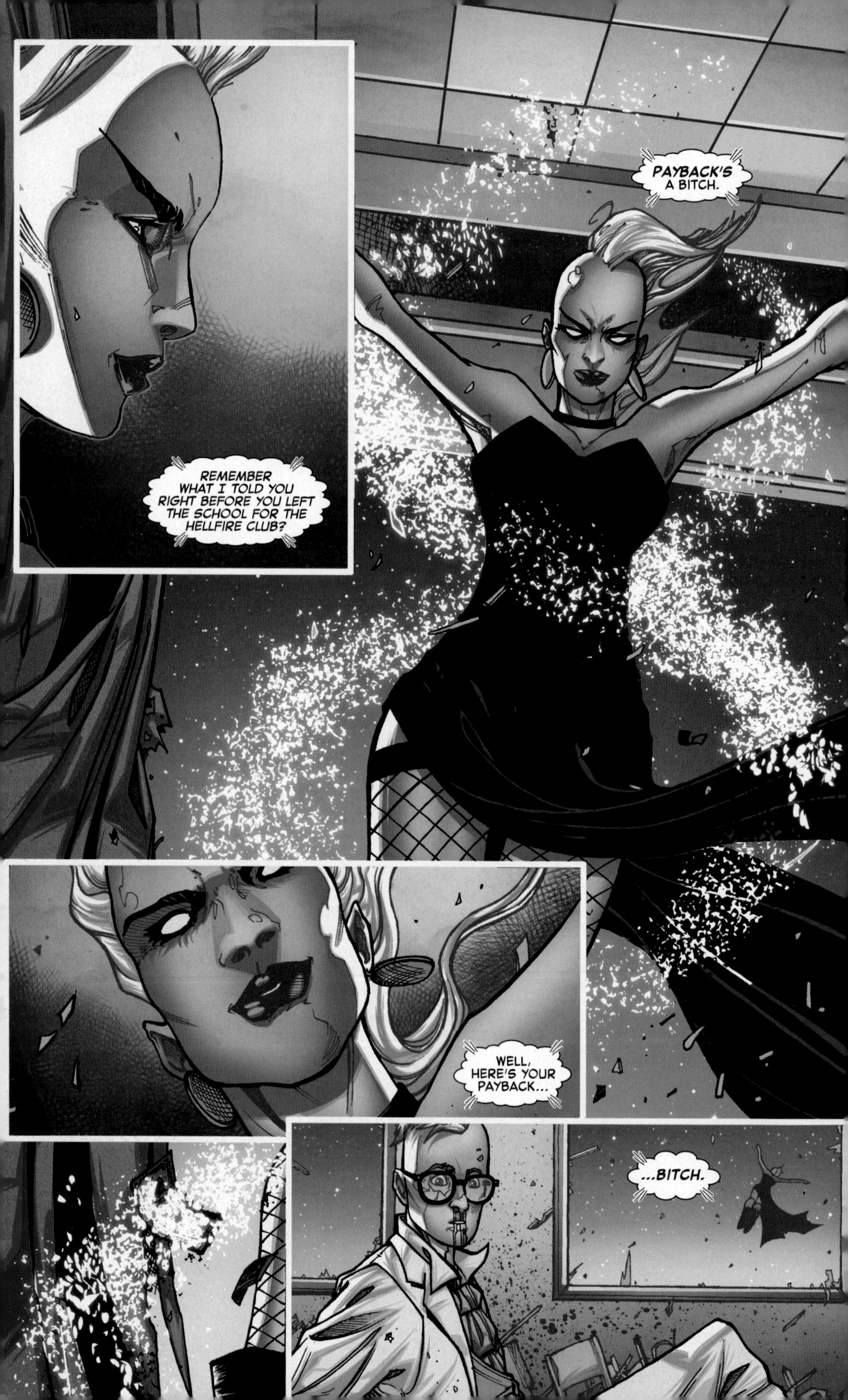
REMEMBER WHAT I TOLD YOU RIGHT BEFORE YOU LEFT THE SCHOOL FOR THE HELLFIRE CLUB?
PAYBACK'S A BITCH.
WELL, HERE'S YOUR PAYBACK...
...BITCH.

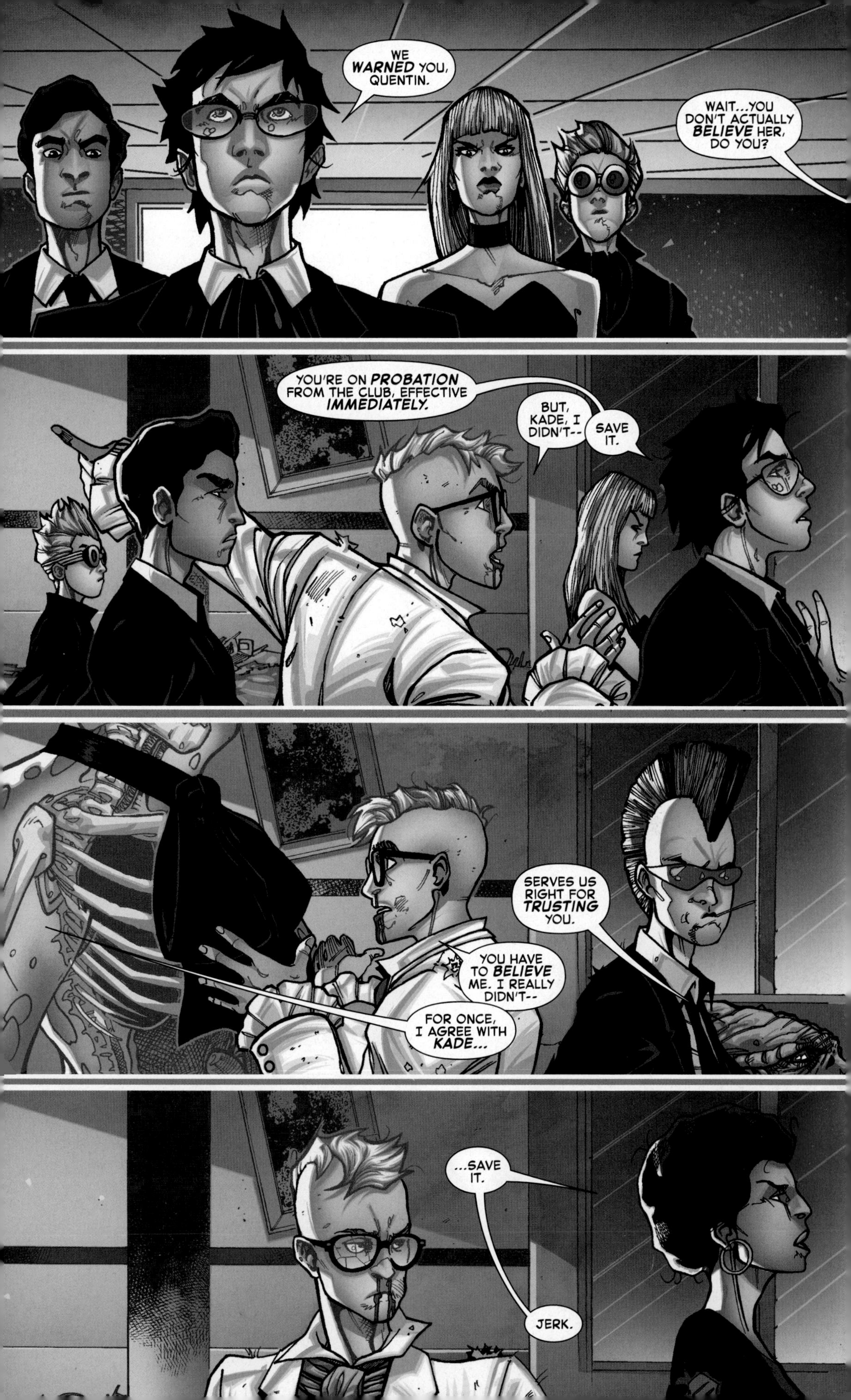
WE WARNED YOU, QUENTIN.
WAIT...YOU DON'T ACTUALLY BELIEVE HER, DO YOU?
YOU'RE ON PROBATION FROM THE CLUB, EFFECTIVE IMMEDIATELY.
BUT, KADE, I DIDN'T--
SAVE IT.
SERVES US RIGHT FOR TRUSTING YOU.
YOU HAVE TO BELIEVE ME. I REALLY DIDN'T--
FOR ONCE, I AGREE WITH KADE...
...SAVE IT.
JERK.

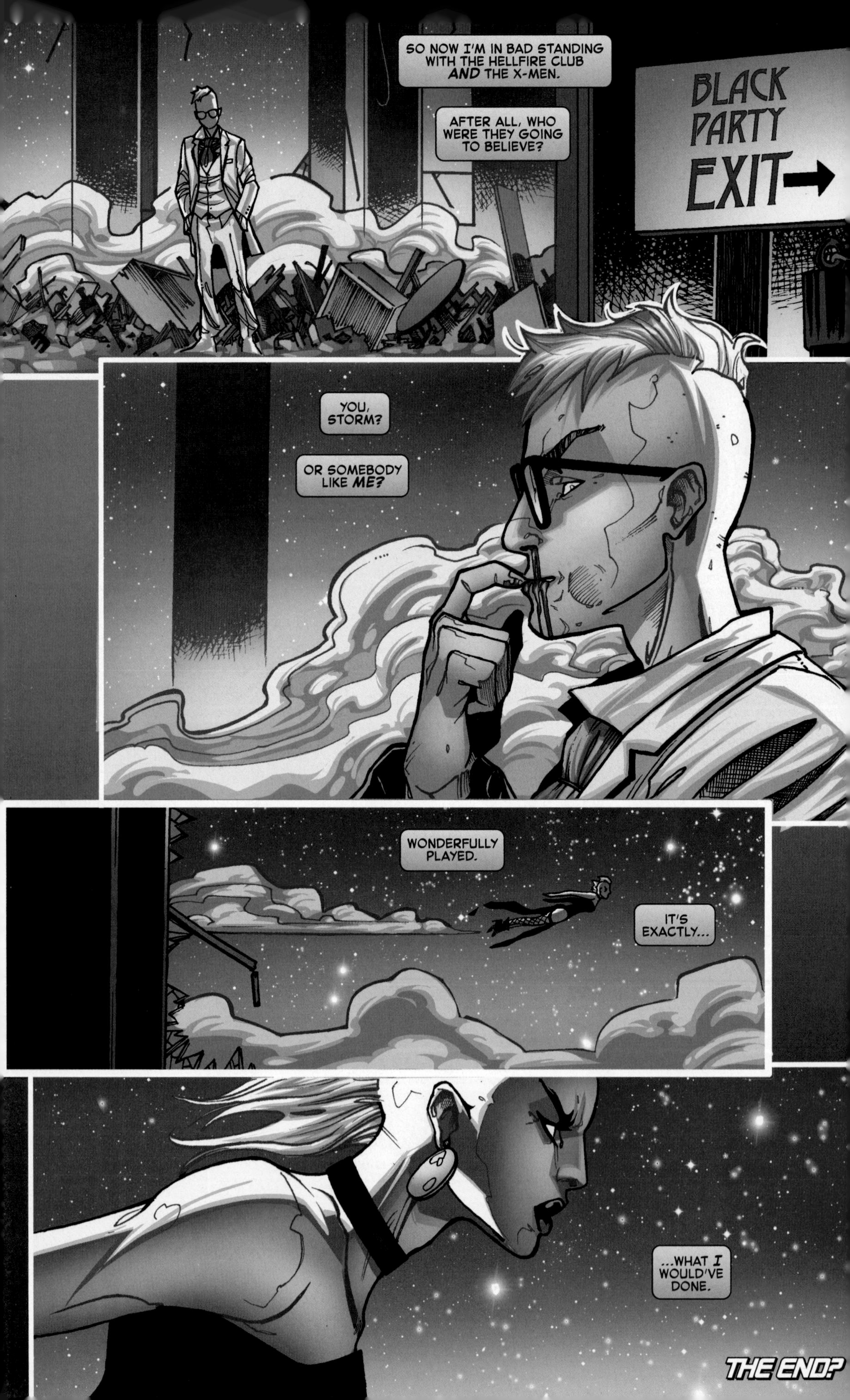

SO NOW I'M IN BAD STANDING WITH THE HELLFIRE CLUB AND THE X-MEN.
AFTER ALL, WHO WERE THEY GOING TO BELIEVE?
BLACK PARTY EXIT
YOU, STORM?
OR SOMEBODY LIKE ME?
WONDERFULLY PLAYED.
IT'S EXACTLY...
...WHAT I WOULD'VE DONE.
THE END?

001

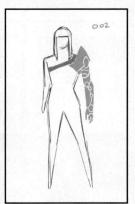

002

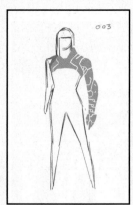

003

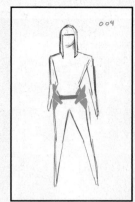

004

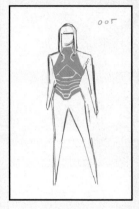

005

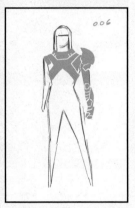

006

007

a1

a2

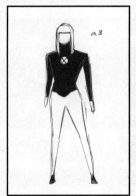

a3

a4

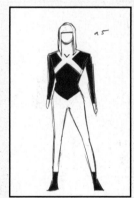

a5

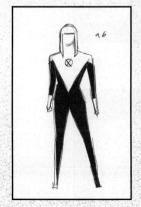

a6

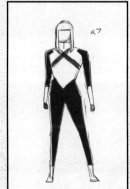

a7

b1

HISAKO DESIGNS BY KRIS ANKA

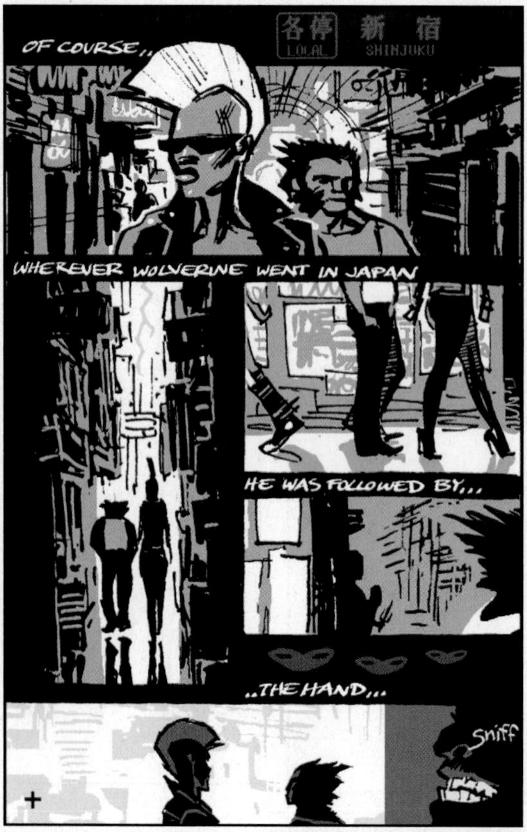
各停
LOCAL
新宿
SHINJUKU
OF COURSE,,
WHEREVER WOLVERINE WENT IN JAPAN
HE WAS FOLLOWED BY,,,
..THE HAND,,,
Sniff

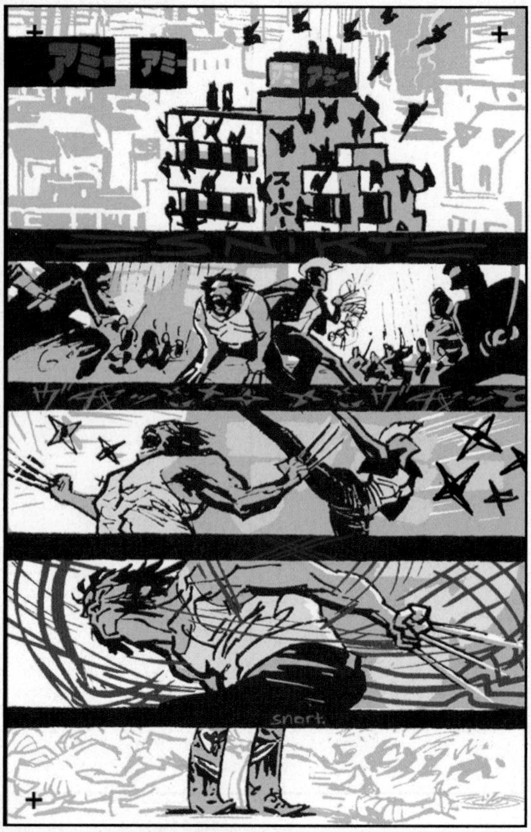
アミー
アミー
snort.

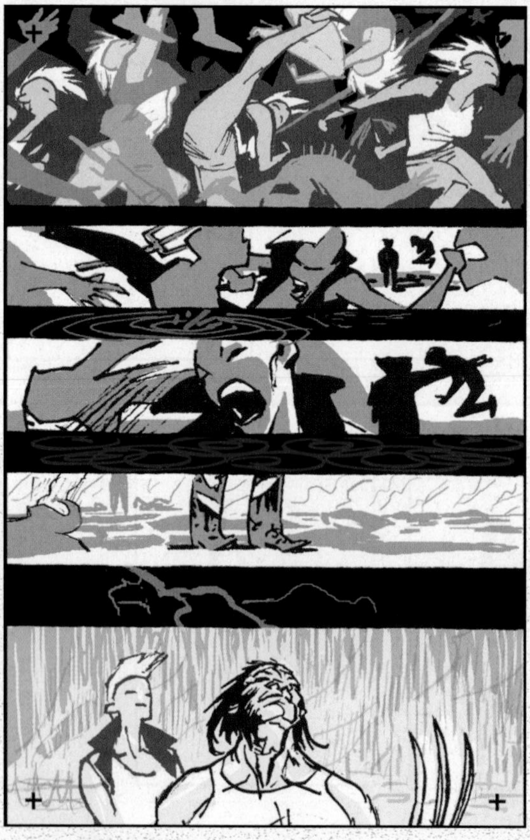

#11, PGS. 15-17 LAYOUTS BY CHRIS BRUNNER

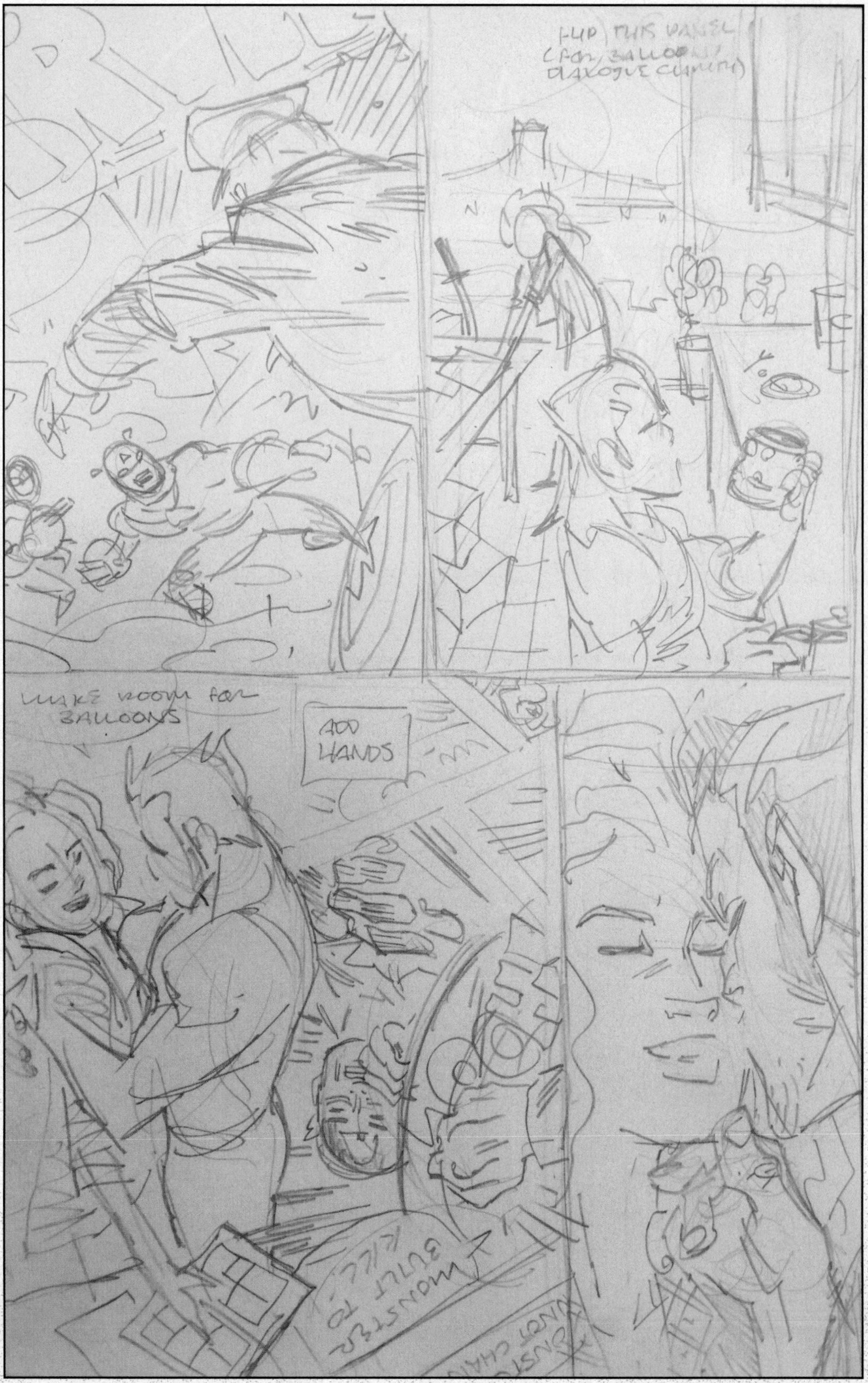
FLIP THIS PANEL
MAKE ROOM FOR BALLOONS
ADD HANDS

#11, PG. 1 LAYOUTS BY BEN CALDWELL

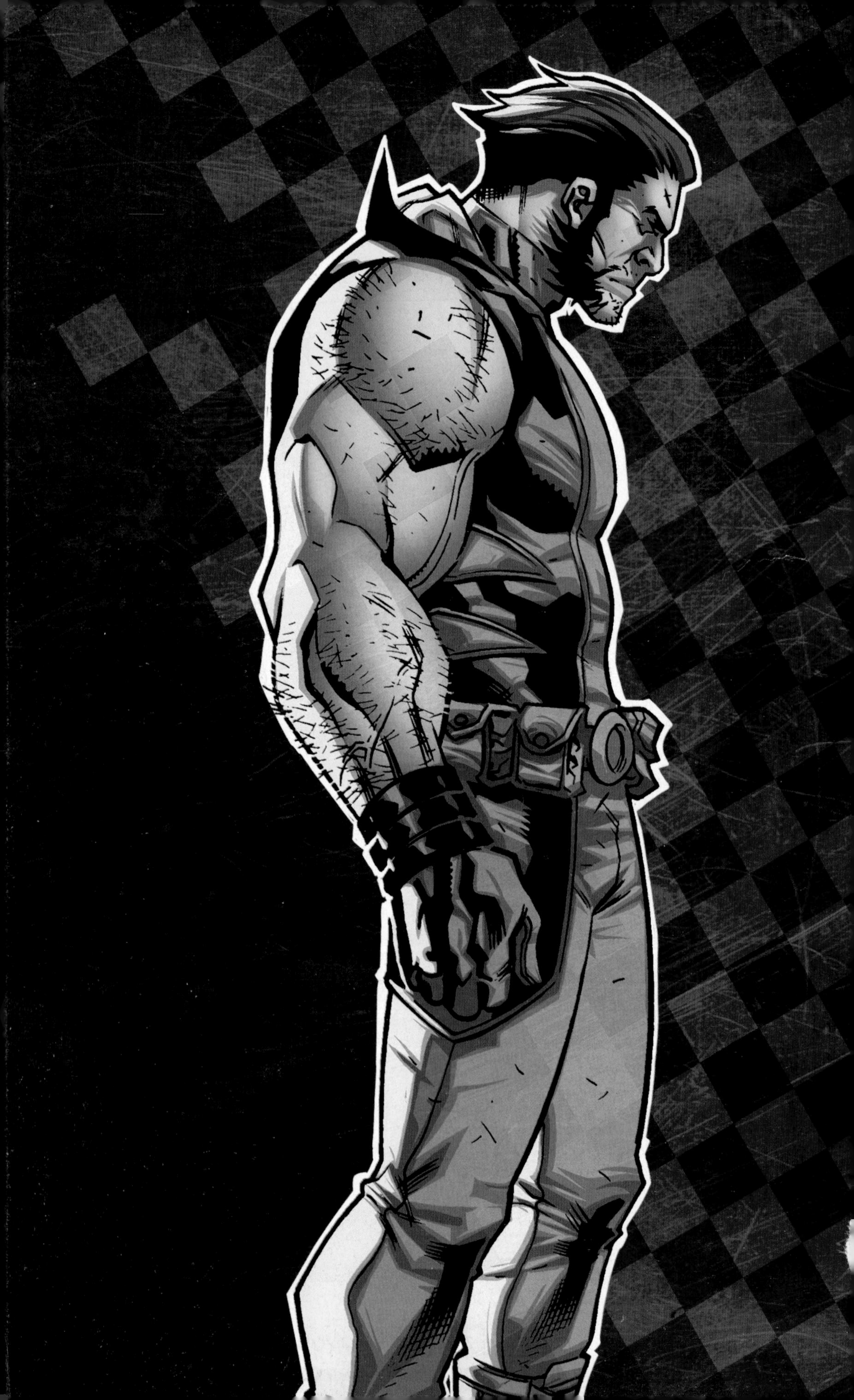